LAW AND LEGALITY
IN THE OTTOMAN EMPIRE
AND REPUBLIC OF TURKEY

LAW AND LEGALITY IN THE OTTOMAN EMPIRE AND REPUBLIC OF TURKEY

Edited by Kent F. Schull,
M. Safa Saraçoğlu,
and Robert Zens

Indiana University Press

Bloomington & Indianapolis

This book is a publication of

Indiana University Press
Office of Scholarly Publishing
Herman B Wells Library 350
1320 East 10th Street
Bloomington, Indiana 47405 USA

iupress.indiana.edu

© 2016 by Indiana University Press

All rights reserved

No part of this book may be reproduced or utilized in any form or by any means, electronic or mechanical, including photocopying and recording, or by any information storage and retrieval system, without permission in writing from the publisher. The Association of American University Presses' Resolution on Permissions constitutes the only exception to this prohibition.

The paper used in this publication meets the minimum requirements of the American National Standard for Information Sciences—Permanence of Paper for Printed Library Materials, ANSI Z39.48–1992.

Manufactured in the United States of America

DOI: 10.2979/lawandlegality.0.0.01

Library of Congress Cataloging-in-Publication Data

Names: Schull, Kent F., editor. | Saracoglu, M. Safa., editor. | Zens, Robert W., editor.
Title: Law and legality in the Ottoman Empire and Republic of Turkey / Edited by Kent F. Schull, M. Safa Saracoglu, and Robert Zens.
Description: Bloomington : Indiana University Press, 2016. | Includes index.
Identifiers: LCCN 2015037652 | ISBN 9780253020925 (pbk. : alk. paper) | ISBN 9780253021007 (electronic)
Subjects: LCSH: Law—Turkey—History. | Turkey—History—Ottoman Empire, 1288–1918.
Classification: LCC KKX120 .L39 2016 | DDC 349.56—dc23
LC record available at http://lccn.loc.gov/2015037652

1 2 3 4 5   21 20 19 18 17 16

Contents

	Introduction · Kent F. Schull & M. Safa Saraçoğlu	1
1	Reaching the Flocks: Literacy and the Mass Reception of Ottoman Law in the Sixteenth-Century Arab World · Timothy J. Fitzgerald	9
2	Ottoman Legal Practice and Non-Judicial Actors in Seventeenth-Century Istanbul · Hadi Hosainy	26
3	Defining Village Boundaries at the Time of the Introduction of the *Malikane* System: The Struggle of the Ottoman State for Reaffirming Ownership of the Land · Michael Nizri	43
4	Economic Interventionism, Islamic Law and Provincial Government in the Ottoman Empire · M. Safa Saraçoğlu	65
5	Reorganization of the Sharia Courts of Egypt: How Legal Modernization Set Back Women's Rights in the Nineteenth Century · Kenneth M. Cuno	92
6	Regulating Land Rights in Late Nineteenth-Century Salt: The Limits of Legal Pluralism in Ottoman Property Law · Nora Barakat	108
7	The *Mecelle*, Sharia, and the Ottoman State: Fashioning and Refashioning of Islamic Law in the Nineteenth and Twentieth Centuries · Samy Ayoub	129
8	Criminal Codes, Crime, and the Transformation of Punishment in the Late Ottoman Empire · Kent F. Schull	156
9	Refugees, Locals and "The" State: Property Compensation in the Province of Izmir Following the Greco-Turkish Population Exchange of 1923 · Ellinor Morack	179
	Index	201

LAW AND LEGALITY
IN THE OTTOMAN EMPIRE
AND REPUBLIC OF TURKEY

Introduction

Kent F. Schull & M. Safa Saraçoğlu

THIS EDITED VOLUME is an expansion of the *Journal of the Ottoman and Turkish Studies Association*'s Spring 2015 issue "Law and Legality in the Ottoman Empire and Republic of Turkey" edited by Kent F. Schull (Binghamton University, SUNY), M. Safa Saraçoğlu (Bloomsburg University), and Robert Zens (Le Moyne College). It represents the wide range of excellent work being done in the field of Ottoman and Turkish socio-legal history. This volume includes a number of articles that were initially presented as part of a four-panel session at the 2013 annual conference of the Middle East Studies Association (MESA) entitled, "Law, Legality, and Legitimacy in the Ottoman Empire." The "embedded workshop" focused on the complex relationship between law, legality, and legitimacy with the particular goal of understanding the transformation of "how law was legitimized" over the course of Ottoman history. Twenty-five presenters and discussants participated in the four panels containing topics related to socio-legal history throughout the empire's existence.

Part of the pretext of the workshop was to view "law" as representing a formal, institutional normative order. The formalization of law is a political and cultural process that requires different groups negotiating how to articulate a formal version of "existing norms." This view also adapts David Garland's "multidimensional interpretative approach, which sees punishment as an over determined, multifaceted social institution" to law, legality, and legitimization.[1] This adaptation allows us to view law, legality, and legitimacy as "social artifacts" that embody and regenerate wider cultural categories and serve as a means of achieving particular legal ends. Laws, legality, and legitimacy cannot be explained by their instrumental purposes alone, but must also take into account cultural style, historical tradition, and dependence upon institutional, technical, and discursive conditions. They are part of a broader institution, administered by the state, but also grounded in wider patterns of knowing, feeling, and acting that depend upon these social roots for their continuing legitimacy and operation. It is also grounded in history, similar to all social institutions; modern legal codes, practices, and systems are historical outcomes that are imperfectly adapted to their current situation—a product of tradition as much as present policy. There are

---

1. David Garland, *Punishment and Modern Society: A Study in Social Theory* (Chicago: University of Chicago Press, 1990), 2.

many conflicting logics that go into law, legality, and legitimacy in any given society. Similar to all social institutions, legal systems shape their environment as much as they are shaped by it. They are not simply dependent variables at the end of some finite line of social and political causation. They interact with their environment, forming part of the mutually constructing configuration of elements that make up the social world.[2]

Due to its political nature, law-making requires justification, which comes in the form of legitimacy. Legitimacy, in this context, emerges as a political concept dealing with a particular political/moral question: "What gives this (or any) particular law-maker the right to demand what one should obey?" The chain of relationship between law, legality, and legitimacy has taken a particular form for several post-enlightenment thinkers. Legality, as something that can be proven through rules of reason, became the basis for legitimacy.[3] While Weber considered this to be one of the defining features of "formal justice," the supposed lack of legal formalism in *"Kadijustiz"* became the distinguishing feature of societies that rely on "substantive justice." The inaccuracy of *"Kadijustiz"*—defined as "informal judgments rendered in terms of concrete ethical or other practical valuations"[4]—has been noted by several scholars, including Iris Agmon, Haim Gerber, Wael Hallaq, Huricihan İslamoğlu, Baber Johansen, David Powers, Lawrence Rosen, and Avi Rubin.[5]

There are at least two factors contributing to the Weberian misperception of the relationship between law, legality, and legitimacy in the Ottoman Empire: it fails to understand the normative consistency in the Ottoman legal system, and it assumes that the peculiar nature of the historical relationship between intellectu-

2. Ibid., 19-22.
3. See Jürgen Habermas, *Legitimation Crisis* (Boston: Beacon Press, 1975), 98; Darrow Schecter, *Beyond Hegemony: Towards a New Philosophy of Political Legitimacy* (Manchester: Manchester University Press, 2005), 30; Carl Schmitt and John McCormick, *Legality and Legitimacy*, trans. Jeffrey Seitzer (Durham: Duke University Press, 2004), 97.
4. Max Weber, *Economy and Society: an Outline of Interpretive Sociology*, 2 vols. (Berkeley: University of California Press, 1978), 976.
5. Iris Agmon, *Family and Court: Legal Culture and Modernity in Late Ottoman Palestine* (Syracuse: Syracuse University Press, 2006); Haim Gerber, *State, Society, and Law in Islam: Ottoman Law in Comparative Perspective* (Albany: State University of New York Press, 1994); Wael B Hallaq, "Was the Gate of Ijtihad Closed?" *International Journal of Middle East Studies* 16:1 (1984): 3-41; Huricihan İslamoğlu, "Intractable Elusiveness of Ottoman Law or Law as the Focus of the Modern Predicament of Ottoman Society," Workshop on Global History of International Law, Interlaken, 19-23 Jan. 2011; Baber Johansen, "Truth and Validity of the Qadi's Judgement: A Legal Debate among Muslim Sunnite Jurists from the 9th to the 13th Centuries," Recht van de Islam 14 (1997): 1-26; David Powers, "Kadijustiz or Qadi-Justice? A Paternity Dispute from Fourteenth-Century Morocco," *Islamic Law and Society* 1:3 (1994): 332-66; Lawrence Rosen, *The Anthropology of Justice: Law and Culture in Islamic Society* (Cambridge: Cambridge University Press, 1989); Avi Rubin, *Ottoman Nizamiye Courts: Law and Modernity* (New York: Palgrave Macmillan, 2011).

als, the religious establishment, and sovereign authority in the "Western world" is universal. We believe that questioning "how law was legitimized" in the Ottoman Empire over the long-run can help avoid this misperception and understand the legal transformation of the empire from the perspective of Islamic law and practice, that is why we invited fellow scholars to discuss the peculiar relationship between laws, legality, and legitimacy in the Ottoman Empire.

We hope that this volume will add to the expanding field of Ottoman socio-legal studies. The reception of law by members of society, its utility and application at the local level are key components of its legitimation. Legal practice in the Ottoman Empire's Sharia and *Nizamiye* courts has received increasingly more attention in the past two decades. In 2008, Iris Agmon and Ido Shahar edited a special issue of *Islamic Law and Society* on the shifting perspectives in the study of Sharia courts. In their introduction, they noted how these courts received very limited attention prior to the 1990s—the journal, as the editors noted, began its life in 1994 as a testimony to this increasing momentum.[6] Although Boğaç Ergene reminds us that Sharia court records were not produced as historical sources; and while these records remain important sources for academic purposes, scholars should avoid making generalizations based on them.[7]

In 2011, Avi Rubin noted a similar lacuna on works related to the nineteenth-century *Nizamiye* courts.[8] Up until very recently our understanding of how these courts functioned was very limited, because of the few records that survive from these courts. While this understanding has somewhat improved thanks to an increasing number of scholars exploring the nineteenth-century provincial judicio-administrative sphere, for the most part, their provincial operations remain a mystery. Proliferating works on the application of law, some included in this volume, point out the complexity of the relationship between legal practices and political economy in the Ottoman provinces. A more nuanced understanding of the complex sets of relations among social actors reveals that it is impossible to think of applied law apart from its social, political, cultural, and economic context.

---

6. Iris Agmon and Ido Shahar, "Introduction," Islamic Law and Society 15 (2008): 9.

7. Boğaç A. Ergene, *Local Court, Provincial Society, and Justice in the Ottoman Empire: Legal Practice and Dispute Resolution in Çankırı and Kastamonu (1652-1744)* (Leiden: Brill, 2003), 207-08. In recent years, *sicil* specialists have emphasized the need to read the sicil as a constructed, rather than a transparent, artifact. See Dror Ze'evi, "The Use of Ottoman Shari'a Court Records as a Source for Middle Eastern Social History: A Reappraisal," *Islamic Law and Society* 5 (1998): 35-57; Najwa al- Qattan, "Textual Differentiation in the Damascus Sijil: Religious Discrimination or Politics of Gender?" in *Women, the Family, and Divorce Laws in Islamic History*, ed. Amira El-Azhary Sonbol (Syracuse: Syracuse University Press, 1996), 191–201.

8. Rubin, *Ottoman Nizamiye Courts*, 9.

In addition to exploring law as practiced in the Ottoman Empire, a different but related line of inquiry helps explain how law was legitimized during the drafting process. In the 1990s scholars including Colin Imber, Haim Gerber, and Lawrence Rosen focused on the organization of the Ottoman judiciary and its complicated relationship between Sharia law and *Kanun*.[9] Our understanding of the early Hanafization process continues to be challenged by new contributions to the field. Scholars, such as Reem Meshal and Guy Burak, propose a more nuanced discursive law-making process in the sixteenth-century Ottoman Empire that should be understood in a comparative manner.[10] While new sets of codes were issued in the seventeenth and eighteenth centuries under the general title "*Kanunname-i Cedid*," more extensive codification efforts took place in the nineteenth century. The foci and rhetoric of the nineteenth-century codification movement was significantly different from earlier efforts—more extensive and seemingly organized according to the principle of division of powers. While these codes have been examined and often cited by scholars who study the nineteenth-century transformation of the empire in the footsteps of Roderic Davidson and Stanford and Ezel K. Shaw, works on the codification movement itself have been limited.[11] Instead, much of the attention has focused on the organizational transformation of the empire during the "so called" Tanzimat era—scholars debate the periodization of this reform era, Western ideological and diplomatic influences, transformation of the central bureaucracy, and resistance from the provinces. These works, however, lack a comprehensive analysis of legal transformation. Fortunately, as this volume attests, legal transformation is now the topic of a number of important recent works. It is now apparent that the reforms of the nineteenth century did not start in 1839 or 1856 as earlier scholars have argued. Instead, these reforms represent a continuum of legal codification movements that stood at the center of broader imperial transformation.[12] This transformation, particularly in the realm of law, did not necessarily mean secularization, but rather proceduralization.[13] In other words, the transformation

---

9. Gerber, *State, Society, and Law in Islam*; Colin Imber, *Ebu's-su'ud: the Islamic Legal Tradition* (Stanford: Stanford University Press, 1997); Rosen, *The Anthropology of Justice*.

10. Reem Meshal, "Antagonistic Sharias and the Construction of Orthodoxy in Sixteenth-Century Ottoman Cairo," *Journal of Islamic Studies* 21:2 (2010): 183–212; Guy Burak, *The Second Formation of Islamic Law: The Hanafi School in the Early Modern Ottoman Empire* (New York: Cambridge University Press, 2015).

11. Roderic H. Davidson, *Reform in the Ottoman Empire: 1856-1876* (Princeton: Princeton University Press, 1964); Stanford J. Shaw and Ezel K. Shaw, *History of the Ottoman Empire and Modern Turkey* (Cambridge: Cambridge University Press, 1976).

12. E. R. Toledano, "Social and Economic Change in the 'Long Nineteenth Century'," in *The Cambridge History of Egypt*, vol. 2, ed. M. W. Daly (Cambridge: Cambridge University Press, 1998), 252–84; Christine M. Philliou, *Biography of an Empire: Governing Ottomans in an Age of Revolution* (Berkeley: University of California Press, 2010).

13. For a good critique of the "secularization" narrative, see Avi Rubin, "Ottoman Judicial Change in the Age of Modernity: A Reappraisal," *History Compass* 7:1 (2009): 119-140. Also,

did not necessarily imply a moving away from *fiqh* or reducing the influence of Sharia courts in the nineteenth century, but the standardization, centralization, and rationalization of law, legality, and legitimization within the hands of the central state at an unprecedented level.

This edited volume consists of nine scholarly articles that represent the field of socio-legal history for Ottoman and Turkish studies. Six of the articles originate from the "embedded MESA workshop." The other three were added later through invitation and at large submissions to the *Journal of the Ottoman and Turkish Studies Association*. While the majority of the articles deal with the late Ottoman Empire and the early Turkish Republic (six out of the nine), three deal with socio-legal issues ranging from the sixteenth through eighteenth centuries. The articles are arranged chronologically in order to demonstrate the sweep and variety of socio-legal projects being carried out in Ottoman and Turkish Studies that intersect issues of property, gender, legal literacy, the demarcation of village boundaries, the codification of Islamic law, economic liberalism, crime and punishment, and refugee rights across the empire and the Aegean region of the Turkish Republic. At the heart of each of these articles is the complicated relationship between law, legality, and legitimization.

In the first chapter, Timothy J. Fitzgerald offers an assessment of the value of literacy (and literacy studies) for the study of law and state formation in the classical Ottoman Empire. It is especially concerned with how questions of literacy might help historians better understand popular or mass engagement with law and politics. It begins by closely surveying existing scholarship related to literacy in the Ottoman context. Fitzgerald then focuses on the Mamluk-Ottoman transition in the Arabic-speaking world, arguing that this deep-rooted period witnessed both expansion and qualitative transformation in the interconnection among law, legitimacy, and textuality. The Ottomans inherited a world in the sixteenth century that was soaked in scribal media, and it came bearing new subjects with high degrees of "legal literacy" in particular. Istanbul sought to reconfigure this world via legal reform and rituals of inscription, realities that both implied and extended access to written texts. Such change was slow, messy, and often resisted. The written did not come to preclude the oral, but trends toward mass document production, the appearance of law courts as "public archives," and the growth and diversification of literacy in an effort to harness the written word for one's own ends are evident. The article concludes by briefly examining how small pieces of evidence from Aleppo, might be studied for their literacy implications.

Hadi Hosainy, in Chapter 2 examines the role played by extra-judicial officers in the Sharia court of seventeenth-century Istanbul. Hosainy makes two central

---

see Ruth Miller, *Legislating Authority: Sin and Crime in the Ottoman Empire and Turkey* (New York: Routledge, 2005).

arguments: that the Ottoman Sharia courts of the period were not immune from the influence of extra-judicial actors even at the imperial capital where the highly centralized Ottoman *ilmiye* hierarchy was based; and that *sicil* studies can prove revealing about court procedures that deviated from conventional practice. Using a micro-level historical analysis, this article examines two court cases from 1666 and 1685 about transgressions against the property and life of two women in the small Bucakbağı neighborhood of Istanbul. Local officers such as the Yedikule fortress warden (*dizdar*) and the neighborhood imam as well as the highest imperial office holders such as the deputy grand vizier (*kaymakam*) and the *kadıasker* were involved in manipulating the court's proceedings in order to accommodate the interests of the men in power. The article, therefore, contributes to the revisionist scholarship challenging the view that early modern Ottoman Sharia courts enjoyed autonomy as a judicial body.

In Chapter 3, Michael Nizri examines four cases in which a need arose to define clearly the boundaries of properties belonging to the endowments of *Şeyhülislam* Feyzullah Efendi (1695-1703). The process of drawing village boundaries not only served the interests of the Ottoman government and the villagers, but also the interests of a land-owning class enabled by *mülk* grants. In response to the introduction of the *malikane* system at the end of the seventeenth century, high-ranking functionaries belonging to the old elites strived to secure rural income by attempting to convert public resources into private property. In this process, the preparation of the demarcation document (*hududname*) was very important. After receiving the official grant, which only mentioned the names of the *mülk* objects, the interested dignitary wanted to be certain of the boundaries of the defined properties, so that his rule over these properties would be full and unconditional. The article shows that, nevertheless, the state always retained ultimate ownership of the land.

In Chapter 4, M. Safa Saraçoğlu argues that intervention into market activity was a common administrative practice in the Ottoman Empire, particularly prior to the nineteenth century. This article focuses on the two key practices of market control, market inspection/inspectors (*ihtisab/muhtasib*) and the setting of price-ceilings (*narh*). A discussion of the basis for these practices in Islamic law is followed by an explanation of their gradual disappearance in the late eighteenth and early nineteenth centuries. Over the course of the nineteenth-century institutional transformation of the Ottoman Empire, a significant role in market control was delegated to the provincial administrative councils, which were commissioned with the task of overseeing economic activity in addition to maintaining a proper environment for the functioning of markets as spontaneous, natural mechanisms. The second half of the article examines this nineteenth-century transformation by analyzing a key 1849 regulation that established a new kind of provincial council (*eyalet meclisleri*) that took over the market related responsibilities of the *muhtasib*.

Kenneth Cuno, in Chapter 5, argues that historians have neglected the reorganization of the Sharia courts in nineteenth-century Egypt, a process that paralleled the reorganization of the Ottoman imperial Sharia court system, and which coincided with the introduction of secular law codes that reduced the jurisdiction of the Sharia courts mainly to family law. New regulations introduced a hierarchical court structure, detailed the qualifications of personnel and the manner of their appointment, set fees, and defined legal procedures. Judges were restricted to Hanafi jurisprudence, insuring greater uniformity in their rulings, and an emphasis on the production of and reliance upon legal documents all but required Ottomans and Egyptians to bring their affairs—especially their family affairs—to the Sharia courts. These regulations affected the substance of Muslim family law as applied, even though it was not codified until the twentieth century. Hanafi law put married women at a disadvantage when seeking to collect arrears of maintenance or to dissolve their marriage due to non-support, desertion, or a husband gone missing. The Ottomans mitigated these disadvantages by allowing the application of Shafi'i and Maliki law, which offered relief to women in these situations. However, in Egypt this was not done until the 1920s.

In Chapter 6, Nora Barakat examines the relationship between different district-level decision-making bodies in the late nineteenth-century Ottoman context. Using Sharia court records and property registers produced in the rural Syrian district of Salt as well as investigations from the district that reached Istanbul, it explores the roles and personnel of various courts and bureaucratic offices involved in allocating rights to landed property and settling disputes over land. Barakat aims to add nuance to recent characterizations of the late Ottoman legal system as pluralistic by exploring the complexities of litigant experience, particularly the practice of forum shopping. The author finds that while state-sanctioned forum shopping in the realm of property law in Salt was limited, litigants did benefit from the Sharia court's acceptance of debt claims to obtain official mention of mortgages contracted outside the property administration's purview on an extra-state land market. The article argues that this market constituted a challenge to the state's attempts to survey and tax every piece of land in the district rather than state-sanctioned legal pluralism. Forum shopping also occurred in a context of bureaucratic expansion, with litigants' experience of and participation in Ottoman governance becoming more intensive through practices of land surveying, registration, and taxation.

Samy Ayoub's article in Chapter 7 addresses one of the key debates in the field of Islamic legal studies concerning the transmutation of Islamic law into state law. Two arguments are advanced in this regard: (1) It is contended that the codification of Islamic law in the late nineteenth century was primarily justified in relation to the existing legal genres within the Hanafi school. The drafters of the *Mecelle* affirmed that it was inspired by the work of the Egyptian Hanafi jurist Zayn Ibn Nujaym (d. 970/1562-3); (2) It is proposed that the emergence of the *Me-*

celle should be understood, not in terms of an epistemic break from the premodern Islamic legal reasoning, but in terms of a continuation and transformation within the legal tradition. The *Mecelle* cannot exist without dependence upon and articulation with previously existing norms and legal literature. The *Mecelle* did not appear *ex nihilo*, as a legal framework alien and opposed to the existing legal literature and legal order, but necessarily emerged out of the existing legal genre of Hanafi legal maxims.

Kent F. Schull, in Chapter 8, investigates the transformation of criminal law, practice, and punishment within the late Ottoman Empire. This article focuses closely on five intertwined aspects of the empire's extensively restructured criminal justice system, namely the concrete links between new penal codes, the extensive delineation of crimes, the adoption of incarceration as the primary form of criminal punishment, incarceration rates for particular crimes, and the deployment of Islamic legal norms and mores to legitimate these reforms. Through the promulgation and then expansion of these new penal codes together with other aspects of its overhauled criminal justice system, the Ottoman administration gradually gained a monopoly over the adjudication of criminal matters. This effectively circumscribed the autonomy of local administrators and Islamic court judges in adjudicating criminal cases and meting out punishments, thus making the prison the primary site of criminal punishment within the empire.

Finally, in Chapter 9, Ellinor Morack studies the application of laws regulating the settlement and compensation of migrants who came to Turkey from Greece in the course of the population exchange. By using petitions and administrative documents, it discusses the questions of legality and legitimacy with regard to two problems: First, the status of exchangees as a group privileged by law, and second, the bureaucratic procedure through which they were given temporary property rights (*tefviz*). The article shows that laws can by no means be taken to be identical with their application, and that various notions of legality and legitimacy were at play, both in different state administrations and among those affected by their policies. It thus makes an important contribution to a better understanding of the relationship between law, state, and society in early Republican Turkey.

These articles collectively demonstrate the rich and vibrant research being done related to law, legality, and legitimacy in Ottoman and Turkish Studies grounded in a socio-legal historical approach.

KENT F. SCHULL is an Associate Professor in the Department of History at Binghamton University and is the editor of *The Journal of the Ottoman and Turkish Studies Association*.

M. SAFA SARAÇOĞLU is an Associate Professor in the Department of History at Bloomsburg University.

1 Reaching the Flocks

Literacy and the Mass Reception of Ottoman Law in the Sixteenth-Century Arab World[1]

Timothy J. Fitzgerald

> *C'est une étrange chose que l'écriture... Le seul phénomène qui l'ait fidèlement accompagnée est la formation des cités et des empires, c'est-à-dire l'intégration dans un système politique d'un nombre considérable d'individus et leur hiérarchisation en castes et en classes... Si mon hypothèse est exacte, il faut admettre que la fonction primaire de la communication écrite est de faciliter l'asservissement.*
>
> Claude Lévi-Strauss[2]

OVER THE PAST few decades, the study of Ottoman law has expanded in ways that defy brief summary. At root, many Ottoman legal historians have drawn inspiration from the concerns and questions prompted by the turn toward social history in the humanities at large. This, combined with more recent imperial and world-history turns, if dizzying, has meant relative boom times for interest in the Ottoman Empire and its legal culture(s) or system(s). One welcome result of all this attention has been the incremental counter-balancing of top-down, center-out type approaches to legal history with ones that highlight the determinative role played by ideas, institutions, and peoples beyond—sometimes far beyond—the imperial capital at Istanbul. Moreover, the interdisciplinary field of inquiry captured by the rubric "legal pluralism" has at last made serious inroads into Ottoman (and Islamic) legal studies, complicating our understanding of the legal

---

1. I would like to thank *JOTSA*'s anonymous reviewers. Their thorough and probing comments helped improve this piece and, as importantly, will inform a larger project I am undertaking related to this material.
2. Claude Lévi-Strauss, *Tristes Tropiques* (Paris: Librairie Plon, 1955), 342–44.

scene in beneficial ways and rendering the Ottoman Empire more intelligible to those analyzing law and politics elsewhere and undertaking comparative study.[3]

Despite having attained such critical mass, gaps and limits—some maintained by the inertia of venerated traditions in Ottoman studies, some shaped by the nature of available source material—leave plenty of work to do in grasping Ottoman law in the fullest sense. One key area of under-development involves accessing the meanings of law, legality, and legitimacy for most subjects of the empire: the literate, semi-literate, or illiterate masses, those typically consolidated, in the view of governing elites, according to their tax-paying identity as the empire's "flocks" (*reaya*). In fairness, the clarion call of social history to bring most people into view has been taken up by research using the voluminous Ottoman law court records, cadastral surveys, and documents produced by the varied petitioning processes employed across the empire. Such research has yielded visibility and agency to a great many living in and around Ottoman domains who might otherwise have never been known to posterity. Moreover, research has shown that while these many lowly persons were shaped by the institutions they engaged—their voices altered by those who represented them and by those who recorded their words and deeds—we also now know that their legal preferences, and the traffic they generated, conditioned law and politics in basic ways. Most would now accept that the law, in any Ottoman (or even Islamic) context, was not merely the byproduct of juristic determination or ruling fiat but an evolving constellation of structures and discourses that resulted from the complex interplay of many actors, state and non-state, elite and non-elite.

Still, one wonders: can more be done to understand what Ottoman law might have meant to the vast majority of people living with its daily consequences? How was law, or in its broader formulation "justice," consumed? And, in what ways might Ottoman lawmakers have recognized and responded to this mass audience? This paper proposes a few lines of approach to these questions by drawing upon a large body of research—under-exploited by Ottomanists—in literacy. After closely surveying the existing scholarship, the study will turn to the sixteenth-century conquest of the Mamluk Sultanate and the incorporation of much of the Arab world into the Ottoman Empire. The Mamluk-Ottoman transition was a moment of transformative expansion in terms of the interconnection among law, legitimacy, and textuality. It also represents an ideal setting in which to test the hermeneutic value of literacy as a lens on the period's central developments. The study will finish by briefly sampling how small pieces of historical evidence

---

3. For a recent intervention, see Karen Barkey, "Aspects of Legal Pluralism in the Ottoman Empire," in *Legal Pluralism and Empires, 1500–1850*, ed. Lauren Benton and Richard J. Ross (New York: New York University Press, 2013), 83–107; also, see Ido Shahar, "Legal Pluralism and the Study of Shari'a Courts," *Islamic Law and Society* 15:1 (2008): 112–41.

might carry unnoticed literacy implications. In case study fashion, special attention is paid to the experience of Aleppo and its inhabitants.

To be sure, there are other ways to examine mass sentiment and how it was perceived by those in authority without simply relying on the potentially idiosyncratic characterizations of elite commentators. Public architecture, visual art, and material culture are fruitful avenues, rarely taken with questions of law and order in mind. Communal action (support or resistance) can be studied from a variety of perspectives in a way that yields genuine insight into the identities of unnamed actors.[4] But "new literacy studies" hold special promise.[5] Questions of literacy nurture fresh thinking about the very sources with which historians, especially legal historians, presume a fair degree of familiarity. And in so doing, they present tantalizing opportunities to synthesize typically disparate areas of research.

Literacy has not been wholly neglected in Ottoman historiography. In the 1990s, two special issues of *Revue des mondes musulmans et de la Méditerranée* collected an impressive spread of research on orality, writing, reading, and book and manuscript cultures in the Ottoman Empire.[6] More recently, Benjamin Fortna has studied reading in the late empire as it related to changes in technol-

---

4. For example, see Antonis Anastasopoulos, ed., *Political Initiatives 'From the Bottom Up' in the Ottoman Empire* (Rethymno: Crete University Press, 2012); Eleni Gara, M. Erdem Kabadayı, and Christoph K. Neumann, eds., *Popular Protest and Political Participation in the Ottoman Empire* (Istanbul: Istanbul Bilgi University Press, 2011).

5. New literacy studies is a vast and variegated field, and not so "new" anymore, having engendered its own revisions and offshoots since emerging at the end of the twentieth century. The field is also entangled with equally sprawling areas variously labeled "history of the book," "history of written culture," and the "sociology of texts." In recent decades, these fields saw important development by anthropologists and French historians, though their influence has extended across many disciplines and areas of inquiry. In broad terms, research has challenged conventional binaries (literate vs. illiterate, written vs. oral, etc.) while emphasizing literacy practices, identity formation, and social power. For an introduction, see James Collins, "Literacy and Literacies," *Annual Review of Anthropology* 24 (1995): 75–93; Brian V. Street, ed., *Cross-Cultural Approaches to Literacy* (Cambridge: Cambridge University Press, 1993); Walter J. Ong, *Orality and Literacy*, new ed. (London: Routledge, 2002), first published in 1982; Alexis Weedon, ed., *The History of the Book in the West: A Library of Critical Essays*, 5 vols. (Farnham: Ashgate, 2010); David Finkelstein and Alistair McCleery, eds., *The Book History Reader*, 2nd ed. (London: Routledge, 2006); idem, *An Introduction to Book History* (London: Routledge, 2005); Guglielmo Cavallo and Roger Chartier, eds., *A History of Reading in the West*, trans. Lydia G. Cochrane (Amherst: University of Massachusetts Press, 2003); Roger Chartier, *Lectures et Lecteurs dans la France d'Ancien Régime* (Paris: Éditions du Seuil, 1987); Robert Darnton, *The Literary Underground of the Old Régime* (Cambridge: Harvard University Press, 1982); Jack Goody, *The Logic of Writing and the Organization of Society* (Cambridge: Cambridge University Press, 1986).

6. Frédéric Hitzel, ed., *Livres et lecture dans le monde ottoman*, in *Revue des mondes musulmans et de la Méditerranée* 87–88 (1999); Nicolas Vatin, ed., *Oral et écrit dans le monde turco-ottoman*, in *Revue des mondes musulmans et de la Méditerranée* 75–76 (1995).

ogy, education, and commerce, and to discourses of modernization and national identity formation.⁷ Nelly Hanna has undertaken pioneering work on literacy in pre-nineteenth-century Egypt, and Cairo in particular. Hanna has argued for literacy's variety, ubiquity, and social embeddedness. "Artisan literacy" developed in connection with elementary schooling, trade, Sufism, coffeehouses, and what she calls the "legalistic culture" cultivated by Ottoman law and bureaucracy.⁸ Dana Sajdi's fascinating examination of "nouveau literacy" proceeds in a similar vein. Sajdi submits that a critical mass of commoners in the early modern Levant, aspiring to greater social mobility, approximated the *'ulamā'*, appropriated the Arabic chronicle, and produced a distinctive kind of written text, something at once richly traditional and "entirely new."⁹ One should also note Brinkley Messick's work that—though not primarily concerned with bottom-up literacy—still represents some of the most rigorous and theoretically-informed research available on "textual domination," law, and authority in a Muslim-majority society, past or present.¹⁰

The work of Leslie Peirce and, more recently, Reem Meshal comes closest to the core concerns of this study (though neither gives much attention to literacy per se). Both authors have grappled with the causes and consequences of the classical Ottoman state's intensifying use of written records and related rituals of inscription as instruments of power. Peirce and Meshal have also explored how Ottoman subjects sought to manipulate writing for their own ends. In sixteenth-century Aintab, Peirce has observed that "inscription [such as that resulting from a cadastral survey] was an act of possession" that "archived" and "immobilized" subject populations in ways that often engendered resistance, renegotiation, and even textual "reconquest" (another cadastral survey).¹¹ In such an environment, individuals—even the technically illiterate—wielded to the extent possible written records to buttress an immense variety of legal claims; they further came to understand the prevailing "hierarchy of documents," where some records had more authority and influence than others. While the importance of orality did

---

7. Benjamin C. Fortna, *Learning to Read in the Late Ottoman Empire and the Early Turkish Republic* (Basingstoke: Palgrave Macmillan, 2011).

8. Nelly Hanna, "Literacy Among Artisans and Tradesmen in Ottoman Cairo," in *The Ottoman World*, ed. Christine Woodhead (Abingdon: Routledge, 2012); idem, "Literacy and the 'Great Divide' in the Islamic World, 1300–1800," *Journal of Global History* 2 (2007): 175–93; idem, *In Praise of Books: A Cultural History of Cairo's Middle Class, Sixteenth to the Eighteenth Century* (Syracuse: Syracuse University Press, 2003).

9. Dana Sajdi, *The Barber of Damascus: Nouveau Literacy in the Eighteenth-Century Ottoman Levant* (Stanford: Stanford University Press, 2013).

10. Brinkley Messick, *The Calligraphic State: Textual Domination and History in a Muslim Society* (Berkeley: University of California Press, 1993).

11. Leslie Peirce, *Morality Tales: Law and Gender in the Ottoman Court of Aintab* (Berkeley: University of California Press, 2003), 279–81.

not disappear in law and politics, those with direct control over the written word accrued increasing social power.[12] In examining Cairo, Meshal has similarly emphasized a profound shift in Ottoman attitudes and compulsory practices that resulted in the "mass production" of legal documents and their innovative association with the courthouse or "public archive"—perhaps the first in Islamic history, she submits.[13] For Meshal, these transformations resonated with others: the early modern expansion of the state, the redefinition of the public and private spheres, and the drift from subject to "proto-citizen."[14]

But, given the extent and diversity of Ottoman history, one is struck by how partial such coverage is. Ottoman literacy studies, thin to begin with, largely remain tethered to interest in how the Middle East might or might not have gained access to modernity through the (belated) appearance of print capitalism, reforms in mass education, and the emergence of a Western-style reading public.[15] Beyond this, the focus has been on new or newly-discovered forms of cultural production: unexpected authors and modes of self-expression. Accordingly, attention has gravitated to the "history of the book" in a limited sense.[16] Such work,

12. Ibid., 282–84.
13. Reem Meshal, *Sharia and the Making of the Modern Egyptian: Islamic Law and Custom in the Courts of Ottoman Cairo* (Cairo: American University in Cairo Press, 2014), 103–39.
14. Ibid., 125–39, passim.
15. For a provocative challenge to the conventional wisdom on the impact of print in Islamic/Ottoman history, see Dana Sajdi, "Print and Its Discontents: A Case for Pre-Print Journalism and Other Sundry Print Matters," *The Translator* 15:1 (2009): 105–38; idem, *The Barber of Damascus*, 205–12. Also, see Orlin Sabev's (Orhan Salih) measured and sifting assessment, "A Virgin Deserving Paradise or a Whore Deserving Poison: Manuscript Tradition and Printed Books in Ottoman Turkish Society," in *Friars, Nobles and Burghers—Sermons, Images and Prints: Studies of Culture and Society in Early-Modern Europe, In Memorium István György Tóth*, ed. Jaroslav Miller and László Kontler (Budapest: Central European University Press, 2010), 389–409. For an alternative formulation of the significance of "paper without print" (and a response to the search for nascent "public spheres" in the non-West), see Rosalind O'Hanlon, "Performance in a World of Paper: Puranic Histories and Social Communication in Early Modern India," *Past and Present* 219:1 (2013): 87–126. In a similar vein, Nile Green has argued that the period of "print absence" in India was in part related to the "conceptual location of knowledge in authoritative persons" (e.g., Sufis) with whom any text needed to be associated to have meaning; in other words, "books were considered less as independent sources of knowledge than as appendages to the personal pedagogical relationships through which knowledge was transferred and within which writing served to provide only one dimension of the knowledge being transferred," *Making Space: Sufis and Settlers in Early Modern India* (New Delhi: Oxford University Press, 2012), 201, 203.
16. See George N. Atiyeh, ed., *The Book in the Islamic World: The Written Word and Communication in the Middle East* (Albany: State University of New York Press, 1995), a foundational collection of essays little concerned with literacy as such. This quality (along with a heavy interest in printing) is reflected in a more recent volume of reprints assembled by Geoffrey Roper, ed., *The History of the Book in the Middle East* (Farnham: Ashgate, 2013). Also, see Alper Çeker, ed., *Türk Kitap Medeniyeti: Turkish Book Civilization* (Istanbul: Kultur, 2008),

while vital, is often bedeviled by questions of representativeness. Whose literacy, by any understanding, is at issue? Most peoples'? A certain class's? An outlying vanguard's? Or rearguard's? A few remarkable individuals'? What, if any, larger social, cultural, and political changes are afoot? And how can these be measured and soundly characterized? This is why it is important to simultaneously explore many kinds of literacy, involve many kinds of evidence, and to think more intently about both authorship *and* audience, about both the production *and* consumption of the written word—recalling that nearly always many more could read than could write.[17] Lastly, following Peirce and Meshal, a role for the state and imperial politics must be brought into the picture more fully, an endeavor that not only adds a critical dimension to literacy studies but also promises to give the approach wider resonance. A first step is to direct our attention deeper into the Ottoman, even pre-Ottoman, past. A second step is to reevaluate the evidence for its literacy implications. Nelly Hanna has done the most work along these lines, but her agenda could be stretched further in time and space and connected to different topics like political legitimacy and state formation. This paper undertakes such a preliminary investigation by re-examining the Ottoman conquest of Mamluk lands.

Texts, Text Producers, and Legal Literacy: The Mamluk Background

Though a robust field in its own right, the history of the Mamluk Sultanate has yet to be given its due by Ottoman historians. While the conservative nature of Ottoman "methods of conquest" is a well-established dogma in the field, suggesting a profound need to examine what came before, scholars have generally followed the Ottomans' own dismissive rhetoric about a long-declining, corrupt, and generally ineffective Mamluk state based in Cairo. Disinterest has extended to Mamluk society and culture. Yet scholars of Ottoman-Arab history and of Ottoman law stand to learn much from the Mamluks, and the vigorous field of Mamluk studies.[18]

---

and the articles collected under the heading "Libraries and Books in the Ottoman Empire" in *The Great Ottoman-Turkish Civilisation*, vol. 4, *Culture and Arts*, ed. Kemal Çiçek (Ankara: Yeni Türkiye, 2000), 867–903.

17. It is striking that Sajdi, for example, claims she is not charting a rise in literacy as much as a "rise in authority in new social groups;" moreover, one of her study's "main points" is to "dissociate book authorship from technical literacy," *The Barber of Damascus*, 9.

18. Recent work by Guy Burak and Cihan Yüksel Muslu suggest an exciting and broad-based challenge to the status quo might be afoot. Burak has attempted to place well-known Ottoman legal developments (e.g., *kanun* and the elevation of the Hanafi *madhhab*) in deep-rooted pre-Ottoman (often Mamluk) contexts, see his "Between the *Kānūn* of Qāytbāy and Ottoman *Yasaq*: A Note on the Ottomans' Dynastic Law," *Journal of Islamic Studies* 26:1 (2015): 1–23; idem, *The Second Formation of Islamic Law: The Hanafi School in the Early Modern Ottoman Empire* (Cambridge: Cambridhe University Press, 2015). Muslu has undertaken

By all indications, the late Mamluk world that the Ottomans would inherit was one soaked in written texts—be they religious, literary, epistolary, governmental, commercial, and/or legal. This reality does not surprise medievalists who have debated how far back in time to push a shift in mentalities, technologies, and politics that favored the expansion of scribal media and reading in the core areas of the Islamic world.[19] Konrad Hirschler has concluded that "the two interrelated developments of textualisation and popularisation thus profoundly transformed cultural practices linked to the production, transmission and reception of texts in Egypt and Syria over the Middle Period," as traders, craftsmen, and others chipped away at the scholarly elite's "near monopoly" on the written word.[20] Of particular interest to early-modernists is the presence of document types from the Mamluk period sometimes thought to be unique, or at least uniquely-abundant, under the Ottomans—for example, endowment deeds, tax registers, military land grants, and law court records.[21] Study of these documents supports the aggregate impression that much was at stake, for many different kinds of people, in the production and consumption of written records. Some have seen in these developments, for Islamic societies and others around the world, a rise in "pragmatic literacy."[22]

---

pioneering study of Mamluk-Ottoman relations using both Arabic and Ottoman sources and reaching well before the events of the early sixteenth century, see her *The Ottomans and the Mamluks: Imperial Diplomacy and Warfare in the Islamic World* (London: I.B. Tauris, 2014).

19. Konrad Hirschler, *The Written Word in the Medieval Arabic Lands: A Social and Cultural History of Reading Practices* (Edinburgh: Edinburgh University Press, 2012); Gregor Schoeler, *The Genesis of Literature in Islam: From the Aural to the Read*, ed. and trans. Shawkat Toorawa, revised ed. (Edinburgh: Edinburgh University Press, 2009); Adrian Gully, *The Culture of Letter-Writing in Pre-modern Islamic Society* (Edinburgh: Edinburgh University Press, 2008); Shawkat Toorawa, *Ibn Abī Ṭāhir Ṭayfūr and Arabic Writerly Culture: A Ninth-Century Bookman in Baghdad* (London: Routledge, 2005); Jonathan Bloom, *Paper Before Print: The History and the Impact of Paper in the Islamic World* (New Haven: Yale University Press, 2001). Also, see Ghislaine Lydon, "A Thirst for Knowledge: Arabic Literacy, Writing Paper, and Saharan Bibliophiles in the Southwestern Sahara," in *The Trans-Saharan Book Trade: Manuscript Culture, Arabic Literacy and Intellectual History in Muslim Africa*, ed. Graziano Krätli and Ghislaine Lydon (Leiden: Brill, 2011), 35–72.

20. Hirschler, *The Written Word*, 197, 200.

21. For an introduction to this wide world, see Christian Müller, *Der Kadi und seine Zeugen: Studie der mamlukischen Haram-Dokumente aus Jerusalem* (Wiesbaden: Harrassowitz, 2013); Lucian Reinfandt, "Mamlūk Documentary Studies," in *Ubi Sumus? Quo Vademus? Mamluk Studies: State of the Art*, ed. Stephan Conermann (Goettingen: Vandenhoeck & Ruprecht, 2013): 285–309; Frédéric Bauden, "Mamluk Era Documentary Studies: The State of the Art," *Mamluk Studies Review* 9:1 (2005): 15–60.

22. Richard Britnell, "Pragmatic Literacy Beyond Latin Christendom," in *Pragmatic Literacy, East and West: 1200–1330*, ed. Richard Britnell (Woodbridge: Boydell Press, 1997), 167–88—other chapters in this volume will be of comparative interest, too. The study of literacy and its expansion in connection with law and government runs deep in European history; for example, see Rosamond McKitterick, ed., *The Uses of Literacy in Early Medieval Europe* (Cam-

A look at the late Mamluk legal scene is especially revealing. That the Mamluks supported, in major cities, judges of the four predominant Sunni legal communities (*madhhabs*) is well-known. This arrangement not only multiplied the production of legal texts, but the encouraged forum-shopping cultivated the spread of "legal literacy," which I imagine to be a form of knowledge that combines access to the meanings of written texts with a complex awareness of distinctions in legal principles, procedures, and outcomes. This kind of literacy is attested to, as it is under the Ottomans, by the variety of people interacting with the legal system (and the textual evidence left by such interaction). But the late Mamluk legal system was more diffuse still as Circassian *amīr*s, chamberlains (*ḥājib*s), and other *siyāsa*-practitioners further multiplied options for conflict resolution, to the extent that they drew criticism for treading upon the jurisdictions of judicial regulars (like judges, jurisconsults, and market inspectors).[23] While such a diffusion of justice is usually (mis)perceived as a straightforward symptom of Mamluk chaos and decline, a result of this scene must have been the intensification of "textual domination," which in turn implies a diffusion of forms of literacy among a wider public forced to cope with such legal complexity and uncertainty. The vibrant endowment (waqf) scene that cut across all levels of society, for example, was in part motivated by interest in securing assets in an environment where confiscations and special exactions were not uncommon.[24] It is worth noting that the late Mamluk regime was not exactly content to see textual domination extend as far as it did. Sultans repeatedly attempted to rein in legal affairs by restricting the number of judges and deputy judges and by regulating their activities.[25] Such initiatives presage similar steps taken by Ottoman governing agents in the immediate post-conquest years.

Let me make this a bit more concrete by focusing briefly on those who actually produced (and consumed) legal documents. Professional scribes, witnesses, and notaries were among judges' most important auxiliaries. Though representing the lower rungs of the judicial hierarchy, these text producers acted as gatekeepers to the world of inscribed law vis-á-vis the broader public. Wit-

---

bridge: Cambridge University Press, 1990) and *idem*, *The Carolingians and the Written Word* (Cambridge: Cambridge University Press, 1989).

23. Yossef Rapoport, "Royal Justice and Religious Law: *Siyāsah* and Shari`ah under the Mamluks," *Mamluk Studies Review* 16 (2012): 71–102; Robert Irwin, "The Privatization of 'Justice' Under the Circassian Mamluks," *Mamluk Studies Review* 6 (2002): 63–70.

24. Ira Lapidus, *Muslim Cities in the Later Middle Ages* (Cambridge: Cambridge University Press, 1967), 77; Toru Miura, "Administrative Networks in the Mamlūk Period: Taxation, Legal Execution, and Bribery," in *Islamic Urbanism in Human History: Political Power and Social Networks*, ed. Sato Tsugitaka (London: Routledge, 1997), 62–3.

25. `Alī al-Jawharī ibn al-Sayrafī, *Nuzhat al-nufūs wa al-abdān fī tawārīkh al-zamān*, ed. Hasan al-Habashī (Cairo, 1970–1994), 3:239–40; Muhammad b. Ahmad ibn Iyās, *Badā'i` al-zuhūr fī waqā'i` al-duhūr*, ed. Muhammad Mustafā, 2nd ed. (Cairo, 1960–1992), 3:259.

nesses or notaries (*shuhūd, 'udūl, shurūtīs*) were especially important because they combined in their functional identities the twin imperatives of attesting to and inscribing legal testimony. By the fourteenth and fifteenth centuries, being a *shāhid* was a widespread and deeply-rooted vocation.[26] For many, having one's *'adāla*—rectitude and, concomitantly, capacity to serve as an official witness—certified and documented was a rite of passage, setting one on the path of a career in law and learning. When not directly assisting a judge, witnesses were busy drawing up legal documents and signing or certifying them at their stalls (*hawānīt, dakākīn*) and benches (*masātib*) for a fee.[27] That these individuals were many in number and operated with considerable influence and independence is attested to by their frequent appearance in contemporary biographical literature, the salience of notary-manuals (*kutub al-shurūt*) as a genre of Mamluk legal literature,[28] the common injunction in judges' appointment documents that they regulate witnesses tightly,[29] and by episodic regime intervention to severely punish miscreant *shuhūd*. Ibn Khaldūn, who served as Cairo's Maliki chief judge in the early Circassian period, recorded his energetic attempts to reform the wayward notaries under his watch.[30] Ibn Iyās pointed to their significance and organization in noting a leader of witnesses (*ra'īs al-shuhūd*).[31]

These late Mamluk scribes/notaries/witnesses were nodes of literacy—legal literacy in particular, but not only. They produced written documents in great quantity and variety that met the demands of a complex society. Indeed the texts they handled attained such importance that there was considerable incentive to forge and otherwise abuse them, hence the many protections against document

---

26. Muhammad Amīn, "Al-Shāhid al-'adl fī'l al-qadā' al-islāmī: dirāsa tārīkhiyya ma' nashr wa tahqīq isjāl 'adāla min 'asr salātīn al-mamālīk," *Annales Islamologiques* 18 (1982): 1–20; Emile Tyan, *Le Notariat et le régime de la preuve par écrit dans la pratique du droit musulman* (Beirut, 1945); Müller, *Der Kadi un seine Zeugen*, 280–319, passim. Meshal refers to witnesses in this period as "[fusing] speaking and writing," *Sharia and the Making of the Modern Egyptian*, 121ff.

27. For example, Ibn al-Sayrafī, *Inbā' al-hasr bi-abnā' al-'asr*, ed. Hasan Habashī (Cairo, 1970), 306, 450; Shams al-Dīn Muhammad al-Sakhāwī, *al-Daw' al-lāmi' li-ahl al-qarn al-tāsi'* (Beirut, 1992), vol. 1, pt. 2, 310; vol. 2, pt. 3, 92; vol. 4, pt. 7, 2.

28. Wael B. Hallaq, "Model *Shurūt* Works and the Dialectic of Doctrine and Practice," *Islamic Law and Society* 2:2 (1995): 109–34. Hallaq underscores the importance of witness-notaries: "It was no doubt the *faqīh*-cum-*shurūtī* who ran the world of documents and documentary evidence in the *qādī*'s court, in particular, and in society at large" (115).

29. Ahmad b. 'Alī al-Qalqashandī, *Subh al-a'shā fī sinā'at al-inshā* (Cairo, 1964), vol. 11, 186, 192–3, esp. 197, 413; vol. 12, esp. 47–8, 52; vol. 14, 341, 343, 345.

30. Ibn Iyās, *Badā'i' al-zuhūr*, vol. 1, pt. 2, 522; Morimoto Kosei, "What Ibn Khaldun Saw: The Judiciary of Mamluk Egypt," *Mamluk Studies Review* 6 (2002): 109–31, esp. 112–15.

31. Ibn Iyās, *Badā'i' al-zuhūr*, 3:443.

manipulation indicated in notary-manuals such as al-Asyūṭī's *Jawāhir al-'Uqūd*.³² But the literacy implications of Mamluk documentary culture are not limited to the legal sphere. A splendid illustration of such wider significance involves the journal, *al-Ta'līq*, produced by the late fifteenth- early sixteenth-century Damascene Ibn Ṭawq, a Shāfi'i scribe and notary of modest social standing.³³ Here is someone at the very edge of the Islamic legal universe who, inspired by the traditional Arabic chronicle, found a voice in producing a rich and extensive personal diary.³⁴ The diary makes plain the transferability of affiliations and abilities from one sphere to another. At the same time, it appears literacy was not of one kind even for a single person, pointing to the artificialness of the categories and typologies often employed to understand the phenomenon. Moreover, Ibn Ṭawq's work of *yawmiyyāt*, if only one case, attests to how literacy and the world of law might combine to give access to the hearts and minds of the common folk.

Assessing the Ottoman Evidence: Textual Domination, Archives, Language

The Ottomans, then, did not come to govern virgin lands beginning in 1516–17. The Arabic-speaking world of the former Mamluk Sultanate was thoroughly steeped in written records, especially those of a legal nature. The legalistic culture and "*Schriftlichkeit*"³⁵ now associated with the spread of literacy in the Ottoman period were in great part inherited, as were the attendant literacies. The process of constructing and legitimating the Ottomans' own "textual polity," pace Messick, would not be about creation *ex nihilo* but about refashioning, even winnowing, the mass of accumulated tradition and inscribed material now within Istanbul's purview. To be sure, fundamental importance was assigned to elaborating lofty political ideologies, and to gaining control over newly available revenues, resources, and communication networks. But such priorities proved inseparable from dominating the world of texts, including numerous text producers and even

---

32. Muhammad b. Ahmad al-Asyūṭī, *Jawāhir al-'uqūd wa mu'īn al-qudāh wa'l-muwaqqi'īn wa al-shuhūd*, ed. Mas'ad 'Abd al-Hamīd Muhammad al-Sa'danī (Beirut, 1996), 1:16; cf. M. T. Clanchy, *From Memory to Written Record: England 1066–1307*, 2nd ed. (Oxford: Wiley-Blackwell, 1993), 318–27, where he argues forgers "are best understood not as occasional deviants on the peripheries of legal practice, but as experts entrenched at the centre of literary and intellectual culture" (319).

33. Ahmad b. Muhammad Ibn Ṭawq, *Al-Ta'līq*, 4 vols., ed. Ja'far al-Muhājir (Damascus: Institut Français de Damas, 2000–); Torsten Wollina, "Ibn Ṭawq's *Ta'līq*: An Ego-Document for Mamluk Studies," in *Ubi Sumus? Quo Vademus? Mamluk Studies*, 337–62.

34. Dana Sajdi, in dutifully tracing the genealogy of her eighteenth-century "nouveau literates," notes Ibn Ṭawq's journal as "perhaps the earliest (extant) manifestation of a nonscholarly diary," *The Barber of Damascus*, 126.

35. Müller, *Der Kadi und seine Zeugen*, 502.

more numerous text consumers. Documents, in other words, were essential to empire-building.[36]

That the Ottomans sought to concentrate legal authority and activity in the hands of Hanafi judges dispatched throughout the empire has long been accepted as a pillar of Istanbul's legal-imperial policy. We now view this impulse more complexly given recent interest in legal pluralism, informal (extra-judicial) dispute resolution, and findings that many others (e.g., governors) remained heavily involved in activities sometimes thought to be monopolized by judges. But a basic concern to focus and streamline legal activity on the part of the Ottomans has withstood such revisions. This concern appears even more starkly in the sixteenth-century Arab world where it was set against the diffusion of justice that had evolved under the Mamluks. Such a concern did not always translate into smooth institution-building, as efforts to arrange judges, law courts, and legal fees in early Ottoman Cairo make clear.[37] Ottomanization, by any understanding, took time. An under-appreciated piece of the Ottomans' post-conquest reforms was the closure of witnesses/notaries' places of work in newly-annexed cities. Though sometimes mentioned in passing as evidence of Ottoman interest in empowering judges and in transferring notarial business to their courts, the implications of this move were wider still. Recall the robust presence of professional witnesses and notaries in late Mamluk society. Ending their independent activity meant a rupture in legal access for many subjects of empire. It meant Ottoman law courts would need to absorb a massive workload pertaining to mundane legal matters that was no longer subcontracted. It meant the many notaries and witnesses of the former Mamluk state would need to find employment and recast their identities.[38] And it suggested, in a basic way, the validity and authority of pre-Ottoman legal documents were in question.

Ottoman initiatives cascaded as changes presented challenges that shaped the need for further adaptation. Thus, despite the well-rehearsed nature of the

---

36. For a look at this dynamic in the contemporary Spanish Empire, which holds many intriguing resonances with the Ottoman experience, see Sylvia Sellers-García, *Distance and Documents at the Spanish Empire's Periphery* (Stanford: Stanford University Press, 2014).

37. Annemarie Schimmel, "Kalif und Kadi im spätmittelalterlichen Ägypten," *Die Welt des Islams* 24 (1942): 1–128, esp. 84–93; Abdul-Karim Rafeq, "The Opposition of the Azhar 'Ulamā' to Ottoman Laws and Its Significance in the History of Ottoman Egypt," in *Etudes sur les villes du Proche-Orient, XVIe-XIXe Siècle: Hommage á André Raymond*, ed. Brigitte Marino (Damascus: Institut français du Proche-orient, 2001), 43–54.

38. To cite one example, ʿAlī b. Hasan al-Sarmīnī (d. 1523), who drafted legal documents at a stall near Aleppo's "hall of justice" (*dār al-ʿadl*) under the Circassians, began producing copies of the Quran and teaching children at a school near Bāb Antākiyya once the Ottomans closed witnesses' shops—Najm al-Dīn Muhammad al-Ghazzī, *Kawākib al-sāʾira bi-aʿyān al-miʾa al-ʿāshira*, ed. Jirbrāʾil Sulaymān Jabbūr (Damascus, 1979), 1:268–9. One wonders if, upon closer study, the reabsorption of such individuals will always appear so seamless.

Ottoman conquest ritual, governance in the Arabic-speaking world exhibited an ad hoc and experimental quality, especially in the first several decades. Importantly, much of this process played out in the world of legal texts. Ottoman law codes articulated the evolving substance of *kanun* while in their very form revealing that the extension of state power would be felt in writing, as the inscription (or codification) of law. While sultanic law codes existed before the Ottomans, one should pause to recognize this basic way in which Istanbul raised the stakes of legal literacy in the core areas of the Middle East. Negotiation over the applicability of various taxes, for example, would take place not just between regime agents and local representatives, but intertextually, hence the need to reissue law codes as events unfolded. The first provincial codes for Aleppo reveal different stages of a protracted back-and-forth over the application of the tithe (*'öşür*) tax to endowed and freehold properties.[39] The widespread uproar stirred by the bridal tax (*resm-i 'arūs*) was not just due to the financial burden imposed but to the unprecedented requirement that marriages be validated in writing, at the permission (*isti'dhān*) of the Hanafi judge, and in full cognizance of the state.[40] These developments made their way into coordinate texts and genres, such as Arabic chronicles, biographical dictionaries, and poetry, revealing how far flux in the world of law pervaded popular consciousness. For many, writing signified government attempts at control and extraction. Literacy was needed to resist the written word.

The study of literacy reminds us to be as concerned with the act of recording and the handling of records as with the literal meaning of the records themselves. Recent observers, seeking to explain the abundance of Ottoman law court records while accepting their substantial pre-Ottoman lineage, have suggested that the Ottomans shaped their judges' written output into a "public" record, or, "dictated that the *diwan*s should be deposited in the public domain."[41] But to call these documents "public" does not do enough to differentiate their management (or the nature of access to them) from what came before. A more useful

---

39. Ahmed Akgündüz, *Osmanlı Kanunnâmeleri ve Hukukî Tahlilleri* (Istanbul: Osmanlı Araştırmaları Vakfı, 1990–1994), 5:649/655, 651/656, 660/662.

40. Radī al-Dīn Muhammad b. Ibrāhīm b. al-Hanbalī, *Durr al-habab fī ta'rīkh a'yān Halab*, ed. Mahmūd Ahmad al-Fākhūrī and Yahyā Zakariyā 'Abbāra (Damascus, 1972–1974), vol. 1, pt. 2, 649–50. Also, see Abdul-Karim Rafeq, "The Syrian 'Ulamā', Ottoman Law, and Islamic Sharī'a," *Turcica* 26 (1994): 9–32; Nelly Hanna, "The Administration of Courts in Ottoman Cairo," in *The State and Its Servants: Administration in Egypt from Ottoman Times to the Present*, ed. Nelly Hanna (Cairo: American University in Cairo Press, 1995), 46–7.

41. Leslie Peirce, "A New Judge for Aintab: The Shifting Legal Environment of a Sixteenth-century Ottoman Court," in *Dispensing Justice in Islam: Qadis and Their Judgments*, ed. Muhammad Khalid Masud, Rudolph Peters, and David S. Powers (Leiden: Brill, 2006), 72; Wael B. Hallaq, "The Qāḍī's Dīwān (Sijill) before the Ottomans," *Bulletin of the School of Oriental and African Studies* 61:3 (1998): 435.

concept, and one that finds much casual use among legal historians, is "archive." The term should carry meanings of 1) the aggregation of regime agents' (e.g., judges') documentary output; 2) the physical space where these documents were maintained; 3) the norms and practices governing the preservation of and access to these documents; and 4) the politicized assertion of control over the menu of text-dependent legal instruments used by an ascendant state's subjects and the creation of related knowledge.[42] It appears the Ottomans came to conceive of archives, especially judicial archives, in this four-dimensional manner, which itself appears derivative of Ottoman "kanun-consciousness." Halil İnalcık has observed that, in cases leaning on unspecified aspects of customary law (*'örf*), judges were to seek Istanbul's direction, rule according to imperial orders, and then make a written record of their decisions in court record books (*sicils*) so that such decisions could function as legal precedent—and thus, judges were further ordered to not take their *sicils* once dismissed from office.[43] Under the Ottomans, a judge's *dīwān* became less his private judicial archive to be copied and transferred in some part (*tasallum*) to a successor and more the ever-accumulating corpus of regime-regulated (public) legal records to which individual judges (and others) both referred and added while in office. This transformation appears linked to inertia in favor of fixing places of adjudication, "courthouses."[44] However, while it is tempting to identify a Weberian impersonalization of judicial office in this process of archive-building, one should not push the observation too far, especially in places where Ottoman government was still settling. Judges did not function mechanistically. As Najwa al-Qattan has argued, they remained "interpreters, keepers, and archivists of the law," performing these tasks with

---

42. For a searching study of the concept of "archive" in the Ottoman context, see Meshal, *Sharia and the Making of the Modern Egyptian*, 105, 111–14, 125ff. The fourth dimension noted is especially important and one Ottomanists have been slow to perceive; it involves examining the archives as a historically contingent subject, and not only as a source of information. The work of Ann Laura Stoler is vital in this regard—see her *Along the Archival Grain: Epistemic Anxieties and Colonial Common Sense* (Princeton: Princeton University Press, 2009); idem, "Colonial Archives and the Arts of Governance," *Archival Science* 2 (2002): 87–109. For rich material on archival practices (state, village, family, and merchant) from around the premodern world, see *Redefining the Archives History: Multilateral Comparative Study on Archives during the Medieval and Early Modern Period* (Tokyo: National Institute of Japanese Literature, 2010).

43. Halil İnalcık, "Suleiman the Lawgiver and Ottoman Law," *Archivum Ottomanicum* 1 (1969), 117; cf. the procedure set down in Silistre's *kānūnnāme* in Ömer Lutfi Barkan, *XV ve XVI Asırlarda Osmanlı İmparatorluğunda Ziraî Ekonominin Hukukî ve Malî Esasları* (Istanbul: Bürhaneddin Matbaası, 1943), 1:276.

44. Nelly Hanna, "The Administration of Courts in Ottoman Cairo," 46; H. İnalcık, s.v. "Mahkama," *EI*[2]; Meshal, *Sharia and the Making of the Modern Egyptian*, 111–14.

both predictability and idiosyncrasy.⁴⁵ There was, moreover, considerable variation across space and time. Efforts to control and reform the production of legal records continued through the nineteenth century, reflecting an ongoing process of negotiation among central and local interests.⁴⁶ Even in the late empire, it is not always clear where a judge performed his duties.⁴⁷

Boğaç Ergene has entered this conversation with the important suggestion that for all their abundance, written records had limited use as evidence in actual court litigation where oral testimony held primacy.⁴⁸ Yet one wonders if this is to underestimate the potency of legal documents as instruments of social power not just within but outside the court. The prevalence of cases bearing on public morality underlines the probability that interaction with the court was a performative ritual, and written records created "facts," as Leslie Peirce would have it, that affected social relations in the present and for all posterity.⁴⁹ Moreover, one should not expect the written to preclude the oral. Even in societies with a deep literate tradition, the shift toward a pervasive documentary culture and practical literacy took time and was characterized by a nagging mistrust of the written word.⁵⁰

---

45. Najwa al-Qattan, "Inside the Ottoman Courthouse: Territorial Law at the Intersection of State and Religion," in *The Early Modern Ottomans: Remapping the Empire*, ed. Virginia H. Aksan and Daniel Goffman (Cambridge: Cambridge University Press, 2007), 201–12.

46. Iris Agmon, "Record Procedures and Legal Culture in the Late Ottoman Shari'a Court of Jaffa, 1865–1890," *Islamic Law and Society* 11:3 (2004): 333–77; Brigitte Marino, "Les Correspondances (*murāsalāt*) adressées par le juge de Damas à ses substituts (1750–1860)," in *Études sur les villes du Proche-Orient, XVIe-XIXe siècle*, 99; cf. the shifting archival practices and evolving role of *escribanos* in the Spanish Empire, Sellers-García, *Distance and Documents*, 141–83.

47. Iris Agmon has argued that the Ottoman government's control over pre-Tanzimat law courts was "loose," leaving them to be economically "self-sufficient" and comparatively independent. Judges, she claims (*contra* Weber), continued to personify their courts. Agmon adds that these circumstances are reflected in the absence of information about a court's specific location in its records, thus "in spite of the profound institutionalization the *shari'a* court underwent during the Tanzimat, it did not become identified with a location or with a structure built according to a specific style that would symbolize its authority," *Family and Court: Legal Culture and Modernity in Late Ottoman Palestine* (Syracuse: Syracuse University Press, 2006), 69.

48. Boğaç Ergene, "Evidence in Ottoman Courts: Oral and Written Documentation in Early-Modern Courts of Islamic Law," *Journal of the American Oriental Society* 124:3 (2004): 471–91.

49. Peirce, *Morality Tales*, 88–9. For a similar argument made with regard to late medieval Marseille, see Daniel Lord Smail, *The Consumption of Justice: Emotions, Publicity, and Legal Culture in Marseille, 1264–1423* (Ithaca: Cornell University Press, 2003).

50. Clanchy, *From Memory to Written Record*, 294ff., passim; Ong, *Orality and Literacy*, 95ff., 113–15, 171–72; Hirschler, *The Written Word*, 197. To appreciate the durability of orality in Islamic legal cultures, one should also recall the commingling of oral and inscribed practices in the transmission of knowledge—Messick, *The Calligraphic State*, 75ff.; Seyyed Hossein Nasr, "Oral Transmission and the Book in Islamic Education: The Spoken and the Written Word,"

The earliest extant Ottoman law court records in the Arab world show something of this archive-making process, especially in Aleppo where I have studied the records most closely. A look at these less regularized records also yields insight into prevailing kinds of literacy. It should first be noted that Aleppo's earliest records (from the 1540s) post-date Ottoman conquest by nearly three decades, suggesting a drive to secure archives and recordkeeping practices took time even in areas set out for tight control.[51] The earliest content includes imperial commands (*awāmir*) regarding tax collection and the imprisonment of deviants and an expected range of court cases emphasizing financial matters like debt collection and estate distribution.[52] Also included are a few late Mamluk waqf deeds,[53] indicating the process of pre-conquest document authentication stretched on for many years, and perhaps revealing how hesitant some Aleppines were to turn over their financial records.

One striking feature of these early documents is that a single folio could contain entries in Arabic and Ottoman produced by multiple hands, without an obvious pattern. With most of the material in Arabic, the appearance of certain entries in Ottoman seems explicable given their intersection with the state's core prerogatives. This would be true, for example, regarding an entry involving an Aleppine Jew who suspiciously fell to his death from the roof of a house, and an entry related to the activity of the city's market inspector (*ihtisāb amīnī*).[54] Yet Ottoman-language entries did not only pertain to criminal acts or the work of government agents. Nor were Arabic-language records restricted to mundane affairs and the local common folk.[55] It appears, rather, that the language of record

in *The Book in the Islamic World*, 57–70; Georges Vajda, *La Transmission du savoir en Islam VIIe-XVIIIe siècles*, ed. Nicole Cottart (London: Variorum, 1983). Also, see Nicolas Vatin "Remarques sur l'oral et l'écrit dans l'administration ottoman au XVIe siècle" and Işik Tamdoğan-Abel, "L'écrit comme échec de l'oral? L'oralité des engagements et des règlements à travers les registres de cadis d'Adana au XVIIIe siècle," in *Oral et écrit dans le monde turco-ottoman*, 143–54 and 155–65, respectively.

51. Cairo's are older, starting in 1527; Damascus's are younger, starting in 1583.

52. Aleppo Law Court Register (LCR) 3, pp. 81–2, nos. 448–54. Note the so-called "Mamluk section" of Aleppo's fourth register almost certainly contains forged documents—or at least forged dates. I have not yet determined why this would be so.

53. For example, Aleppo LCR 72, p. 349, no. 965, an endowment deed dated to 1496. Endowment information was also collected as part of separate waqf surveys. In a review of four undated registers kept at Aleppo's Directorate of Pious Foundations, I identified over eighty waqfs that were established before the Ottoman arrival—most were from the Circassian Mamluk period, three preceded the Mamluks, with one dated 1167–8 (Aleppo Directorate of Pious Foundations Register 1, p. 23.). The earliest register appears to be the result of an inspection undertaken around the start of the seventeenth century.

54. Aleppo LCR 1, p. 94, no. 846; 1, p. 100, no. 915.

55. Cf. entries connected to the activity of Aleppo's special supervisor of endowments pertaining to the holy cities (*nāzir* [or *mutawallī*] *awqāf al-Haramayn al-Sharīfayn*), e.g., Aleppo LCR 4, p. 298, no. 1579.

was affected by the needs and literacies of the parties involved. In entries for 2 July 1550, for example, one finds a short series of single-lined cases pertaining to simple financial dealings. One entry involves the transfer of "one sheep and one lamb" between two regular folk and is written in Ottoman; the immediately previous and following cases are in Arabic.[56] Why enter this case in Ottoman? Why vary the language of record for these comparatively insignificant matters at all? Could it be that a document in a particular language would be more useful to the parties involved, implying some kind of practical, textual literacy? Situations like this surface frequently in Aleppo's sixteenth-century law court records.

Further circumstantial evidence for literacy is found in the regular presence of translators or interpreters at Aleppo's *mahkama* (they often appear among listed witnesses, *shuhūd al-ḥāl*).[57] Did translators only facilitate oral and aural access to Ottoman law, or did they not help generate the written records demanded by a legally-literate, polyglot society?[58] Indeed it seems that translators were important and potentially controversial personalities in early Ottoman Aleppo. One Yūsuf b. Aḥmad, known as Ibn al-Mihmandār (d. 1528), served several of the city's judges until he was implicated in the killing of the Ottoman land-and-tax surveyor assigned to the region and executed by the governor.[59] The construction of the Ottomans' textual polity was not to be meddled with!

Conclusion

The study of mass literacy in any premodern setting is a daunting task. To begin, there was never one homogenous mass, even when elite discourse insisted on such an entity. Nor was there one kind of literacy; there were many, and of types sometimes hard to describe. One is further challenged by the evidence, which is more about absences than presences. The need to make large, often risky, inferences based on shreds of evidence is all but unavoidable. The rough-and-ready, if controversial, use of signatures to determine literacy rates across contemporary Europe has no obvious equivalent in the Ottoman world.[60] And still, the data can be accumulated.[61] Nelly Hanna has set a good model here in not relying on any

---

56. Aleppo LCR 1, p. 45, nos. 446–48.

57. In fact, an "'Alī al-Turjumān" is listed as a witness to a case documenting the "smell of wine" on two persons taking place on the same day as the transaction noted above (no. 449).

58. See Kemal Çiçek, "Interpreters of the Court in the Ottoman Empire as Seen from the Sharia Court Records of Cyprus," *Islamic Law and Society* 9:1 (2001): 1–15. Çiçek's useful introduction, however, does not say much about interpreters' direct involvement in the production of written records.

59. Ibn al-Hanbalī, *Durr al-habab*, vol. 2, pt. 2, 589–90.

60. Martyn Lyons, *A History of Reading and Writing in the Western World* (Basingstoke: Palgrave, 2010), 88–93.

61. Recent interest in manuscripts' paratextual elements is promising in this vein. Hirschler, though focused in his own research on earlier periods, has expressed hope that "the countless

one kind of evidence in painting her picture of a variously-literate early-modern Cairo. Indeed an aggregation of different kinds of data and probable interpretations to create an overall impression seems most likely to match the messy reality that must characterize the "most people" literacy studies chase after.

In Ottoman history, this project has only just begun. Yet, if tardy, it has an auspicious beginning. The Ottoman past harbors a pervasive legal culture and is comparatively rich in texts, conditions the state played no small role in nurturing. It did not, however, proceed in unfettered fashion. The inherited traditions of pre-Ottoman societies shaped what was possible in law and politics. And for peoples already long accustomed to textual domination, especially in the world of law they daily encountered, the consequences of widespread literacy would be that much more profound. These were exactly the circumstances the Ottomans faced upon conquering the core Arab lands in the sixteenth century. One hopes that closer examination of this period, with questions of literacy in mind, will reveal more of how most of Istanbul's new subjects experienced this world-historical transition, as well as more of how the Ottoman Empire sought to accommodate the masses it meant to govern.

TIMOTHY J. FITZGERALD is an Assistant Professor in the Department of History at James Madison University, Harrisonburg, VA.

---

notes on manuscripts including those of individual reading (*mutāla'a*), ownership statements (*tamlīk/tamalluk*) and endowment attestation (*waqfīya/tahbīs*)" might yield good information on pre-print reading culture under the Ottomans, *The Written Word*, 199; see also Andreas Görke and Konrad Hirschler, eds., *Manuscript Notes as Documentary Sources* (Beirut: Orient-Institut, 2011). For fascinating work of this kind related to a late Ottoman judge and his manuscript collection, see Tatjana Paić-Vukić, *The World of Mustafa Muhibbi, A Kadi from Sarajevo*, trans. Margaret Casman-Vuko, Tatjana Paić-Vukić, and Miroslav Vuko (Istanbul: Isis Press, 2011), 69ff.

2 Ottoman Legal Practice and Non-Judicial Actors in Seventeenth-Century Istanbul[1]

Hadi Hosainy

ON 31 AUGUST 1666, the Istanbul Court exonerated the imam of the Bucakbağı neighborhood of the homicide of a woman named Ayşe, daughter of Abdullah. The homicide took place a day earlier at the house of the imam, Mustafa Efendi. A grand vizieral order (*buyruldu*) was already issued for the investigation and registration (*keşif ve tahrir*) of the case. Accordingly, the court sent a group of investigators to the location of the homicide, i.e., the house of the mentioned imam. At the head of the investigating team were a high-ranking judge from the court and the chief police officers of Istanbul. They examined (*mu'âyene*) the dead body of Ayşe and arrived at several findings. *İsmail Beşe, the elder son of the imam, had loaded a gun and put it at a window sill. In the meantime, Ayşe went to the imam's house for some business. When the minor son of the imam tried to put a copy of the Quran on the same sill where the gun had been placed, he unintentionally touched the trigger. The gun went off and the bullet hit the right side of Ayşe's neck and came out the other side. The investigating team concluded that this was the cause of Aşye's death.*[2]

About two decades later on 23 October 1685, the *kadıasker* of Rumeli Ahmed Efendi held a hearing to adjudicate a dispute over some waqf property in the neighborhood of Bucakbağı. The founder of the waqf was a certain Fatma Hatun bint Ali, who had designated the income of the endowed property for her freed slaves and their issue. The trustee of the waqf, Ahmed Ağa, sued a certain el-Hac Mustafa bin Abdullah for having appropriated the endowed property, demolished some of the buildings, and built in its place a commercial fruit and vegetable garden. Ahmed Ağa added that the defendant had admitted his usurpation in front of some neighbors. El-Hac Mustafa denied the accusations and claimed that he had bought and owned the mentioned property. Then Ahmed Ağa produced two witnesses who testified that el-Hac Mustafa had admitted his usurpa-

---

1. This work was supported by TÜBİTAK and Sabanci University.
2. İstanbul Şeriye Sicili (İŞS) 18:63a.

tion. The *kadıasker* then sent a committee to the Bucakbağı neighborhood to investigate the integrity of the witnesses. The neighborhood residents testified to the trustworthiness of the two witnesses, after which the court decided the case in the plaintiff's favor. The trustee won this case on behalf of the woman Ayşe who was the primary beneficiary of the endowed property.[3]

What did the law mean for the two Ayşes of this marginal neighborhood? The second case, in which the fortress warden acted as a litigant, had indeed been initiated years earlier by the waqf beneficiary Ayşe. There are significant time gaps between el-Hac Mustafa's initial usurpation of the waqf property, Ayşe's litigation, and finally the warden's involvement. In addition to the warden, the offices of the grand vizier and the Rumeli *kadıasker* were involved in the case. Similarly in the case of Ayşe the slain, in addition to the Istanbul *kadı*, the offices of the grand vizier and the chief police officers were involved in a relatively insignificant case. What role did the extra-judicial actors play in the entire court process?

The two *sicil* entries might initially appear as ordinary as the other thousands of entries that were registered in the period between the two cases. Yet, a close look at them gives the historian some significant hints about the decision-making process of the Ottoman *kadı*. Contrary to some Ottoman legal studies arguing that the Ottoman *kadı* court was strictly bound by legal principles and, therefore, was an ideal site for the alleviation of some structural inequalities, I argue that the *kadı* court did not only follow legal principles but was also sensitive to the social norms and political realities of the day.[4] Through the in-depth analysis of the cases, I examine the role of the *kadı* court as well as the extra-judicial actors such as the grand vizier, imam, and fortress warden (*dizdar*) in the investigation and adjudication of crimes.

The Court and Beyond

The traditional Ottoman legal historiography minimizes the role of the extra-judicial actors. Haim Gerber, for example, argues that the Ottoman legal system was a bureaucratic/rational one based on well-defined legal principles and procedures; the *kadı* assumed primarily an adjudicative rather than mediating or conciliatory role, and judicial discretion was limited by the substance of law providing a certain amount of predictability to judicial outcomes.[5] Discrimination based on gender, faith, one's freedom or slave status, and one's *askeri* or *reaya* status were explicitly prescribed in the imperial *kanunname*s and decrees

---

3. İstanbul Bab Şeriye Sicili (İBŞS) 46: 39b-40b.
4. The historiography on the subject is discussed below.
5. Haim Gerber, *State, Society, and Law in Islam: Ottoman Law in Comparative Perspective* (Albany: State University of New York Press, 1994), 17-22.

as well as the *fiqh* manuals and fatwa compilations.[6] Despite that, traditional Ottoman legal studies claim that the legal system treated litigants fairly according to Islamic legal principles. They argue that the Ottoman legal administration was sophisticated enough to distinguish the role of the judiciary from that of the executive officers; the latter were responsible to execute the judicial decisions while having minimal impact on the process of adjudication.[7] These legal historians have substantiated their arguments with either the prescriptive *kanun* texts or the *sicil* cases in which women, non-Muslims, and/or taxpaying subjects won in their litigation against men, Muslims, and/or members of the *askeri* class.[8]

The early modern prototype of the Ottoman *kadı*, therefore, appears to be an independent judge immune to any influence from external norms and factors. Haim Gerber, for example, maintained that his research did not corroborate the idea that "the kadi adjudicated with any element of sensitivity to local structure or the social origins of litigants."[9] Ahmet Akgündüz, similarly, asserted that Ottoman *kadı*s precisely applied Islamic law in their adjudications.[10] Ekrem Ekinci likewise emphasized the independence of the Ottoman *kadı*, upon whom even the notarial witnesses (*şuhûd el-hâl*) had no influence.[11] In other words, although legal substance and procedure were inherently discriminatory, "rule of law" was maintained through both a well-defined body of legal rights and duties as well as a centralized legal administration, at least in the seventeenth and eighteenth

---

6. Madeline Zilfi, *Women and Slavery in the Late Ottoman Empire* (New York: Cambridge University Press, 2010), 9–21; Joseph Schacht, *An Introduction to Islamic Law* (Oxford: Oxford University Press, 1964), 126–33.

7. Ekrem Buğra Ekinci, *Ateş İstidası: İslam-Osmanlı Hukukunda Mahkeme Kararlarının Kontrolü* (Istanbul: Filiz Kitabevi, 2001), 92–4; M. Aydın, "Mahkeme," *İslam Ansiklopedisi* (Istanbul: Türkiye Diyanet Vakfı İslam Ansiklopedisi Genel Müdürlüğü), 27:342.

8. For women as litigants, see Ronald C. Jennings, "Women in Early 17th-Century Ottoman Judicial Records: The Sharia Court of Anatolian Kayseri," *Journal of Economic and Social History of Orient* 18:1 (1975): 53–114; Haim Gerber, "Social and Economic Position of Women in an Ottoman City, Bursa 1600–1700," *International Journal of Middle East Studies*, 12:3 (1980): 231–44; Fariba Zarinebaf-Shahr, "Women, Law, and Imperial Justice in Ottoman Istanbul in the Late Seventeenth Century," in *Women, the Family, and Divorce Laws in Islamic History*, ed. Amira El Azhary Sonbol (Syracuse: Syracuse University Press, 1996), 81–95; for the fair treatment of non-Muslims, see Ahmet Akgündüz, *Pax Ottoman: Osmnalı Yönetiminde Gayrimüslimlerin Yönetimi* (Istanbul: Timaş Yayınları, 2008), 37–47; Nevzat Erken, "18. yy'ın Yarısında Üsküdar'da Müslim-Gayrimüslim İlişkileri: Şeriyye Sicilleri ve Müdevvel Kaynaklar Işığında" (PhD diss., Marmara Üniversitesi, 2012). For irrelevance of one's *reaya* or *askeri* status in litigation, see Haim Gerber, *State, Society, and Law in Islam*, 55–7.

9. Haim Gerber, *State, Society, and and Law in Islam*, 17.

10. Ahmet Akgündüz, *Osmanlı Kanunnameleri ve Hukuki Tahlilleri*, (Istanbul: Fey Vakfı Yayınları, 1990), 1:43–4.

11. Ekinci, *Ateş İstidası*, 96.

centuries.¹² Such a view renders the entire extra-judicial actors examined here including the imam, the *dizdar*, and the grand vizier irrelevant to the judicial process.

The literature on Ottoman law, however, is not limited to the monolithic narrative of the "rule of law." Some revisionist studies have questioned Gerber's portrayal of the Ottoman court as a scene of formalistic judicial activities in which the judge based his equitable decisions on a well-defined set of legal principles resulting in predictable decisions. Such studies have shown that the *kadı*'s only function was not issuing verdicts in a zero-sum game of adjudication; rather, they were involved in extra-judicial activities such as mediation and arbitration.¹³ The court and judicial decisions were influenced by social norms surrounding the courthouse. Canbakal and Ergene argue that the social status of litigants had a significant impact on judicial verdicts.¹⁴ Kuran and Lustig observe the institutionalization of judicial biases against non-Muslim merchants and in favor of state officials in seventeenth-century Istanbul.¹⁵ My article is a contribution to the revisionist literature examining the role of the privileged legal and non-legal actors in the investigation and adjudication of transgressions.

The registration of the extra-judicial actors' intervention in the two court cases examined here is exceptional due to the inherent legal ambiguity of such interventions. The Sharia prescribed a well-defined set of procedural laws which excluded the intervention of political office-holders.¹⁶ Yet, the Ottomans had integrated the court system into the bureaucracy and, therefore, the *kadı*s as employees of the sultan took decrees issued by him or his deputies seriously. Such executive interventions in the court system, however, formed an anomaly that prompted contemporary debate and criticism. Ottoman subjects complained about *ehl-i örf* (executive officers) and their interference with the judicial pro-

---

12. Ahmet Akgündüz explicitly used the concept *hukukun üstünlüğü* (rule of law) to describe the legalistic nature of the Ottoman state. Akgündüz, *Pax Ottoman*, 33–34.

13. Boğaç Ergene, "Pursuing Justice in an Islamic Context: Dispute Resolution in an Ottoman Court of Law," *Political and Legal Anthropology Review* 27:1 (2014): 51–71; idem, "Why Did Ümm-i Gülsüm Go to Court," *Islamic Law and Society* 17:2 (2010): 215–44; Aida Othman, "'And Amicable Settlement is Best': *Sulh* and Dispute Resolution in Islamic Law," *Arab Law Quarterly* 21:1 (2007): 64–90.

14. Hülya Canbakal, *Society and Politics in an Ottoman Town: 'Ayntâb in the 17th Century* (Leiden: Brill, 2007), 123–49; Boğaç Ergene, *Local Court, Provincial Society and Justice in the Ottoman Empire: Legal Practice and Dispute Resolution in Çankırı and Katamonu (1652–1744)* (Leiden: Brill, 2003), 66–74.

15. Timur Kuran and Scott Lustig, "Judicial Biases in Ottoman Istanbul: Islamic Justice and its Compatibility with Modern Economic Life," *Journal of Law and Economics* 55:3 (2012): 631–66.

16. Shacht, *An Introduction to Islamic Law*, 188–98.

cess of the *kadı*s in order to secure unjust verdicts.[17] The *ulema*, particularly in the post-classical Ottoman period, tried to limit the arbitrary executive decrees within the confines allowed by the sharia.[18] That might explain the relative dearth of information in the court registers about the intervention of extra-judicial actors in the courts' legal proceedings.

The near-silence of the archival sources about such interventions should not lead one to conclude that they were absent. Rather, applying "another way to read the sources"[19] should help us challenge the ideological biases of our sources in reconstructing the history of legal practice, which might not necessarily correspond with prescribed legal procedure. Rather than finding trends based on a vast number of court cases, I chose to focus on a detailed examination of two cases that would appear on the face of it marginal, exceptional, and therefore not worthy of close study, but actually reveal, in Zilfi's words, "much about the ordinary as well as the uncommon in social encounters across normative divides."[20] The experiences of the two Ayşes are representative of situations in which legal norms failed to serve the interests of those in power, who were led to exert influence on the judicial process in order to secure outcomes favorable to them.

In this article, I use a micro-level analysis to shed further light onto the relationship between the law, on the one hand, and everyday socio-economic realities and social norms on the other. I argue that when legal principles and procedure contradicted the existing norms of the community, litigation could achieve little without both the litigants' willingness to consider the concerns and sensitivities of the community and their capacity to employ them to their own benefits. In a society of "classical patriarchy," women had to develop bargaining strategies involving men of power in order to achieve desired legal outcomes.[21] In the absence of men of power that could support marginal women's cases, the legal system behaved less than impartially. In what follows, I first reconstruct the political and social relationships among the residents of the small and "marginal"

---

17. Suraiya Faroqhi, "Political Activity among Ottoman Taxpayers and the Problem of Sultanic Legitimation (1570–1650)," *Journal of the Economic and Social History of the Orient* 35:1 (1992): 18–9.

18. For the rise of the sharia in the seventeenth century, see Uriel Heyd, *Studies in Old Ottoman Criminal Law* (Oxford: Oxford University Press, 1973), 152–57. For a more comprehensive analysis of the post-classical legal transformation, see Baki Tezcan, *The Second Ottoman Empire: Political and Social Transformation in the Early Modern World* (New York: Cambridge University Press, 2010), 14–45.

19. Ehud Toledano, *As If Silent and Absent: Bonds of Enslavement in the Islamic Middle East* (New Haven: Yale University Press, 2007), 34.

20. Madeline Zilfi, "Goods in the *Mahalle*: Distributional Encounters in Eighteenth-Century Istanbul," in *Consumption Studies and the History of the Ottoman Empire, 1550–1922: An Introduction*, ed. Donald Quataert (Albany: State University of New York Press, 2000), 291.

21. Deniz Kandiyoti, "Bargaining with Patriarchy," *Gender and Society* 2:3 (1988): 274–90.

neighborhood of Bucakbağı. I then analyze the ways the court interacted with and accommodated the norms generated by the complex web of relationships in the neighborhood.

The Neighborhood

The small neighborhood of Bucakbağı was located close to the Yedikule Tower in the southwestern suburbs of the city.[22] The neighborhood was not named after a monumental building such as a well-known grand mosque (*cami'*); rather, it took its name from a little mosque (*mescid*) whose founder is quite unknown. Unlike ninety percent of Istanbul's neighborhoods, the most well-known name of the neighborhood was not identical with that of the founder; rather, it was named after a garden (*bağ, bağçe*).[23] Emine Hatun was probably the founder of the mosque and the neighborhood was occasionally known by her name.[24] The late eighteenth-century author Ayvansaraylı Hafız Hüseyin Efendi, however, mentions another woman, Rukiye Hatun, as the founder.[25] The waqf surveys of 1546 and 1600, however, do not mention either Emine Hatun or Rukiye Hatun as a founder in the Yedikule area.[26]

The neighborhood might have appeared sometime between 1546 and 1600. There is no reference to Bucakbağı in the 1546 Istanbul waqf survey. Eight out of the ten waqfs in the adjacent Yedikule neighborhood were cash waqfs.[27] By 1600, the Yedikule neighborhood had four more new endowments, all of which were residential houses.[28] The Bucakbağı neighborhood appeared in three deeds of these new endowments, though in passing notes. In the first two of them, the Bucakbağı mosque or its imam is not mentioned. The third one was founded in 1575, which provides the first piece of evidence for the existence of the Bucakbağı mosque and a sense of neighborhood identity. A convert female named Münev-

---

22. From the neighborhood and the mosque close to Yedikule, only the altered name of Bucakbaşı Street survives. According to Behar, the neighborhoods close to the city walls were of lower socio-economic status. Cem Behar, *İstanbul'un bir Mahllesinin Portresi: 16.-19. Yüzyıllar* (Ankara: Yeni Reform Matbaacılık, 2006), 34.

23. İnalcık, "İstanbul," 231.

24. İBŞS 46: 39b-40b refers to an imam of the Emine Hatun mosque in the Bucakbağı neighborhood. In a detailed survey conducted in the late nineteenth century, the name of neighborhood is mentioned as "*Bucakbağı nam-ı diğer Emine Hatun Mahallesi*," N.A. *Dersaadet ve Bilad-ı Selase'de Mevcud Nüfusun İstatistik Cetvelidir* (Istanbul: Matbaa-ı Osmaniye, 1302/1885), 86.

25. Ayvansarayı Hüseyin Efendi, *Hadikat'ül-Cevami*, (Istanbul: Matba'a-i 'Âmire, 1281), 62.

26. The waqf survey of 1649 seems to be a facsimile copy of the 1600 survey. Compare BOA, TT 1115 with Mehmet Canatar, ed., *İstanbul Vakıfları Tahrîr Defteri: 1009 (1600) Tarîhli* (Istanbul: Fetih Cemiyeti, 2004), 647–48.

27. Ömer Lutfi Barkan and Ekram Hakkı Ayverdi, eds., *İstanbul Vakıfları Tahrîr Defteri 953 (1546) Tarîhli* (Istanbul: Baha Matbaası, 1970), 390–91.

28. Canatar, *İstanbul Vakfıları*, 647–48.

ver Hatun bint Abdullah endowed a house, which adjoined on two sides the house of a certain Mahmud Çelebi, and on the other two the house of a certain Mehmed bin Musa and the local road. The waqf was a typical family waqf to support the founder as long as she lived, and then her husband, and then her heirs. After the extinction of her line of heirs, the imam of the "Bucakbağçe" neighborhood was to benefit from the house. She appointed the neighborhood residents as the *hasbi* (non-paid) overseers of the waqf.[29] The endowment, in this way, wove a complicated web of relationships of rights and responsibilities within the emerging neighborhood. The endowed property would provide support for the neighborhood's imam as the head of the neighborhood, who was apparently the waqf's trustee as well.[30] On the one hand, in return for the benefit he received from the neighborhood's waqf, the imam was deemed accountable to his own community (*cemaat*), i.e., the fellow residents of the neighborhood. On the other, the residents had the collective responsibility to oversee the waqf in return for the communal services the imam provided.

The neighborhood seems to have started to flourish in the second half of the seventeenth century. The first evidence of the existence of a large property in the Bucakbağı neighborhood comes from an endowment deed in 1646. The future chief white eunuch Bosnevi Hasan Ağa endowed a huge property containing a double-story building with multiple rooms, a huge pool, two water mills and a garden. The endowed property was surrounded by the Yedikule Fortress, an endowed vegetable garden, and residential properties.[31] One adjacent property was an endowed house for the imam of the Bucakbağı neighborhood mosque. The *sicil* shows that from the mid-seventeenth century onward, the residents of the Bucakbağı neighborhood frequented the Istanbul courts to litigate their disputes or notarize their transactions, including the sale of their houses or the founding of waqfs.[32]

Bucakbağı was a socially mixed neighborhood accommodating both members of the *askeri* as well the taxpaying subjects. In addition to the future chief white eunuch, the ex-governor of Trabzon, Mehmed Pasha, resided in a property he owned in Bucakbağı in 1633.[33] When the Istanbul court sent its officials to ascertain the integrity of the two witnesses in a case, three residents of the neighborhood with the title of *bey* and one member of the *ulema* (*efendi*) testi-

---

29. Ibid., 647.

30. The trustee is not explicitly mentioned but a comparison with similar waqfs and the fact that there is no payment to be given to a trustee suggest that the resident of the house would also be the trustee.

31. One adjacent residential property belonged to the incumbent chief white eunuch Abdurrahman bin Abdurrahim. For the chief white eunuch, see Mehmed Süreyya, *Sicill-i Osmanlı*, ed. Nuri Akbayar (Istanbul: Numune Matbaacılık, 1996), 1728.

32. See İBŞS 46: 39b-40a; İBŞS 54: 7a, 22a-b; BOA TT 116, pp. 310, 313.

33. Rumeli Sadaret Mahkemesi Sicili (RSMS) 56:31a.

fied. There were some non-*askeri* residents of higher socio-economic background either known as merchants (*tüccar*) or bearing the titles of *çelebi* and *el-hac*.[34] As a neighborhood in the furthest corner of the walled city and close to the city walls, Bucakbağı accommodated also a good number of people from the lower classes.[35] The greater Yedikule area attracted many immigrants primarily from the Balkans as well as the north of the Black Sea, who made their living working as laborers in the vegetable gardens.[36]

In addition to the fruit and vegetable gardens, perhaps the most significant feature of Bucakbağı's topography was the adjacent Yedikule Fortress.[37] For the residents of the neighborhood, as for other nearby neighborhoods in the area, Yedikule was more than a prison or a defensive fortress on the southwestern edge of the walled portion of the peninsula. Yedikule and its personnel were quite integrated into the social and economic life of the people living in the area.[38] Within the fortress was a mosque of which only a minaret survives.[39] The imam and muezzin of the mosque, who were timariots and official members of the fortress,[40] were also financially supported by the endowments in the surrounding neighborhoods. In return, the fortress officials functioned as the trustees or overseers (*nazırs*) of the endowments.[41]

The Fortress Warden in the Court

A good example showing the extent of such a symbiotic relationship between the officials of the Yedikule Fortress and the residents of the neighborhood is the second court case mentioned at the beginning of this paper. The female benefi-

---

34. İBŞS 46:39b-40a. For more information about the Ottoman titles, see Ömer Barkan, "Edirne Askeri Kassamına Ait Tereke Defterleri," *Belgeler* 3 (1966): 15–6.
35. Behar, *İstanbul'un bir Mahllesinin Portresi*, 34.
36. İBŞS 3:92b; Aleksander Sopov and Ayhan Han, "Osmanlı İstanbul'unda Kent İçi Tarımsal Toprak Kullanımı ve Dönüşümleri: Yedikule Bostanları," *Toplumsal Tarih* 236 (2013): 36.
37. See Antoine Ignace Melling, *Voyage pittoresque de Constantinople et des rives du Bosphore*, (Istanbul, 1969) n. 48.
38. Eldem maintains that the Yedikule Fortress personnel included a warden (*dizdar*), a superintendent (*kethüda*), six sergeants (*bölükbaşı*), and about fifty privates (*neferat*). Unfortunately he does not mention neither the source nor date for this figure. Halil Ethem Eldem, *Yedikule* (Istanbul: Kanaat Kütüphanesi, 1932), 26. Oğuzoğlu gives similar information about late seventeenth-century Konya: The Konya Fortress had a warden, a superintendent, an imam, a muezzin, and 117 privates in 1690. Yusuf Oğuzoğlu, "17. Yüzyılın İkinci Yarısında Konya Şehir Müesseseleri ve Sosyo-Ekonomik Yapısı Üzerine bir Araştırma" (PhD diss., Ankara University, 1981), 75.
39. The Yedikule mosque survived until the early twentieth century. See Eldem, *Yedikule*, 25.
40. Oğuzoğlu, "Konya Şehir Müesseseleri," 75–6.
41. Barkan and Ayverdi, *İstanbul Vakıfları*, 647–48; İBŞS 46: 39b-40b.

ciary of the family trust sued el-Hac Mustafa for the usurpation of the endowed property. When the case was dropped based on a legal procedural argument, she employed the warden who happened to be the trustee of the endowment. About seven decades earlier, the wise female founder of the endowment had appointed not a particular person, but the incumbent holder of the *dizdar* office at the adjacent Yedikule Fortress in return for some income. Through employing a resourceful executive officer who was physically accessible to the endowment beneficiaries, the founder had insured the integrity of the endowment against possible transgressors and usurpers.

While the warden resided in the proximity of the endowed property, the beneficiaries had reasons not to involve him in the administration of the endowment as long as it functioned smoothly. The trustee was usually paid a portion, and sometimes a considerable amount, of the endowment income. In addition, Ayşe Hatun, the sole beneficiary of the endowment mentioned in the *sicil*, might have been reluctant to involve the trustee in the administration of the waqf income. Were there other beneficiaries that might have had a claim to income from the endowed property? Were there any legally invalid settlements among the beneficiaries so that the entire income of this endowment would go only to Ayşe Hatun? With the dearth of information in our *sicil* case, one could only speculate about Ayşe's reluctance to involve the trustee in the actual administration of the waqf.

Ayşe had not asked for the help of the trustee since at least twelve years earlier, when the resourceful defendant Mustafa had initially appropriated the endowed property. Ayşe might have hoped that she and Mustafa could agree on the terms of a settlement. Any such hopes were lost some four years before, when Mustafa decided to transform the appropriated endowed property into a commercial garden. Even then Ayşe did not ask the warden to act as the legal trustee of the waqf. She rather decided to sue Mustafa in court, which proved to be a failure. Mustafa came with a legal argument based on the law of procedures, maintaining that Ayşe, as the beneficiary, could not be a party (*khasm*) to the dispute. The case was not even heard and therefore she did not have the chance to provide any evidence. It was only then that Ayşe decided to ask the warden to intervene on her behalf.

The involvement of the warden proved quite effective as he aggressively mobilized his resources to defeat the defendant Mustafa. The lawsuit initiated by the trustee cannot be viewed as an appeal for two reasons. One, the plaintiff was different and, therefore, it was considered a new case. Two, the original case was dropped based on legal procedure, which rendered it null and void, and the hearing never took place; the decision basically ruled that Ayşe Hatun could not initiate the lawsuit in the first place. The trustee's lawsuit, therefore, could be heard again by any of the judges or deputy judges of Istanbul.

The trustee Ahmed Ağa, like any other Ottoman subject, could directly apply to the *kadıasker* court.[42] He instead decided to take the case to the *kadıasker* court through an order from the highest political authority of the empire. Ahmed Ağa secured two consecutive decrees by the deputy grand vizier, Mustafa Pasha, ordering the Rumeli *kadıasker*, the second-in-rank in the *ulema* hierarchy after the *şeyhulislam*, to adjudicate the case. The first decree was issued some two months prior to the court hearing and the second one only about ten days before the hearing. After the defendant's denial, Ahmed Ağa produced two witnesses from the Bucakbağı neighborhood, the imam and a merchant. They both testified that they had heard the defendant admit that the real property in question actually belonged to the waqf. The *kadıasker* then sent a commission to the neighborhood to investigate the integrity of the witnesses. After the verification of their integrity, Ahmed Ağa won the case.

One would look in vain for any deviation from legal principles in the record of the case. The initial case issued by Ayşe Hatun, the beneficiary, was null and void based on the majority opinion of the Ottoman jurists. Although a minority of jurists argued for the legality of the beneficiary's competence to initiate a lawsuit on behalf of the waqf in question, the dominant view was that the trustee enjoyed the sole right to act as a party to such disputes.[43] Later Ottoman jurists, however, preferred the opinion that beneficiaries could initiate lawsuits as well.[44] The scribe of the *sicil* of the case was aware of the legal argument among the jurists and therefore made sure to justify the earlier court decision, mentioning that it was the preferred jurisprudential opinion (*kavl-i müfta bihi*) not to accept the beneficiary as a party to the dispute. After the defendant's denial of wrongdoing, the court asked the plaintiff to provide evidence. The evidence was the oral testimony by the neighborhood imam and the merchant. The integrity of the witnesses was verified by the testimony of Bucakbağı residents. Therefore, the *sicil* case shows that the final verdict was based strictly on the legal substance and the *kadıasker* strictly followed the laws of procedure.

The problem with this conclusion is that the *sicil* was supposed to produce the exact same conclusion. We do not know some legally irrelevant, although important, information such as what happened in the previous twelve years between Ayşe Hatun and el-Hac Mustafa; why Ayşe Hatun did not initiate a lawsuit for a few years; if Ayşe Hatun was ignorant about the legal procedure in her first attempt to sue Mustafa; and if there were any deals between Ayşe Hatun and the

---

42. Mustafa Şentop, *Osmanlı Yargı Sistemi ve Kazaskerilik* (Istanbul: Klasik, 2005), 136–37.
43. Ahmet Akgündüz, *İslam Hukukunda ve Osmanlı Tatbikatında Vakıf Müessesesi* (Ankara: Türk Tarih Kurumu, 1988), 329–30.
44. Ali Haydar Efendi, *Dürerü'l-Hukkâm: Şerhu Mecelleti'l-Ahkam* (Istanbul: Osmanlı Yayınevi), 4:209–10.

warden in order to convince him to intervene on her behalf. For the purpose of this article, I ask if the warden's military status and the fact that he could arrange for executive orders as well as decide the adjudication venue had any impact on winning the case. The *sicil*s, quite intentionally, do not give answers to such questions. What we do know from the entry, however, is that the warden had raised the stakes from the previous lawsuit initiated by Ayşe Hatun. She had only asked for and would have been satisfied with the return of the waqf property to her. What the warden wanted and the judge granted was the maximum of what he could achieve. In addition to the return of the waqf property, he demanded that Mustafa demolish the commercial establishment, restore the waqf buildings to their original form, and compensate the waqf with the income for the past twelve years. True, winning the case was legally impossible without the intervention of the trustee; the warden's intervention, however, had produced an outcome more desirable than for which Ayşe Hatun could have hoped or achieved even if she legally could have sued Mustafa.

The Imam and the Court

Extra-judicial actors made their existence and influence felt in the case of Ayşe's homicide as well. The grand vizier, or his deputy, sent an order to the judge of Istanbul to conduct an investigation of the homicide. The judge, therefore, sent a committee, including the *subaşı* and *asesbaşı* of Istanbul, to the crime scene. They found that the homicide had in fact happened accidentally and reported their observations to the court to be registered accordingly. In what follows, I will examine the role played by different actors and their impact on the process and the final findings of the investigation.

In theory, the Sharia located homicide in the domain of private law. The kin of the victim had the right to initiate the legal process, and once an intentional homicide was proved, the kin had the right to arrive at an amicable settlement (*sulh*) with the killer or to ask for retaliation.[45] In practice, however, disputes over homicide were not totally left to be settled in the private domain. Although the office of public prosecutor was absent, the early modern Ottoman criminal legal system had created some financial incentives for the executive officers to initiate judicial lawsuits against criminal suspects.[46] Therefore, *kadı* courts were usually informed about homicides through either the people involved in the case or the executive officers.

There was a difference between the role played by the executive officers in Istanbul and their counterparts in the provinces. The seventeenth-century evidence from the provinces demonstrates the active involvement of executive officers such as the *subaşı*, *mütesellim*, and governor in informing the court and

45. Schacht, *Introduction to Islamic Law*, 184–85.
46. Heyd, *Studies in Old Ottoman Criminal Law*, 66, 277.

demanding an investigation.[47] Furthermore, they or their representatives were present in almost every investigative team dispatched to examine severe crimes.[48] The interaction between the *kadı* court and executive officers in Istanbul, however, was minimal. The few cases of homicide that came to the attention of the Istanbul *kadı* were primarily brought forward by private individuals who were personally involved rather than the executive officers. Furthermore, the executive officers of Istanbul were not part of the investigative team dispatched by the *kadı* to the crime scene.[49]

The Istanbul *kadı* court was rarely involved in the examination and adjudication of criminal cases. Alternative venues of adjudication, including the imperial divan, the Friday divan, and the Wednesday Assembly in addition to the offices of the *bostancıbaşı*, *subaşı*, *asesbaşı*, and the *janissary ağa*, could act quite independently from the court in dealing with such cases. The executive officers arrested the suspects, after which they either directly imposed a punishment on them or referred them to some of the alternative venues of adjudication.[50] The exact process of investigation and adjudication of homicide cases by the alternative venues are yet to be studied.

Such a division of labor reduced the role of the *kadı* to a notarial one, if any, in the cases of homicide. The investigative team sent by the *kadı* had a simple role of observing and reporting on the crime scene. The examination of a murdered body was quite technical and limited to observations regarding the visible condition of the body, including the injuries and bruises. For example, one day after the mother of Mehmed Siyavuş died, on 12 June 1661, her son came to

---

47. Gerber, "Sharia, Kanun and Custom," 143–44; Özen Tok, "Kayseri Kadı Sicillerindeki Yaralanma ve Ölüm Vakalarıyla İlgili Keşif Raporları (1650–1660)," *Sosyal Bilimler Enstitüsü Dergisi* 22:1 (2007): 331–32; Sibel Kavaklı, "Ölüm ve Yaranlanma Olayları ile İlgili Keşif Hüccetlerinin Değerlendirilmesi: Onyedinci Yüzyıl Amasya Şer'iyye Sicillerinden Örneklerle," *History Studies* 5:3 (2013): 120–24. The involvement of the executive officers in bringing cases to the attention of the *kadı* occurred so often that Gerber suggested that the *subaşı* represented an embryonic form of prosecutor ("Sharia, Kanun, and Custom," 143).

48. Işık Tamdoğan, "Qadi, Gonvernor and Grand Vizier: Sharing of Legal Authority in 18th Century Ottoman Society," *AJAMES* 27:1 (2001): 248; Kavaklı, "Onyedinci Yüzyıl Amasya," 125–26; Tok, "Kayseri Kadı Sicillerindeki Yaralanma ve Ölüm Vakaları," 331–32; Ronald C. Jennings, "Kadı, Court, and Legal Procedure in 17th C. Ottoman Kayseri: The Kadı and the Legal System," *Studia Islamica* 48 (1978): 166–67.

49. İŞS 9:20a, 57b, 185a; İŞS 12:46b; İŞS 18:168b.

50. İBŞS 46:17a. BOA D.BŞM.d 956 includes many cases of arrest and prosecution by executive officers such as the janissary *ağa* or *bostancıbaşı* without feeling the need to involve the *kadı*. Also, see Fariba Zarinebaf, *Crime and Punishment in Istanbul, 1700–1800* (Berkeley: University of California Press, 2011), 133–40. Eyal Ginio observes that the executive officers of Salonica in the eighteenth century arrested and adjudicated criminals without involving the *kadı*; see "The Administration of Criminal Justice in Ottoman Selânik [Salonica] during the Eighteenth Century," *Turcica* 30 (1998), 203–04.

the court and accused Mehmed, son of Kalaycızade Mahmud Efendi, of breaking into his mother's house and injuring her with a sword. Ten days later, she died. The court dispatched an investigative team to her house. They examined her body and recorded two sword cuts on her head, two on her back, four on her right thigh, one on her left thigh, and one on her left heel. Beyond this technical registration of the visible wounds on the victim's body and the fact that she had been killed, the team did not elaborate any further about how, why, and when she was killed.[51] Similarly, on 5 December 1661, the tenant of a bread oven, Bayram, an Armenian, reported the accidental death of his employee, another Armenian named Mardros, the previous night. Bayram requested the examination of the body. The dispatched team examined the body and noted that he was found apparently caught within the wheel operating the mill and that he suffered contusions on his head and left arm. Once again, the examination team did not record anything beyond the fact that the cause of death was the employee's falling down. No comment was made on whether he had fallen by himself or was pushed by someone into the mill.[52]

Considering the minimal role the executive officers played in the Istanbul court and the technical report drawn by the examination team dispatched by the court, the case of Ayşe's homicide appears quite extraordinary. The central government, the executive officers, and the *kadı* were immediately involved in a relatively insignificant case of a kinless victim. The *kadı* dispatched an examination team including the two chief police officers of the capital, namely the *subaşı* and the *asesbaşı*. The team not only observed the bruises and scars on the body of the slain Ayşe but also wrote an unusual report about how the incidents of the previous day led to her killing.

The language of the *sicil* was meticulously crafted to exonerate the imam, removing any suspicion around him and his son. After the victim was identified, the *sicil* immediately referred to the imperial order issued for the investigation of the case. The wording of the order as reformulated by the court scribe was as follows: "A *buyruldu* has been issued to investigate the case of Ayşe bint Abdullah who was unintentionally killed by gunfire in the house of Mustafa Efendi, the imam of the neighborhood." This entrance into the case gives the impression that the imperial order had acknowledged the unintentional nature of the homicide.

Both the suspect imam and the dispatched court representative were members of the *ulema* and were well aware of the Islamic legal substance and procedure as well as Ottoman legal practice pertaining to homicide. Intentional killing (*katl 'amd*) could result in retaliation (*qisas*), that is, the execution of the murderer. In this case in which the victim had no apparent kin to demand retaliation, the Ottoman sultan had the right to decide the punishment of the individual who

51. İŞS 9:20a.
52. İŞS 9:185a.

intentionally killed an heirless person.⁵³ Muslim jurists prescribed three objective criteria for the assessment of intention in homicide, namely "type of action, instrument or weapon used . . . , and the general context."⁵⁴ If the action generated injury, if the instrument used was a lethal one, and if the context was such that homicide was expected, then the intention of the killer was to be verified. In the case of Ayşe's homicide, someone had taken the action of firing the gun, a lethal weapon. In other words, one could argue that the first two criteria were present. We do not know much about the context since the *sicil*, perhaps intentionally, is silent about it. The situation of the imam or of his adult son was even more precarious as suspects since Ottoman criminal legal practice could arrest and sentence even suspects of murder to the galleys.⁵⁵

The scenario offered by the suspect imam, however, made sure there was minimal liability for Ayşe's homicide.⁵⁶ The gun was loaded by the imam's elder son, and the minor son was trying to locate a copy of the Quran close to the gun when he unintentionally touched the trigger. This story kept the two adult members of the family, who could be prosecuted for their actions due to their legal competence (*ehliyet*), out of the case. Furthermore, this scenario ruled out also the possibility of quasi-intentionality in Ayşe's homicide, which would result not only in the payment of blood-money, but also in expiation which would require the killer to manumit a slave.⁵⁷ For quasi-intentionality, it is enough if someone actually used a lethal weapon, regardless of the intention or context. In our story, if the imam or his elder son had fired the gun, both blood money and expiation would be necessary. The *sicil* story, however, recounted that the trigger had been touched and not pulled by a legally incompetent minor son. The punishment, therefore, was the minimum that could be inflicted in any case of homicide, that

---

53. Menteşizade Abdurrahim, *Fetava-yı Abdurrahim*, İstanbul Müftülüğü Kütüphanesi, no. 76, p. 145a; J. N. D. Anderson, "Homicide in Islamic Law," *Bulletin of the School of Oriental and African Studies* 4 (1951): 814.

54. Paul Powers, "Intentionality in Medieval Islamic Law" (PhD diss., University of Chicago, 2001), 198–99.

55. İdris Bostan, *Osmanlı Bahriye Teşkilatı: XVII. Yüzyılda Tersane-i Amire* (Ankara: Türk Tarih Kurumu Basımevi, 1992), 215. BOA Cevdet Adliye 3562 informs about the arrest and imprisonment of a suspect. A certain Mustafa son of Arab, who was the suspect (*mezınna*) in the homicide of a servant of the *menzilci* of Mudanya, was jailed in Istanbul. Later on, he was released on 9 Za 1119/2 March 1708 by the surety of two janissary officers, guaranteeing the suspect's presence whenever summoned by legal officers.

56. Islamic law recognizes liability for all cases of homicide no matter if the killer had the intention or used any lethal weapon. The intention would determine the type of legal consequence for the killer. See Powers, "Intentionality," 204.

57. Powers, "Intentionality," 194–204.

is, the payment of blood-money, in this particular case of kinless Ayşe, to the *beytülmal*.[58]

Conclusion

The cases of the two Ayşes suggest that the portrayal of the early modern Ottoman *kadı* requires further modifications in the historiography. The problems with the "rule of law" discourse are at least partially source-based. Court records, as one of the primary sources of early modern Ottomanists, are not mere descriptions of what happened in the courtrooms. Rather, scribes excluded legally irrelevant details of context regarding the lawsuits at hand. Whatever happened in the courtroom, including the litigation, defense, confession, testimony, and verdicts, was summarized in a way that would confirm legal substance and procedure. Therefore, reading court records to see the existence of "rule of law" would lead a historian into a teleological trap.[59] Yet, the "chaotic" and unedited nature of these court summaries helps historians single out colorful realities of social life.[60] Micro-historical studies of the last decade, particularly regarding gender relationships, have proved productive in reading between the lines of the court records and overcoming such source-based problems.[61]

The very adjudicative role of the Ottoman *kadı* has been questioned by certain studies. After Rosen's ethnographic study in which he claims that the modern Moroccan qadi does not issue verdicts but rather situates litigants in the position to re-negotiate their relationships,[62] it took Ottomanists decades to make similar observations about the Ottoman *kadı*. Ghazzal argues that much of the litigation in the Ottoman *kadı* court was indeed fictitious and that such litigation

---

58. Ömer Nasuhi Bilmen, *Hukuk-ı İslamiyye ve Istılahat-ı Fıkhiyye Kamusu* (Istanbul: İstanbul Üniversitesi Hukuk Fakültesi, 1950), 3:161.

59. Nikki Keddie, "Problems in the Study of Middle Eastern Women," *International Journal of Middle East Studies* 10:2 (1979): 225–40. Keddie suggests students of court records to consider the reality on three levels, "the law, the court decision, and what happened" and be cautious about what goes beyond the second level. As a solution, she suggests that historians can benefit from the anthropological studies, and particularly the anthropological observation that court records did not necessarily match the reality on the ground (p. 229).

60. Dror Ze'evi, "Women in 17th-Century Jerusalem: Western and Indigenous Representatives," *International Journal of Middle East Studies* 27:2 (1995): 169.

61. Leslie Peirce, *Morality Tales: Law and Gender in the Ottoman Court of Aintab* (Berkeley: University of California Press, 2003); Iris Agmon, *Family and Court: Legal Culture and Modernity in Late Ottoman Palestine* (Syracuse: Syracuse University Press, 2006); idem, "Women, Class, and Gender: Muslim Jafa and Haifa at the Turn of the 20th Century," *International Journal of Middle East Studies* 30:4 (1998): 477–500. For methodological debates, see Iris Agmon, "Muslim Women in Court According to the *Sijill* of Late Ottoman Jaffa and Haifa," in *Women, the Family and Divorce Laws in Islamic History*, 112–25.

62. Lawrence Rosen, *The Anthropology of Justice: Law as Culture in Islamic Society* (New York: Cambridge University Press, 1989), 65.

was either a re-working of the terms of an already existing agreement between the two parties or indeed a negotiation between the two.[63] Similarly, Ergene depicts a portrait of the *kadı* who took extra-legal factors as well as actors who were involved in extra-judicial bargaining seriously in his decision making process.[64]

My analysis of the two *sicil* cases corroborates the argument that the *kadı* was not an impartial third party who was bound only by legal principles. Rather, the *kadı* in both his notarial and adjudicative functions acted as an integral part of the society and therefore sensitive to the political realities and social norms of the day. In the case of Ayşe the beneficiary of the waqf, the case as it was initiated by Ayşe was dropped by the Istanbul *kadı*. Later on, with the involvement of the grand vizier and the fortress warden, the *kadıasker* ruled strongly in favor of Ayşe, restituting all her violated rights which was possibly beyond her imagination. Fatma, the female founder of the waqf, had perhaps anticipated the prospective transgressions against the endowed property and, therefore, had appointed the incumbent warden as the official administrator and protector of the waqf. While the property rights of both men and women were guaranteed by Islamic legal principles, legal practice provided some venues for further negotiation of such rights. The court, even the one in the imperial capital, at least for a certain number of cases, was a site where different disputing parties mobilized their political and social capital to maximize their bargaining power and to secure the optimal result.

In the case of Ayşe the slain, extra-judicial actors such as the grand vizier and the chief police officers were involved as well but this time in favor of her murderer(s). The court in its notarial capacity violated its well-established tradition of merely registering the visible conditions of death. With the further centralization of Ottoman criminal legal administration, homicide could not go unnoticed, especially when it happened in the capital.[65] The imam, therefore, mobilized his resources to secure the intervention of the grand vizier, the *kadı*, and the chief police officers on his behalf. He managed to bend the traditional judicial procedure in order to emerge exonerated from an otherwise highly suspicious situation which could result in severe punishment of the imam or his son.

The language of the *sicil* used in the registration of the case of Ayşe the slain is, however, an anomaly. The record deviates from the standardized form of criminal documents, in which the *kadı* plays only the role of the notary. The *kadı* court untypically shifted from a notarial to an adjudicative role and arrives at a conclusive verdict. The problem was that adjudication required two parties

---

63. Zouhair Ghazzal, *The Grammars of Adjudication: The Economics of Judicial Decision Makin in fin-de-siécle Ottoman Beirut and Damascus* (Beirut: Institut Français du Proche-Orient, 2007), Chapter 3.
64. Ergene, "Pursuing Justice."
65. Zarinebaf, *Crime and Punishment*, 162.

(*khasm*) while no one litigated on behalf of Ayşe the slain. Such a procedural and bureaucratic anomaly was possible under the particular circumstances of the case. The social status of the imam as member of the *ulema* might have had an impact on the decision-making process of the *kadı*. The imam did not leave it to chance and solicited a grand vizieral order that inserted some political pressure on the *kadı*. On the other hand, Ayşe the slain, who was a single convert female of unknown reputation, did not have any (male) heir to litigate on her behalf. The *kadı*, therefore, had a strong incentive to bend the customary law that required merely his notarial function in serious criminal cases.

The two cases analyzed here show that the early modern Ottoman *kadı* court was quite integrated within the society. As much as the court could influence the lives of Ottoman subjects, it was susceptible to the influences from the society. The *kadı* court, therefore, played complicated and sometimes contradictory roles in bringing about social justice. On the one hand, strict legal principles limited judicial discretion to a certain degree that could result in the mitigation of some structural inequalities based on one's sex or gender. On the other hand, the *kadı* court could actually enhance the same inequalities through considering the political realities and social norms in making their final decision.

HADI HOSAINY is a PhD candidate in the Department of History at the University of Texas at Austin.

3 Defining Village Boundaries at the Time of the Introduction of the *Malikane* System

The Struggle of the Ottoman State for Reaffirming Ownership of the Land[1]

Michael Nizri

SINCE LAND FORMED the major economic resource for centuries, providing a large share of people's income and an important part of government's taxes, the Ottoman state and Hanafi jurists had to deal with problems and issues relating to ownership, land management, access to agricultural surplus, and the settlement of disputes.[2] As power relations shifted among various forces—the state, provincial administrators, local notables, owners of "free-hold" properties, waqf founders, peasant cultivators, and so forth—the rules of landed property were occasionally recast by legal thinkers and the central government.[3] After all, as Sabrina Joseph asserts, "the law is a dynamic discourse, an integral part of the historical process, which is responsive to existing reality and actively engaged in shaping and re-shaping this reality. Thus, the law, similar to relations of power, is constantly being renegotiated."[4]

Legal norms relating to landed property were formulated on the basis of Islamic law (sharia) and Ottoman imperial regulations *(sing. kanun)* defined in sultanic decrees and derived from local and customary usage as well as administrative exigencies. They emphasized first and foremost the role of the state or the ruler as the source of property rights (the right to make decisions regarding the

---

1. I would like to express my deepest thanks both to Kent F. Schull and the article's anonymous reviewers.
2. The Ottomans officially adopted Hanafi jurisprudence.
3. Baber Johansen, *The Islamic Law on Land Tax and Rent* (London: Croom Helm, 1988); Huri İslamoğlu-İnan, *State and Peasant in the Ottoman Empire* (Leiden: Brill, 1994), 56–61; Martha Mundy and Richard Saumarez Smith, *Governing Property, Making the Modern State: Law, Administration and Production in Ottoman Syria* (London: I.B. Tauris, 2007), 11–39; Sabrina Joseph, *Islamic Law on Peasant Usufruct in Ottoman Syria* (Leiden: Brill, 2012).
4. Joseph, *Islamic Law*, 4.

land). These rights did not entail absolute claims over a certain property. Rather, they described differentiated and particularistic claims of revenue and subsistence. Not only rights to revenues, to the use of the land, and to its title were differentiated, but each claim could also be assigned to different claimants under various categories of property.[5]

Thus, landholding arrangements were intertwined with revenue-holding rights and taxpaying obligations. State lands (*miri*) were those arable lands, mainly grain-producing fields, where peasants had rights of possession, tenancy, and use of the farmlands, provided they worked them and paid their taxes. The state/public treasury retained ownership (*rakaba*) and distributed the rights of possession and usufruct as separate elements. Still, in practice, cultivators did have a hold over their land depending on its type and what it produced. For example, orchards and vineyards cultivated by peasants constituted private property. Furthermore, cultivators working on other types of state lands could sell, bequeath, mortgage, or pawn their usufruct rights.

Mülk lands in the Ottoman context did not entail "free-hold" or absolute ownership to land as absolute rights over revenues, such as the right to sell or bequeath those rights. Only properties categorized as *mülk* could be made into an endowment. In waqf-owned land, ownership was supposedly transferred to God in perpetuity while its revenues were dedicated to pious purposes. Each endowment was managed by a *mütevelli* who was responsible for the collection and distribution of the revenues produced. Cultivators on endowed lands had the same status as cultivators on *miri* lands, though they were entitled to additional tax-exemption privileges.

Finally, in the *timar* system holdings of various sizes were allocated to military and administrative officers in exchange for extracting taxes and participating in military campaigns. The sultan's order officially confirming the grant did not usually confer ownership of the land, but only the right to enjoy its fruits for a set period. Similar to waqf, in the *timar* system ultimate ownership and usufruct were clearly separated.[6]

---

5. İslamoğlu-İnan, *State and Peasant*, 58.

6. For a description of the Ottoman land regime, see Johansen, *The Islamic Law on Land Tax*, 80–125; Joseph, *Islamic Law*, 27–188; Mundy and Smith, *Governing Property, Making the Modern State*, 11–39; İslamoğlu-İnan, *State and Peasant*, 56–77; idem, "Property as a Contested Domain: A Reevaluation of the Ottoman Land Code of 1858," in *New Perspectives on Property and Land in the Middle East*, ed. Roger Owen and Martin P. Bunton (Cambridge: Harvard CMES, 2000), 3–61; Halil İnalcık, "The Ottoman State: Economy and Society, 1300–1600," in *An Economic and Social History of the Ottoman Empire, 1300–1914*, ed. Halil İnalcık and Donald Quataert (Cambridge: Cambridge University Press, 1994), 103–31; Dror Ze'evi, *An Ottoman Century: The District of Jerusalem in the 1600s* (Albany: State University of New York Press, 1996), 115–39.

All in all, the Ottoman land regime recognized multiple layers of ownership. It is important to note that multilayered, shared claims to land were continuously renegotiated and redefined in the face of an ever-changing reality. The relationship between the contending parties was largely determined by the political and economic power of the relevant parties existing in a historically specific context, as well as the legal norms developed by the administration and Muslim jurists.[7] Due to the importance of land as the major economic source, any change in the systems of land tenure had significant repercussions at every level of society. One such change, to be discussed later, was the gradual abandonment of the *timar* system in favor of tax farming.

In this complex land regime, villages constituted the defining units with regard to taxation and the award of new lands for almost the entire existence of the empire.[8] A village was not only a place where people dwelt, but also an important fiscal/administrative, territorial, and communal unit with defined boundaries of arable land, pastures, and tax liability. For the Ottomans, the decisive factor in defining a rural settlement as a village was the existence of agriculturally based continual human settlement. A settlement was registered as a village in the imperial Ottoman registers only if it had a cemetery, a water source, pastures (for draft animals and livestock), a meadow, a harvest floor, and fixed boundaries that could be verified by the testimony of reliable local witnesses. All of this was important to the survival of the village as an economic unit. Thus, as noted by Halil İnalcık, one could say that the guiding principles in establishing villages were tradition and the imperial concern for maintaining a tax base.[9] The latter principle was crucial, considering that the Ottoman economy depended primarily on agriculture and livestock, the main sources for village subsistence and for generating revenues.

In this matter, it was of vital importance to delimit the borders of the villages, pastures, fields, and forests. Those who had recourse to village revenues as part of a military fief, *mülk*, or waqf land, had to know the exact area granted.[10] Agricultural tithes, as well as taxes on summer and winter pastures, grazing grounds, mills, and so forth were charged according to village boundaries.

---

7. İslamoğlu-İnan, "Property as a Contested Domain," 3, 7, 11, 16, 26; Johansen, *The Islamic Law on Land Tax*, 3.

8. In the second half of the nineteenth century, some of the emphasis in the fiscal/administrative logic shifted to larger units, such as the *sancak*. For example, see Jun Akiba, "From Kadi to Naib: Reorganization of the Ottoman Sharia Judiciary in the Tanzimat Period," in *Frontiers of Ottoman Studies: State, Province, and the West*, ed. Colin Imber and Keiko Kiyotaki (London: I.B. Tauris, 2005), 1:43–60.

9. İnalcık, "The Ottoman State: Economy and Society," 174.

10. Ibid., 175; Osman Gümüşçü, "The Concept of Village Boundary in Turkey from Ottoman Times to the Present," *Archivum Ottomanicum* 24 (2007): 42–3.

Normally, the Ottomans adopted the existing village borders determined by their predecessors.[11] Yet occasionally, there were cases where villages boundaries were not clearly defined, or disagreements about them arose. This often led to land disputes among the landholders themselves or between them and neighboring villages or government officials.[12]

Indeed, different sources, such as judicial court records (*sicils*), testify to the many disputes that arose between villagers and elites over boundaries and landholding rights. Local judges, who had formal adjudication rights over both the officials and the peasants, were responsible for resolving disputes over boundaries. They (or their representatives) would visit the disputed site to investigate. After checking the records of the landowners and consulting with disinterested and trustworthy local persons, they would produce a document defining and demarking the village boundaries mainly through locally known physical markers, such as trees, rocks, streams, rivers, water canals between mountain ranges, and so on. Later on, due to the importance of the subject, it was the sultan himself who issued a demarcation document (*hududname* or *sınırname*) to the relevant people, based on the original judicial document. Copies of those documents were preserved at the office of the registry of landed property (*defterhane*), both in Istanbul and in the relevant province.[13] It is worth mentioning that apart from the local courts there were alternative sites for dispute resolution, both official (the governor, for example), and unofficial (the community's conflict resolution mechanisms, for example). Usually, litigants brought their disputes to provincial courts if they thought their claims would fall on sympathetic ears.[14]

Even today villages in Turkey keep *hududname*s that were issued during the early years of the Turkish Republic on the basis of the Ottomans' *hududname*s. Ottoman documents, till this day, still play an important role in resolving disputes between villages in contemporary Turkey regarding the ownership of pastures, meadows, fields, and so on. Furthermore, if there is a disagreement

---

11. İnalcık, "The Ottoman State: Economy and Society," 175; Gümüşçü, "The Concept of Village Boundary," 39, 43; Gabor Agoston, "A Flexible Empire: Authority and its Limits on the Ottoman Frontiers," *International Journal of Turkish Studies* 9:1–2 (2003): 27–8.

12. İnalcık, "The Ottoman State: Economy and Society," 175–76; Gümüşçü, "The Concept of Village Boundary," 40.

13. İnalcık, "The Ottoman State: Economy and Society," 175; Gümüşçü, "The Concept of Village Boundary," 40–1, 44–5; Amy Singer, "Transcrire les frontières de village," in *Lucette Valensi à l'oeuvre, Une histoire Anthropologique de l'Islam mèditeranèen*, ed. François Pouillon and Lucette Valensi (Paris: Editions Bouchene, 2002), 133–43; Mübahat Kütükoğlu, «Hududname,» *Türkiye Diyanet Vakfı İslam Ansiklopedisi* (1998): 18:304.

14. Boğaç A. Ergene, *Local Court, Provincial Society and Justice in the Ottoman Empire: Legal Practice and Dispute Resolution in Çankırı and Kastamonu (1652–1744)* (Leiden: Brill, 2003), 107–08, 170–88. Also, see Ronald C. Jennings, «Limitations of the Judicial Powers of the Kadi in 17th Century Ottoman Kayseri,» *Studia Islamica* 50 (1979): 151–55.

between two villages over boundaries then the process of dispute resolution still resembles past Ottoman practices.[15]

Notwithstanding the current continuation of these Ottoman practices, scholars have paid scant attention to the Ottoman system of establishing village boundaries, even though this practice was vital in terms of the empire's economy, administration, and legal system. The purpose of this article is to shed further light on the practice of establishing village boundaries in the Ottoman Empire. This issue raises interesting questions, among them: 1) What are the benefits of examining *hududname*s and *temlikname*s (deeds to formal possession of property granted by the sultan) as documents of legal disputes?; 2) How were Islamic law, *kanun*, local practices, and pre-Ottoman norms in the Ottoman land regime reflected in the legal process of boundary demarcation?; 3) To what extent did the palace placate the Ottoman high elite's demands to convert public resources into private property with the emergence of the *malikane* system at the close of the seventeenth century?

To this end, I have utilized documents that are attached to the endowment deeds (sing. *waqfiyya*) of Şeyhülislam Feyzullah Efendi (1695–1703), namely *hududname* and *temlikname/mülkname*.[16] The endowment deed in itself generally provides a minimal description of the outline of the lands, as the focus is on the types of properties and their annual yields. However, the aforementioned documents, provide clear definitions of ownership and property lines, in order to prevent any confusion with regard to the right of the owner to revenue-yielding properties. Specifically, they concern four places in which the need arose for a clear definition of the boundaries of some properties belonging to the endowments of Feyzullah Efendi: the village and salt works of Kömör, the Gönelü salt works (all three located in the province of Erzurum), and the village of Muazamiye (located in the province of Damascus).

In what follows, I briefly introduce Feyzullah Efendi and the main sources, describe the shift from an agrarian system based on *timars* to one based on tax farming and its repercussions, analyze the four cases mentioned above, and discuss the possible implications of property boundary demarcation for the state, elites, and villagers.

Feyzullah Efendi and His Proximity to the Palace

Feyzullah Efendi was a very interesting and controversial figure. He was born in 1638 in the city of Erzurum. In 1669, through his patron's intercession (Vani Efendi), he was appointed to the dignified position of tutor (*hoca*) to young

---

15. Gümüşçü, "The Concept of Village Boundary," 47–9; Osman Demir and Yakup Emre Çorhulu, "Determining the Property Ownership on Cadastral Works in Turkey," *Lands Use Policy* 26 (2008): 112–15, 117–19.
16. Başbakanlık Vakıflar Genel Müdürlüğü, Register no. 571, 104–34 (hereafter BVGM).

Prince Mustafa. No doubt, this was the first major turning point in Feyzullah's career. He held this post for 17 years, during which he developed a very strong and affectionate relationship with the future sultan. Indeed, after Sultan Mustafa II ascended the throne in February 1695, he reappointed his beloved mentor as *şeyhülislam* (Feyzullah was first appointed *şeyhülislam* in 1688), thus making him the head of the *ilmiye* (the Ottoman academic-judicial-religious establishment).

Feyzullah Efendi served as *şeyhülislam* during the entire reign of Sultan Mustafa II (1695–1703). The intimacy between the two and the great influence the *şeyhülislam* had on the sultan allowed the former to exercise authority beyond the usual norms. Not only did Feyzullah Efendi achieve an iron grip on the affairs of the religious institution, but he also wielded great control over the political sphere. With the support and encouragement of the sultan, who made an effort to weaken the power of the vizier and pasha households, the *şeyhülislam* was authorized to intervene in the management of state affairs, so much so, that he also came to dominate the central administration, too. Feyzullah also possessed an insatiable greed demonstrated by his ability to accumulate enormous amounts of wealth and property. This greed and influence eventually led to his violent demise in 1703 during the "Edirne Incident."[17]

The Sources

Şeyhülislam Feyzullah Efendi established endowments in Istanbul, Edirne, Erzurum, Damascus, Mecca, Medina, and Jerusalem for the maintenance of institutions such as mosques, *medreses*, and schools as well as fountains. In each case, Feyzullah Efendi did not allocate revenue-yielding properties of his own to finance the beneficiaries at the time he created these waqfs. Instead, Sultan Mustafa II gave properties to the *şeyhülislam* as revenue sources to support the endowments established by the latter. As different boundary problems arose at the beginning of the process, various documents were produced in order to try to solve these issues.

A *hududname* was issued whenever there were disputes over land boundaries. Generally speaking, this document mentions the reason(s) for delimiting the boundaries of the waqf landed properties and the names of all those involved in the process. It also defines the perimeter of the village on four sides (north, south, east, and west) on the basis of topographical features and buildings. The popula-

---

17. On Feyzullah Efendi and his special status within the Ottoman government, see Michael Nizri, *Ottoman High Politics and the Ulema Household* (Basingstoke: Palgrave Macmillan, 2014); Rifaat Ali Abou-El-Haj, *The 1703 Rebellion and the Structure of Ottoman Politics* (Istanbul: Nederlands Historisch-Archaeologisch Instituut, 1984); Orhan F. Köprülü, "Feyzullah Efendi," *İslam Ansiklopedisi* (1948): 4:593–600.

tion of the land was counted and registered as well.[18] In our case, two *hududname*s were issued by the sultan. The first refers to the boundaries of the village of Muazamiye (issued at the beginning of May 1696), and the second refers to the boundaries of the properties belonging to the imperial treasury in Erzurum, including Gönelü salt works as well as the salt works and village of Kömör (issued on 7 May 1697).[19]

As for the *temlikname*, it was customary for high dignitaries to apply for *temlik* (formal possession of property). The applicant (grand vizier, vizier, princess, and so on) would declare that he/she needed the revenue of a public land (mainly a village or villages) to establish a major pious endowment. As a reward for the applicant's good services and loyalty, the sultan would issue a title deed granting ownership of the land. By so doing, the public land was converted into registered and inheritable property. The title deed also defined the boundaries of the property belonging to the waqf. Everything within these boundaries, along with the land, belonged to the grantee. That meant that the latter could bequeath the property, sell it, bestow it, or make it into an endowment. Moreover, the state renounced all rights to the land, such as tax collection and law enforcement. Central and local authorities were required to abstain from interference in the affairs of *mülk* owners.[20] It should be stated that the Ottoman rulers followed their predecessors in employing *temliks* by bestowing exemptions and immunities on land revenue and peasant labor in order to ensure the support of their local notables.[21]

Yet, the state's renunciation of rights could be reversed. There was always a possibility that *mülk* lands, and even waqf lands, would revert back to their original *miri* status by a sultanic order under certain conditions (uncultivated land, for example). Thus, the renunciation of rights was conditional. In this matter, Moutafchieva adds that state properties were not acquired by means of Islamic law of purchase and sale, in which one party had to be the fisc, but were given

---

18. Kütükoğlu, «Hududname,» 303–04; Gümüşçü, "The Concept of Village Boundary," 43–4.

19. BVGM: 571, 113–17.

20. İnalcık, "The Ottoman State: Economy and Society," 120–26; Ömer Lütfi Barkan, «Türk-İslam Toprak Hukuku Tatbikatının Osmanlı İmparatorluğu'nda Aldığı Şekiller: İmparatorluk Devrinde Toprak Mülk ve Vakıfların Hususiyeti,» in *Türkiye'de Toprak Meselesi*, ed. Ömer Lütfi Barkan (Istanbul: Gözlem Yayınları, 1980), 253, 255–62; Vera P. Moutafchieva, *Agrarian Relations in the Ottoman Empire in the 15th and 16th Centuries* (Boulder: East European Monographs, 1988), 61–77.

21. Halil İnalcık, "Autonomous Enclaves in Islamic States: Temliks, Soyurghals, Yurdluk-Ocakhks, Mdlikane-Mukta'as and Awqaf," in *History and Historiography of Post-Mongol Central Asia and the Middle East: Studies in Honor of John E. Woods*, ed. Judith Pfeiffer and S. A. Quinn (Wiesbaden: Harrassowitz, 2006), 112–25; Mehmet İpşirli, "Temlikname," *Türkiye Diyanet Vakfı İslam Ansiklopedisi* (2011): 40:430.

free of charge. Therefore, Islamic legal experts considered them as false and not as a true *mülk*.²² In any case, by the late seventeenth century, *mülk* grants had become a common practice.²³ One such example is a *temlikname* in favor of Feyzullah Efendi. In February-March 1696, Sultan Mustafa II issued the *temlikname* concerning the grant of the village of Muazamiye.²⁴

A *mülkname* document was no different from a *temlikname*. Both documents referred to a sultan's grant of ownership of public assets and were issued similarly.²⁵ Still, it appears that starting from the seventeenth century most of the imperial grants were defined as *mülkname*.²⁶ Mustafa II issued a separate *mülkname* concerning the grant of the Gönelü salt works (at the beginning of June 1695),²⁷ as well as another one pertaining to all revenue sources given to Feyzullah Efendi in Erzurum (February 1697).

The Introduction of the Malikane System and Its Repercussions

An important means by which the central government sought to maintain its ownership of land, and the right to appropriate surplus and reallocate it at will, was the replacing of the *timar* system with tax farming. The former system, which prevailed until the end of the sixteenth century, and continued into the nineteenth century, was based on the allocation of income from fiefs to military and administrative officers, in return for the collection of taxes and for the provision of a small contingent of cavalry. The standard *timar* was a relatively small holding that included one or more villages and was intended to support a cavalryman and band of fighters. The lion's share of the holdings' taxes (in cash or produce) went to the holder of the *timar*, while the surplus was passed on to the Imperial Treasury. *Timar* holders were not the owners of the land. They were only allowed to collect taxes and keep a certain share for themselves. The sultan could divide fiefs as he saw fit, pass them on, or change their definition. Generally, *timar* holders were not allowed to sell their fiefs, divide them or bequeath them to their sons (only with special permission). In addition, their deeds had to be renewed when a new sultan ascended the throne.²⁸

---

22. Moutafchieva, *Agrarian Relations in the Ottoman Empire*, 64.
23. Rifaat Ali Abou El-Haj, *Formation of the Modern State: The Ottoman Empire, Sixteenth to Eighteenth Centuries* (Syracuse: Syracuse University Press, 1991), 120–21.
24. BVGM: 571, 108–09, 112–13.
25. Barkan, "Türk-İslam Toprak Hukuku," 253; İpşirli, "Temlikname," 430; Mehmed Z. Pakalın, "Temlikname," *Osmanlı Tarih Deyimleri ve Terimleri Sözlüğü* (Istanbul: Maarif Basımevi, 1951), 3:455.
26. İpşirli, "Temlikname," 431.
27. BVGM: 571, 109–10.
28. On the *timar* system, see Halil İnalcık, *The Ottoman Empire: The Classical Age, 1300–1600*, trans. Norman Itzkowitz and Colin Imber (London: Weidenfeld and Nicolson, 1973), 104–18; Metin Kunt, *The Sultan's Servants: The Transformation of Ottoman Provincial Govern-*

Starting from the end of the sixteenth century, the Ottoman state gradually abandoned the *timar* system in favor of tax farming (known as *iltizam*), for economic and military reasons. The weakening of the Ottoman economy, the growth of inflation, the slowdown in conquests, as well as changes in the size and readiness of the Ottoman army, made it necessary to raise tax income.[29]

In the tax farming system, sultans farmed out the collection of state revenue or taxes to private bidders through public auction. Various state revenue sources (sing. *mukataa*) were distributed in return for a mutually agreed-upon price: agricultural taxes (such as those related to arable fields), other taxes (such as customs dues or poll tax), or state-owned monopolies (such as salt production). Usually the length of the tax-farming contracts ranged from three to six years. The deal went through after the tax farmer (*mültezim*) received a *berat* (an order from the sultan confirming the receipt of certain privileges) that spelled out his obligations and rights. The *mültezim* was obliged to pay the sum he proposed in return for the tax lease, regardless of the sum he actually collected. He could do so upon payment of a lump sum in advance of the agreed-upon sum or by paying a down payment and the rest in installments. The financial administration demanded that he obtain a counter-signer or post his property as collateral in case he could not meet his contractual obligations. In fact, leasing a tax farm was a gamble, but it could also yield considerable profits if the tax farmer succeeded in collecting more than the sum to which he had committed in his contract.[30]

It often happened that the tax farmer's zeal to recoup his investment harmed agriculture and oppressed the farmers. Therefore, starting in 1695, a new system of tax farming, called *malikane* enabled the tax farming contract to be held for life. In return, the *malikane* holder had to make a larger down payment (*muaccele*) determined by public auction, along with annual sums that were set in advance. The central government hoped that a longer lease period would encourage tax farmers to take an interest in the welfare of the taxpayers. Another important reason for instituting the *malikane* system was tied to the treasury's need to increase its income in light of heavy financial deficits caused by the empire's extensive European wars. The system enabled the center to increase its hold on

---

ment, 1550–1650 (New York: Columbia University Press, 1983), 9–13, 50–1; Hamilton Gibb and Harold Bowen, *Islamic Society and the West* (London: Oxford University Press, 1957), 1:48–52.

29. Halil İnalcık, "Military and Fiscal Transformation in the Ottoman Empire, 1600–1700," *Archivum Ottomanicum* 6 (1980): 283–337; Ariel Salzmann, "An Ancien Régime Revisited: 'Privatization' and Political Economy in the Eighteenth Century Ottoman Empire," *Politics and Society* 21:4 (1993): 398–400.

30. On the *iltizam*, see İnalcık, "Military and Fiscal Transformation," 327–33; Linda Darling, *Revenue-Raising and Legitimacy, Tax Collection and Finance Administration in the Ottoman Empire, 1560–1660* (Leiden: Brill, 1996), 47, 119–60 and passim; Murat Çizakça, *A Comparative Evolution of Business Partnerships* (Leiden: Brill, 1996), 140–59.

the periphery by controlling the distribution of income sources, as well as accommodate provincial elites who were not part of the old distributive networks.[31]

Still, as Ariel Salzmann argues, central-state elites emerged politically and economically stronger through the incessant power struggles between the central state and the old elites. In the last decades of the seventeenth and early eighteenth centuries, the palace surrendered to the demands of the upper strata of the Ottoman state elite—viziers, high-ranking *ulema*, officers, bureaucrats and palace figures, closely tied to the central state itself—for more direct and longer term rights over revenue assignments, in addition to other privileges, such as immunity from taxation. Tax farming enabled central-state elites not only to accumulate wealth but also to establish power centers in the provinces based on the staff needed for operating and managing their revenue sources.[32]

In this context it should be noted that receiving a *malikane* contract on state revenues created certain rights to the source of income. The *malikane* holder (*malikaneci*) could run things as he pleased, subject to the conditions of the contract, while the local judge could only supervise or intervene if his activities exceeded the permissible. The tax farmer could promise the transfer of all or part of the *malikane* rights to his heirs, on condition that they made a new down payment. The *malikaneci* was even entitled to sell the tax source, transfer it, or sub-lease shares to others.[33] More important, some high-ranking figures even attempted, and sometimes succeeded in converting a *malikane* holding into private property.[34] Apparently, the best chance for doing so was the conversion of contracts into endowments.[35]

The Village of Muazamiye (Damascus)

The *malikane mukataa* of Muazamiye was part of the *nahiye* (sub-district) of Qalamun. At that time (1696), it yielded the imperial treasury an annual income of 24,000 *akçe*. At first, Feyzullah Efendi obtained the *malikane* contract of the village of Muazamiye. Afterwards, he asked the sultan to grant him this rev-

---

31. On the shift from short-term tax farming to the long-term *malikane* system, see Salzmann, "An Ancien Régime Revisited," 393–423; Mehmet Genç, "Osmanlı Maliyesinde Malikane Sistemi," in *Türkiye İktisat Tarihi Semineri*, ed. Osman Okyar and H. Ünal Nalbantoğlu (Ankara: Hacetepe Üniversitesi Yayınları, 1975), 231–96.
32. Salzmann, "An Ancien Régime Revisited," 398–409.
33. Çizakça, *A Comparative Evolution*, 159–60, 163; Genç, "A Study of the Feasibility of Using Eighteenth-Century Ottoman Financial Records as an Indicator of Economic Activity," in *The Ottoman Empire and the World-Economy*, ed. Huri İslamoğlu-İnan (Cambridge: Cambridge University Press, 1987), 348, 352, 356.
34. Ariel Salzmann, *Tocqueville in the Ottoman Empire: Rival Paths to the Modern State* (Leiden: Brill, 2004), 98.
35. Ibid; Abou El-Haj, *Formation of the Modern State*, 16, 120–21.

enue source as a *mülk*,³⁶ so that it could be converted into a pious endowment. Following the request, Sultan Mustafa II issued a *temlikname* stating that the village would be transferred to the possession of the *şeyhülislam* and his descendants. The grantee's "freehold" ownership included everything within the long-established boundaries of the village: lands, pastures, summer highland pastures (*yaylak*), meadows, winter quarters (*kışlak*) for animals, mountains, hills, rivers, and wells. Moreover, in order to secure full autonomy for the village lands, the sultan prohibited central and local authorities from intervening. ³⁷

In addition, there is a long list specifying what kind of taxes and dues could be collected by the new owner (or his/her representative). It should be noted that the revenue of the Ottoman Empire consisted of various taxes, dues, fees, and levies on production, trade, and so on. These taxes varied according to locality and group (ethnic and religious groups, for example). We find a distinction between two main categories of taxes: Islamic taxes (such as tithes and poll tax) and state-customary taxes. The latter were detailed in official collections of sultanic edicts (*kanunname*s), attached to cadastral surveys or tax registers.

Our document mentions only that Feyzullah Efendi was entitled to revenues from Islamic taxes (*tekalıf-i şeriyye*) while going into detail regarding revenues derived from state-customary taxes (*tekalıf-i örfiyye*), those taxes which were originally paid under the pre-Ottoman regimes and incorporated into the Ottoman tax system. Among the customary taxes are enumerated the following: sheep tax (*adet-i ağnam*), bachelor tax (*resm-i mücerred*), sheepfold tax (*adet-i ağıl*(, marriage tax (*resm-i arus*), watermill tax (*resm-i asiyab*), farmland tax (*resm-i çift*), fodder tax (*resm-i giyah*), beehive tax (*resm-i küvare*), and tobacco tax (*resm-i duhan*). Irregular and occasional revenues from fines and fees imposed as penalties for misdemeanors and crimes (usually known as *bad-i hava*)³⁸ were also included, such as *cürm-ü cinayet* (tax exacted from known criminals). Furthermore, revenues from the *beytülmal* (public treasury)³⁹ along with property of absent and missing persons⁴⁰ were also included.⁴¹

36. Abdülkadir Özcan, ed., *Anonim Osmanlı Tarihi 1688–1704* (Ankara: Türk Tarih Kurumu, 2000), 224.
37. BVGM: 571, 108.
38. On the *bad-i hava*, see Bernard Lewis, "Bad-i Hawa," *EI*² (1958): 1:850.
39. This term was normally restricted to revenues belonging by law to the public treasury. The most important were properties belonging to missing and absent people and dues for recovering stray cattle, runaway slaves, etc. See Amnon Cohen and Bernard Lewis, *Population and Revenue in the Towns of Palestine in the Sixteenth Century* (Princeton: Princeton University Press, 1978), 73–4, 99.
40. Apparently, if someone's heir was outside the country and his place of residence was unknown, that man was called *mefkud* and his belongings would be left in possession of a custodian for one year, to be handed over thereafter to the public treasury. See Cohen and Lewis, *Population and Revenue*, 99 n. 67.
41. BVGM: 571, 108–09.

The title deed was signed by the sultan in February-March 1696 and witnessed by distinguished persons, such as the grand vizier (Elmas Mehmed Pasha), vizier Hasan, vizier Osman, *defteri (*perhaps *defterdar)* Halil, the Chief Military Judge of Rumelia (Ali Efendi), the Chief Military Judge of Anatolia (Abdullah Efendi), and *tevkii* Ali (the official who drew the sultan's signature). After the imperial order had been composed, witnessed, and signed, it was addressed to the governor and *defterdar* of Damascus, Osman Pasha and Şehdi Mustafa Efendi, respectively.

Shortly thereafter (30 April 1696), Mustafa II sent a messenger, Ahmed Ağa, to present and ratify the sultan's order (*temlikname*) in the court of law of the judge of Damascus under whose jurisdiction the village of Muazamiye fell. But it turned out that old copies of the *hududname*s of the village of Muazamiye could not be found either in Istanbul or Damascus.[42] Simply put, apparently they were lost. This prevented the judge from establishing the exact boundaries of the village mentioned in the decree, causing disputes, because the protection of tax resources depended on the identification of village units.

The boundaries of the village, therefore, once again needed to be reconfirmed based on the testimony of disinterested witnesses from neighboring villages, in accordance with the dictates of the sharia. In fact, as in earlier Islamic practice, there were two kinds of witnesses in Ottoman courts: instrumental/expert witnesses (*şuhudülhal*) and circumstantial witnesses (*udul*). The former stood witness to the legal validity of the particular case, and their names were regularly affixed underneath the written record. It often happened that the *şuhudülhal* belonged to the local notables and carried military and religious titles. As such, they probably had some influence on the court processes. The latter gave testimony to confirm or refute the claims of the litigants, and their names were identified in the main body of the document.[43] In general, the sworn testimony of reliable witnesses traditionally took precedence over written evidence.[44] Boundaries of property could not be fixed without the consensus of neighbors, even when a written document was available. However, as Amy Singer points out, the very existence of the written boundary documents suggests that oral testimony of local experts was insufficient for the Ottoman state and the *kadı* as its representative.

---

42. Ibid., 113.
43. Ergene, *Local Court*, 28–30, 168; Hülya Canbakal, *Society and Politics in an Ottoman Town: 'Ayntāb in the 17th Century* (Leiden: Brill, 2007), 130. On the debate over the group of *şuhudülhal*, see Ergene, *Local Court*, 28–30.
44. Canbakal, *Society and Politics*, 129, 131–32; Amy Singer, "The Mülknâmes of Hürrem Sultan's Waqf," *Muqarnas* 14 (1997): 97; Lucette Valensi, *Tunisian Peasants in the Eighteenth and Nineteenth Centuries*, trans. Beth Archer (Cambridge: Cambridge University Press, 1985), 64, 132; Joseph Schacht, *An Introduction to Islamic Law* (Oxford: Oxford University Press, 1964), 192–93.

In this case, the written expression of the boundaries became a declaration of state authority.[45]

The accepted boundaries of Muazamiye from olden times were defined as follows, based on local topographical features and built structures:

> The boundary on the west begins from the mill and continues toward the mountain called Mt. Qabliyah; and on the south it lies along the wide open area; and on the east it joins the great hills; and on the north it reaches the mountain of Wadi Shadub (Vadi Şedub).[46]

Also, with regard to the river that flowed between the villages of Muazamiye and Qadifeh and served as a natural border on the northern side, it was decided with the help of the witnesses that both villages were equally entitled to use the water.[47]

Immediately afterwards (beginning of May 1696) a land dispute arose between the villages of Muazamiye and Qadifeh that necessitated the issuing of a *hududname* by Süleyman Efendi, the judge of Damascus. The controversial issue concerned the *mezraa*[48] (communally owned arable land) of Botoqya, situated at the northern side of the river that flowed between the two villages. The boundaries of the disputed *mezraa* are described as follows:

> In the western direction, from the poplar trees that are found near Wadi Shadub to the mountain called Mt. Maddah; in the northern direction from the lower edge of Mt. Maddah to Jis Canal; in the eastern direction, the land of the village of Jurud that passes along the Jis Canal; and in the southern direction, a watercourse which is bounded by the village of Muazamiye.[49]

The village of Qadifeh belonged to the endowments of the late Sinan Pasha. The manager (*mütevelli*) of those endowments, Kasım Ağa, claimed that the *mezraa* of Botoqya should not have been included within the boundaries of the village of Muazamiye. Rather, according to the documents at his disposal (*mülkname* and registers of *Defter-i Hakani*—the office where central cadastral registers of the provinces were kept), the *mezraa* in question actually belonged to the village of Qadifeh. Ahmed Ağa, the above-mentioned representative of the sultan, disagreed with Kasım Ağa's claim on the grounds that it was not evident

---

45. Singer, "Transcrire les frontiers," 142. Also, see Jennings, «Limitations of the Judicial Powers,» 173–74.
46. BVGM: 571, 113.
47. Ibid.
48. The *mezraa* was often assigned as part of a timar or a waqf. See İnalcık, "The Ottoman State: Economy and Society," 162–66.
49. BVGM: 571, 113–14.

that the *mezraa* had actually been registered in these documents as the property of Qadifeh village.[50]

An inquiry into the matter revealed that peasants from the villages of Qadifeh and Ayn al-Tin had been cultivating the lands of the *mezraa* in question for some time. Indeed, in some instances, lands were commonly exploited by both villages. Yet, unlike the village of Qadifeh, the village of Ayn al-Tin possessed a document, signed by the former judge of Damascus (Resül Efendi) that stipulated the village of Ayn al-Tin possessed the right to cultivate the land of the *mezraa* through the general consensus of the neighbors (*şöhert ve tevatür*). Furthermore, the villages of Ayn al-Tin and Jurud acknowledged the proprietary right of the village of Muazamiye over the *mezraa*. Moreover, Ahmed Ağa submitted to the judge two court decisions written and signed by two former judges of Damascus in 1686 and 1690, confirming that the *mezraa* of Botoqya belonged to the village of Muazamiye.[51] In principle, according to the precepts of Islamic law, court orders constituted sufficient proof. It was very complicated to appeal or revoke a decision of the court.[52]

Nevertheless, trustworthy local witnesses, from adjacent villages as well as other villages in the district, also testified in court that the disputed land belonged to the village of Muazamiye. Consequently, the *hududname* included the *mezraa* of Botoqya within the boundaries of the village of Muazamiye. The expert witnesses (*şuhudülhal*), whose names followed and who validated the document were Mehmed Vedad Efendi (a former judge of Jerusalem), Ali Efendi (the *mufti* of Damascus), Seyyid Hasan (the son of Ahmed Pasha), and Osman Ağa (*ser muhzır*—chief summoning officer in the court of law).[53]

Even though court records do not normally reveal the legal reasoning behind the court decisions, it may be assumed that in the above dispute a high value was placed on written documents (those court decisions presented by Ahmed Ağa and the cultivators from the village of Ayn al-Tin). If so, this supports Singer's claim that oral testimony of local experts was insufficient for the Ottoman state and the judges who represented it. Written documents proved so indispensable that they remained in constant use. They were essential to verify boundaries and claims to land as well as for reaffirming state authority and sovereignty. The dispute that arose between the manager of Sinan Pasha's endowment (Kasım Ağa) and the sultan's agent (Ahmed Ağa) also supports Mundy and Smith's claim, as well as Joseph's claim, regarding the tensions that existed between imperial and local concepts as to governing rights to land.[54]

50. Ibid., 114.
51. Ibid.
52. Ergene, *Local Court*, 145.
53. BVGM: 571, 114.
54. Mundy and Smith, *Governing Property, Making the Modern State*, 22–3, 28–9, 39; Joseph, *Islamic Law*, 170, 180–81.

Of greater interest is the fact that Sultan Ahmed III decided to return the village of Muazamiye to state control in September 1703, following the deposition of Sultan Mustafa II and the execution of Feyzullah Efendi.⁵⁵ Although the above mentioned village reappeared in the waqf's list of properties during the first half of the reign of Sultan Mahmud I (between 1730 and 1743), who allowed the descendants of the executed *şeyhülislam* to return to the seat of power, it afterwards disappeared from the list.⁵⁶ This shows that *temliknames* had to be confirmed by each new sultan. In this case the attempt of Feyzullah Efendi to convert his *malikane* holding into an endowment failed. This strengthens the assumption of Salzmann, that the conversion of *malikane* contracts into endowments by prominent members of the Ottoman elite did not necessarily guarantee the conversion of a public resource into private property.⁵⁷ In this matter, Huri İslamoğlu-İnan argues that the state made a continuous effort to impose limits on the development of absolute ownership of different land categories, such as *mülk* lands and waqf lands, well into the mid-nineteenth century.⁵⁸

Gönelü Salt Works (Erzurum)

Salt played an important part in people's diet as well as in preserving fish, beef, and vegetables.⁵⁹ The Ottoman government controlled the production and distribution of salt in bounded regions. In principle, salt mines and salt beds were considered to be state property, though the state recognized the freehold rights of privately created salt works in order to ensure its continued supply. In any case, the common practice in most state-controlled enterprises was to empower private contractors with a special deed from the sultan, granting entrepreneurs authority in matters of exploitation and management of state-owned monopolies.⁶⁰

The *mukataa* of the Gönelü salt works (*memlaha*) was part of the *sancak* (district) of Kızuçan. It was among the largest salt works in the province of Erzurum.⁶¹ The family of a certain Ali had long ruled over the district of Kızuçan, and was the owner of all the villages, arable lands, salt works, and pastures in that district. When the area came under Ottoman control, the sultans granted Kızuçan to Ali's family as *ocaklık*.⁶² So, before moving to the presentation of the case itself, a brief explanation of the *ocaklık* system is necessary.

---

55. Başbakanlık Osmanlı Arşivi: Cevdet/Saray/1223.
56. Nezaret Öncesi Evkaf Defterleri, No. 4339, 1; EV.d/10450.
57. Salzmann, *Tocqueville in the Ottoman Empire*, 98.
58. İslamoğlu-İnan, *State and Peasant*, 61; idem, "Property as a Contested Domain," 3–61.
59. İnalcık, "The Ottoman State: Economy and Society," 59.
60. Ibid., 59–60.
61. Neşe Erin, "18. Yüzyılda Erzurum Tuzları: Osmanlı Tüketim Malları Tarihine Bir Katkı," *A.Ü. Türkiyat Araştırmaları Enstitüsü Dergisi* 21 (2003): 224, 227.
62. BVGM: 571, 109.

Apparently, starting from the eleventh century, whole regions were bestowed as a grant of autonomy to powerful tribal Türkmen or Kurdish chieftains in Anatolia by different Islamic rulers. These areas were held for life or were inheritable with certain autonomy vis-à-vis the state. In the sixteenth century, during the first days of the Ottoman-Safavid wars on the eastern frontiers, Sultans Selim I (1512–1520) and Süleyman I (1520–1566) needed the cooperation of local rulers for the region's military defense and socio-political organization. Therefore, they allowed certain Türkmen and Kurdish tribal leaders to preserve their hereditary rights and status in north and southeastern Anatolia. Namely, from the 1530s, as a reward for their service and in recognition of their power, former chieftains were granted some degree of autonomy by the central government in the newly conquered lands with the formation of administrative units of special status, the *ocaklık sancak*s. On the one hand, tax registers were prepared in their *sancak*s, the *timar* system was introduced, and the *sancakbeyi*s were obligated to support the sultan with troops during military campaigns. On the other hand, the hereditary rulers of *ocaklık sancak*s possessed the traditional symbols of power (a drum and a flag), they could be neither dismissed nor appointed to other posts, and the lands were given to them and their descendants with full proprietary rights (by means of *mülkname*s) and could not be given to « outsiders. » That is, the grantees had full rights to sell, donate, or make a waqf out of their landed properties.[63]

Of course, over time the number of *ocaklık sancak*s changed in the eastern provinces depending on changing power relations between the local dynasties and central authorities. It appears that in the seventeenth century, the Ottoman government encountered difficulties in exerting greater control considering the growing number of *ocaklık sancak*s in the area.[64] For example, during the years 1682 to 1702, nine of the seventeen *sancak*s in the province of Erzurum, including Kızuçan, were *ocaklık*.[65]

Thus, at the time of the establishment of Feyzullah Efendi's endowments, it seems that the *ocaklık* status of the district of Kızuçan was becoming stronger. Indeed, it is said that the family of Ali had been holding this district as *ocaklık*

---

63. It should be mentioned that the term *ocaklık* had a very broad application in Ottoman fiscal practice. For instance, it also designated funds set aside to meet various expenses. On the *ocaklık* system see İnalcık, "Autonomous Enclaves," 113, 115, 126–28; Agoston, "A Flexible Empire," 18–29; Michael Robert Hickok, *Ottoman Military Administration in Eighteenth Century Bosnia* (Leiden: Brill, 1997), 42–53; Sabri Ateş, *Ottoman-Iranian Borderlands: Making a Boundary, 1843–1914* (Cambridge: Cambridge University Press, 2013), 34–42; Orhan Kılıç, "Ocaklık," *Türkiye Diyanet Vakfı İslam Ansiklopedisi* (2007), 33:317–18; Géza Dávid, «Administration, Provincial,» *Encyclopedia of the Ottoman Empire* (New York: Facts On File, 2009), 14.

64. Agoston, "A Flexible Empire," 22.

65. Orhan Kılıç, "XVIII. Yüzyılın İlk Yarısında Osmanlı Devleti'nin Eyalet ve Sancak Teşkilatlanması," *Osmanlı* (Ankara: Yeni Türkiye Yayınları, 1999): 6:96.

for more than two hundred years, as different sultans acknowledged the special status of the *sancak* through *berats*.⁶⁶

Hence, it is interesting to discover that the object of the sultan's grant did not convey *miri* status, but *ocaklık* status in the first place. For this reason, when Feyzullah Efendi requested that the sultan confer on him ownership over the Gönelü salt works, so that it could be given to an endowment, a special procedure had to be followed. First, the property in question had to be sold to the imperial treasury, since the *temlikname* system was based on the assignment of *miri* properties. Ali agreed to sell the *memlaha* and its surroundings (ponds and circular level spaces used for spreading salt) for the sum of 2,500 *kuruş*. Upon receipt of the sale deed from the judge of Kızuçan, the sultan issued a *mülkname* in order to transfer ownership rights to Feyzullah Efendi. As soon as the *baş defterdar* (the head of the finance administration) was notified of the sultan's imperial decree, the *şeyhülislam* was registered as the new owner of the Gönelü salt works in the "summary register" (*defter-i icmal*), which lists the distribution of revenue sources by the local fief-holders in accordance with their share of the revenues. In addition, the *mülkname* warns senior officials (viziers, governors, military commanders, and others) against interference in the *memlaha*'s affairs. The title deed was signed by the sultan at the beginning of June 1695 and witnessed by the same eminent functionaries mentioned in the *temlikname* of Muazamiye.⁶⁷ One possible explanation why Mustafa II was willing to make such a great effort is the closeness between him and the *şeyhülislam*, as well as Feyzullah Efendi's tremendous influence.

In May 1697, the sultan also issued a *hududname* which defined the boundaries of all revenue-yielding properties granted to Feyzullah Efendi in the province of Erzurum: Gönelü salt works, Kömör salt works, Kömör village, Timusi salt works, and Sim village. The sultan gave two reasons why the document was necessary. First, the fact that Feyzullah Efendi had earlier been granted ownership over the Gönelü salt works. Second, as in the case of the village of Muazamiye, copies of *hududnames* relating to the boundaries of Kömör village and the Kömör salt works could not be found at the office of the *defterhane* in Istanbul.⁶⁸

Accordingly, the judge of Erzurum began to make inquiries. He sent Abdülbaki Efendi to the Gönelü salt works with the intention of reconstructing its boundaries. Abdülbaki Efendi questioned local experts: Muslims from the district of Kızuçan (Mustafa Efendi, Mehmed Bey, Ali Beşe, Murad Bey and others) and the Christian managers of the *memlaha* (Evans, Osip and Temük). The witnesses agreed that the *mukataa* of the Gönelü salt works was to be included

66. BVGM: 571, 109.
67. Ibid., 109–10.
68. Ibid., 115.

within the boundaries of Gönelü village, and retraced the landmarks along its perimeter on four sides:

> From the path connecting the village of Güne and Erzincan to the spring of Saksan and the mill; and then continuing to the big stream which runs from the direction of the convent and the edge of the stream known as Mezraa Stream; then continuing eastward along the opposite side of the big stream towards the arable field of Toros the Armenian, then to the aforementioned big stream and the edge of the arable field possessed by Ahdik the Armenian; and then reaching the aforementioned path and the boundary of the arable field of Margos the Armenian.[69]

All of these descriptions in total create a kind of map meant to establish the boundaries of properties belonging to the waqf of Feyzullah Efendi. The borders were defined by physical markers—spring, mill, stream, field, road and so on—as they were perceived as permanent, or long-lived enough to be reliable signposts in the event that the border had to be verified,[70] as was the case here. One should take into consideration that Ali's family had been holding this revenue bearing property for more than two hundred years, during which there was no recording of the precise boundaries of the village and the salt works. Therefore, villagers living in close proximity to the boundaries in question, as well as residents of district who were familiar with the landmarks along the perimeter and were aware of any changes that had taken place in the past for various reasons (natural disasters, gradual changes, human intervention, etc.), took part in retracing the exact borders.

In this context, the same local experts were asked to measure the buildings attached to the *memlaha*: one salt well, ten stone ponds (*abdan*), two circular spaces used for spreading out salt (*harman*), and a one-room storehouse. For example, the measurements of the largest stone pond connected to the well were: thirty-three *zira* long (approximately twenty-five meters) and ten *zira* wide (approximately 7.6 meters). At the end of the process, Abdülbaki Efendi sent a delegation of three people (*çukadar* Mustafa Beşe, Mehmed Efendi, and *muhzır* Ali Çelebi) to the court of the judge of Erzurum in order to present and explain his findings. Only then, on the basis of the testimonies provided by knowledgeable local people given in court did the judge of Erzurum prepare a written description of the boundaries.[71]

However, in this case, too, the conversion of the salt works from *mukataa* to *mülk,* so that it could be given to an endowment, did not guarantee absolute ownership of land. It turned out that in 1705, shortly after the *şeyhülislam*'s vio-

---

69. Ibid., 116.
70. Singer, "Transcrire les frontiers," 137; Gümüşçü, "The Concept of Village Boundary," 41–2, 45.
71. BVGM: 571, 116.

lent demise, Sultan Ahmed III decided to restore the Gönelü salt works to state control.[72] According to Feyzullah Efendi's waqf account book of 1743, the customs of Erzurum had been added to the list of properties instead of the revenue source of Gönelü.[73]

The Salt Works and Village of Kömör (Erzurum)

The *mukataa* of Kömör was part of the *nahiye* of Kemah. At that time, it yielded the imperial treasury an annual income of 40,000 *akçe*. At first, in accordance with accepted practice, the sultan issued a title deed granting Feyzullah Efendi ownership of the Kömör salt works, Kömör village, Timusi salt works, Sim village, and Gönelü salt works. All of these revenue-producing properties, except the last, originally belonged to the imperial treasury and were classified as imperial domain (*havass-ı hümayun*). They were granted in exchange for two villages, Şahsula and Büyükyörgiç (both located in the sub-district of Mihaliç—west of Bursa), which had been given to Feyzullah Efendi by Sultan Mehmed IV (1648–87) as *mülk* grants and were at this point reclaimed by the state.[74]

Just like the *mülkname* issued on the matter of the village of Muazamiye, the state officially conceded all rights to the grantee. Hence, Sultan Mustafa II announced that everything within the boundaries of the five *mukataa*s would be the private property of the owner, which included lands, pastures, meadows, summer highland pastures, winter quarters for animals, mountains, hills, rivers, and wells. As for the taxes due to the waqf, they resembled those assigned in the case of Muazamiye. Revenues from taxes on orchards and gardens, not mentioned in the *mülkname* of Muazamiye, were added as well.[75]

Finally, we find the same warning by the sultan against any intervention by powerful people in the affairs of the granted *mukataa*s, be they government officials from the center or from the province. The decree was signed by the sultan in February 1697 and witnessed by high-ranking officials: the grand vizier (Elmas Mehmed Pasha), vizier Hasan, vizier Mahmud (head of the Janissary Corps), Ali Efendi (the Chief Military Judge of Rumelia), Mehmed Efendi (the Chief Military Judge of Anatolia), *defteri* (perhaps *defterdar*) Halil, and *tevkii* Elhac Ali.[76]

Three months later, the sultan issued a *hududname* in which all revenue-yielding properties granted to Feyzullah Efendi in Erzurum were carefully defined. This was done, because the original *hududname* document and its copies defining the boundaries of the salt works and the village of Kömör had been lost. To settle the matter, Feyzullah Efendi nominated Mehmed Efendi, the son of Perviz Efendi, to represent him in the local court. Afterwards, elderly people living

---

72. Erin, "18. Yüzyılda Erzurum Tuzları," 224, 227.
73. Başbakanlık Osmanlı Arşivi: Nezaret Öncesi Evkaf Defterleri, No. 4339, 1.
74. BVGM: 571, 111–12.
75. Ibid., 112.
76. Ibid.

in the immediate proximity to the village (for example, the town of Kemah, the village of Marik, and the village of Timus) were summoned to court to define the ancient boundaries of the two *mukataa*s. Based upon their testimonies and many others, the boundaries of the village and the salt works were reestablished.[77]

Below is the description of the village boundaries:

> Its boundary on the west [begins from] the cemetery of the aforementioned village to Elhac Yunus Bridge; from there, the boundary continues to Körhane Valley and the path leading to the mountain known as Karadonlu; from there, to a place known as Maktbayırı; from there, it continues to a place known as Karataş; from there, to the head of Karasennak; and on the north side [its boundary begins from] the edge of the valley and Kuşak and reaches to Manşger Bridge; from there, it continues to the foot of the mountain known as Saldağı and a place called Kızlıyar; from there, to a place of ruins known as Vanik facing east and Firaz Mountain; from there, it continues to Taşvangil where the summer pastures of the aforementioned village are to be found; from there, it continues to a settlement named Çaylıca; from there, it continues to Kokmuş Spring; from there, it continues to a settlement named of Kuyulu; from there, it continues to Firaz Mountain and Haydar Spring which has long been providing the aforementioned village with water; from there, it continues to a water channel; from there, it continues to Mecnun Salt Mine and the lower edge of a place known as Kızılevler; from there, it continues to the Kuruköprü bridge; from there, it continues to a path leading from [the city of] Erzincan to the town of Kemah; from there, it continues to a private water channel and the aforementioned cemetery as far as the aforementioned village.[78]

At the time, the *mukataa* of the salt works yielded the imperial treasury an annual income of 65,000 *akçe*, and was included within the boundaries of the village. Local experts who had taken part in setting the boundary, namely land assessors and the managers of the *memlaha*, focused their attention on the salt production process. At first, they estimated and testified that the amount of salt water flowing from the two springs of the salt works was approximately three *masure*.[79] Then, they started measuring the relevant facilities. There were two stone ponds attached to the springs. The larger pond's measurements were thirty-two *zira* long (approximately twenty-four meters), twenty *zira* wide (approximately fifteen meters), and one *zire* deep (0.758 cm). The second pond was thirty *zira* long (approximately 22.7 meters), twenty *zira* wide (approximately fifteen meters), and one *zire* deep (0.758 cm). Two more facilities consisted of paved circles used for

77. Ibid., 115.
78. Ibid.
79. According to the Ottoman system of measurement, the rate of flow of water or spring passing through a short pipe, whose inner diameter is twenty-six mm and whose axis is ninety-six mm below the level of water or spring, equals one *lüle*—that is, thirty-six l/min., or fifty-two m³/day. One *masure* equals 1/8 of a *lüle* (4.5 l/min.).

spreading salt. One was made of sundried bricks and twenty-four *göl* (?), and the other was made of sixty-two *göl* (?) (eighty-six *göl* total). Two old houses and a storehouse were also recorded as property of the salt works.[80]

Finally, it is worth noting that the *mukataa*s of the salt works and village of Kömör, similar to the village of Muazamiye and the Gönelü salt works, reverted to state control between 1708 and 1723. Similar to the case of the Gönelü salt works, the customs of Erzurum replaced these sources of income as the new revenue-bearing source. The reason was apparently either a decrease in revenue or a liquidity problem.[81] Thus, of the five revenue-yielding properties granted by Mustafa II to Feyzullah Efendi in the province of Erzurum for the establishment of his endowments, only one endured for a period of 150 years, that of the village of Sim.[82]

Conclusion

As has been shown, on several occasions the interested dignitary, Feyzullah Efendi, initiated boundary demarcation in order to be certain of the boundaries of the granted properties, mentioned in the *temliknames/mülkname*s, so that his powers over these revenue sources would be full and unconditional. A few problems, however, arose pertaining to these properties granted to him by the sultan for the purpose of waqf making. These included old copies of *hududname*s of villages/other revenue-yielding properties having been lost, the occurrence of land disputes, and one of the properties carried the status of *ocaklık* wherein its boundaries had not been defined for more than two hundred years. These disputes necessitated an investigation of the boundaries of these properties and their redrawing.

The person in charge of preparing a document defining village boundaries (or that of other properties) was the local judge (or his representatives). The process of boundary marking had two main stages. First, local experts with the requisite knowledge were summoned to court in order to determine the boundaries of the village. That knowledge was passed from generation to generation predating the Ottoman era. The experts' description of the boundaries was based on established and long-lasting physical markers. Then the judge or his representative visited the relevant site in order to reenact the process by which the village description was initially recorded. Thus, the written description needed to be validated by oral testimony and physical demonstration. On the whole, the legal process of boundary demarcation reflects how land ownership was actually based on several sources of law: Muslim law (sharia), Ottoman regulations (*kanunname*s), pre-Ottoman customs and local customary practices. This was

---

80. BVGM: 571, 115–16.
81. İE: Vakıf/4656, 6901; CEV. Evkaf/15345, 22315.
82. EV. d/12404.

expressed, among other things, by using *temliknames/mülknames*, court decisions, witnesses, oral testimonies, consensus and knowledge of neighbors, and old forms of property ownership (*ocaklık*).

The definition of boundaries served both the Ottoman government and the villagers. Given that the Ottoman economy depended mostly on agriculture and stock raising for generating revenues, a clear demarcation of space was crucially important in terms of administrative practices since tax payment and collection was the nexus of peasant-official interactions. As such, properly determining the size and borders of the village and each of its units (i.e., salt works, arable lands, pastures, and so forth) helped to maintain the tax base and clarify revenue-holding rights and taxpaying obligations.

Also, as the document of delimitation was considered to be valid and authoritative, it enabled village land disputes to be settled on the basis of the boundaries as recorded in the *hududname*. This, in turn, contributed to maintaining social order, given the many disputes over lands between neighboring villages as well as between village communities and elites. Apparently, peasants could benefit from the recognized authority of the judge on their own behalf only by presenting written documents, such as boundary documents in court, or by referring to the relevant text found in the judge's possession.

One other reason for careful attention devoted to village-boundary drawing in the Ottoman context, beyond concerns of the central government and concerns of villages, was the interests/concerns of a land-owning class enabled by *mülk* grants. In response to the introduction of the *malikane* system at the end of the seventeenth century, high-ranking functionaries belonging to the old elites strove to secure rural income for themselves and their descendants by attempting to convert, in stages, public resources into private property. At first, they obtained *malikane* contracts of revenue sources. Then they asked the sultan to change the designation of state revenue sources to *mülk* grants. Finally, some of them even tried to convert *mülk* grants of *malikane* holdings into pious endowments hoping this would guarantee the conversion of state property into a private property.

Yet the case of Feyzullah Efendi demonstrates that even when the sultan granted absolute rights over revenues and immunity from state interference in the form of *temlikname*, there was always a chance that the central government would regain control over *mülk* lands, and even waqf lands. It appears that the state made an ongoing effort to strengthen its position as the source of property rights. Thus, even if at some point the palace surrendered to the demands of highly placed officials to convert a *malikane* contract into private property or a pious endowment, each new sultan could abrogate land titles.

MICHAEL NIZRI is a Lecturer in the Department of Middle Eastern Studies and Israel Studies, Ariel University, Ariel, Israel.

4 Economic Interventionism, Islamic Law and Provincial Government in the Ottoman Empire[1]

M. Safa Saraçoğlu

IN THIS CHAPTER, my intention is to make some observations on the transformation of Ottoman administrative involvement in the functioning of markets from the fifteenth to the nineteenth centuries. My intent is not a comprehensive treatment of the subject, but rather, to raise questions that can help us understand shifts in how markets were conceptualized in the eighteenth and nineteenth centuries. I argue that mechanisms that regulated the conduct of fair and legitimate market place exchange changed significantly in the Ottoman Empire from the fifteenth to the nineteenth centuries, as the rulers gradually abandoned an interventionist policy (using regulatory mechanisms such as price ceilings) in favor of noninterventionist state policies. Administrative intervention in markets was not a process that was easily accepted by medieval *fiqh* scholars, who claimed that it interfered with the free will of individuals in determining and declaring the value of their property. The Ottomans ignored these objections, however, particularly between the sixteenth and eighteenth centuries.

In these centuries the Ottoman state legitimated the use of price ceilings by claiming that such policies promoted a balanced societal order; in contrast, its later noninterventionist attitude was legitimized by the perceived necessity of spontaneous market mechanisms for an equitable system. Both policies had particular institutional configurations that reflected these concerns: market inspectors (*muhtasib*) and price-ceiling policies (*narh*) dominated the earlier period, administrative councils replaced them in the nineteenth century. This shift, I argue, reflects a change in the nature of Ottoman governance that needs to be explored in order to understand connections between the development of free market policies and legal transformation in the empire. I do not seek here to

---

1. Many thanks to the fellows and staff at the Institute of Advanced Studies at Nantes, Andrea Schwartz at Bloomsburg, the participants of the workshop that Kent Schull and I organized at 2013 MESA Conference, and the anonymous reviewers for *JOTSA*. I am grateful to Huricihan İslamoğlu, Boğaç Ergene, and Michael C. Hickey for helping me clarify my arguments.

provide evidence of continuity of intellectual debates between the eighteenth and nineteenth centuries; my goal, rather, is to show that in the course of Ottoman institutional transformation during these centuries, pre-eighteenth-century market control mechanisms were replaced by newly established provincial councils in 1849.

In the first half of this article I focus on pre-eighteenth-century market control mechanisms. A discussion of how Ottoman administrators incorporated market inspection/inspectors (*ihtisab/muhtasib*) and price-ceiling (*narh*) is followed by a contextualization of these practices in the larger complex of sovereign authority, justice, and societal balance. Despite its disputed Islamic legitimacy, *narh* was commonly used in the Ottoman Empire and the *muhtasib*s (market inspectors), as agents of the larger judicio-administrative complex, were actively engaged in its utilization towards maintaining social balance. While in this framework oppression (*zulm*) related to a ruler's inability to maintain the balance in social structuration, its meaning gradually shifted in the eighteenth century. During the eighteenth century, through the works of Ottoman scholars such as Naima, *zulm* increasingly became associated with excessive state intervention in the natural market order. This shift had parallels in Western intellectual debates about the spontaneous nature of markets.

In the second half of the article, I trace the organizational outcome of this ideological shift. In the course of eighteenth and nineteenth centuries, the empire eliminated its established policies of state provisioning and *narh*. Gradually, the imperial center relegated the task of supervising economic activity to provincial administrative councils established in the 1840s. My discussion of the transformation of key Ottoman market control institutions is followed by a contextualization of these changes in a larger complex of authority, security, and information. As the nineteenth-century Ottoman judicio-administrative sphere reorganized around a particular conceptualization of economy, markets became a test ground for measuring the limits of necessary governmental intervention to maintain a spontaneous natural order. Provincial councils, established following an 1849 regulation, played a significant role in this new Ottoman method of governance.

A note about the 1849 regulation and the new provincial councils (*eyalet meclisi*), is in order: I am particularly interested in the rules outlining these councils' authority over the economic sphere and their possible political implications. These councils served as a platform where provincial administrative and judicial issues were discussed with an emphasis on justice. My examination of the 1849 regulations is based on a copy in *Mecmu'a-yı Kavanin*, which was published in 1851.[2] The collection does not have an official title or a cover page, but is struc-

---

2. Ottoman official publications increased significantly in the nineteenth century. In 1851, the imperial printing house, published this 142-page volume of codes—the earliest attempt to

turally and stylistically similar to the *Düstur* series that was published as single volumes in 1862 and 1865 before it became a series in 1872. A revised version of this code was included in those later volumes of *Düstur*.³

Most of the established literature on provincial administration acknowledges the 1849 regulation, but considers 1864 as a more important turning point in provincial administration.⁴ The significance of the 1864 regulation is obvious: it organized the provincial division and the judicio-administrative infrastructure around two interconnected local councils where the notables played important roles.⁵ The "councils" were not new institutions, however.⁶ They had been a part of Ottoman governance culture before 1840 (at the local and imperial level), and the 1849 and 1864 regulations built on familiar notions about how the councils should operate.⁷ The 1849 regulation should be understood in the particular context of local notables' systematic inclusion into Ottoman governance.⁸ Unfortu-

---

collect governmental codes in printed volumes during the Tanzimat. The copy I used has no title page; however, later volumes of *Düstur* (1862, 1865) refer to a volume published at this date. Karakoç refers to it as *Mecmu'a-yı Kavanin*, (A Corpus of Laws) and to the latter two volumes as *Düstûr-ı atîk, sene 1279* and *Düstûr-ı atîk, sene 1282* ("The Old Düstur," 1862 and 1865). Sarkis Karakoç, *Külliyât-ı Kavânîn: Kavânîn ve Nizâmât ve Ferâmîn ve Berevât ve Irâdât-ı Seniyye ile Muâhedât ve Umûma Ait Mukâvelâti Muhtevidir* (Ankara: Türk Tarih Kurumu, 2006). Karakoç's definition, ("a corpus") is mentioned in the cover of the later volumes as the description for the term *Düstur*: "A corpus containing the laws and regulations is called *düstur*."

3. *Düstur* (Istanbul: Matba'a-yı 'Amire, 1862), 486; *Düstur* (Istanbul: Matba'a-yı'Amire, 1865), 870.

4. İlber Ortaylı, *Tanzimat Devrinde Osmanlı Mahalli İdareleri (1840–1880)* (Ankara: Türk Tarih Kurumu, 2000), 43; Musa Çadırcı, *Tanzimat Döneminde Anadolu Kentleri'nin Sosyal ve Ekonomik Yapısı* (Ankara: Türk Tarih Kurumu, 1997), 218–24; Jun Akiba, "The Local Councils as the Origin of the Parliamentary System in the Ottoman Empire," in *Development of Parliamentarism in the Modern Islamic World*, ed. Tsugitaka Sato (Tokyo: The Toyo Bunko, 2009), 183.

5. M. Safa Saraçoğlu, "Some Aspects of Ottoman Governmentality at the Local Level: The Judicio-Administrative Sphere of the Vidin County in the 1860s and 1870s," *Ab Imperio* 8:2 (2008); Beshara Doumani, *Rediscovering Palestine: Merchants and Peasants in Jabal Nablus, 1700–1900* (Berkeley: University of California Press, 1995); Mahmoud Yazbak, *Haifa in the Late Ottoman Period, 1864–1914: A Muslim Town in Transition* (Leiden: Brill, 1998).

6. "Institutions are the 'rules of the game' . . . , the patterns of interaction that govern and constrain the relationships of individuals." Douglass Cecil North, et al., *Violence and Social Orders: A Conceptual Framework for Interpreting Recorded Human History* (New York: Cambridge University Press, 2009), 15.

7. Akiba points out that "during the 18th century, there were provincial councils presided over by governors or judges (*kadı*) and joined by local notables dealing with the assessment and collection of taxes. They were certainly predecessors of the Tanzimat councils, although the latter were innovative in that they became permanent official institutions and officially accepted non-Muslim members." Akiba, "The Local Councils," 179.

8. For an earlier discussion that does not focus on this particular regulation, see: M. Safa Saraçoğlu, "Resilient Notables: Looking at the Transformation of the Ottoman Empire from

nately, very little has been written about the 1849 regulation.[9] In the context of the market related institutional transformation in the Ottoman Empire, these councils replaced the *muhtasib* in supervising the proper functioning of the economic domain, particularly in the provinces. Their responsibilities, outlined in the 1849 regulation, reflected the changing perspectives on what market activity is and how it should be controlled. While more research is needed on the pace and structure of these changes during the eighteenth and nineteenth centuries, this article outlines how the transformation focused on debates about the nature of market activity.

Ihtisab, Value and Narh in Islam

As an Abrahamic religion, Islam associates price of a commodity with assessment and honest declaration of abstract concepts such as value and labor.[10] Islamic scholars have long problematized the essential function of markets, as markets,—which Islamic law treats as public space[11]—play an important role in establishing a just society based upon "commanding right and forbidding wrong" (*al-amr bi'l-ma'ruf wa'l-nahı 'ani'l-munkar*).[12]

---

the Local Level," in *Contested Spaces of Nobility in Early Modern Europe*, ed. Matthew P. Romaniello and Charles Lipp (Burlington: Ashgate, 2011).

9. For the only significant discussion in English, see Akiba, "The Local Councils." There is a German translation by Thomas Scheben, *Verwaltungsreformen Der Frühen Tanzimatzeit: Gesetze, Massnahmen, Auswirkungen: Von Der Verkündigung Des Ediktes Von Gülhane 1839 Bis Zum Ausbruch Des Krimkrieges 1853* (New York: P. Lang, 1991), 288–302. For a Turkish summary, see Çadırcı, *Tanzimat Döneminde Anadolu Kentleri'nin*, 218–24.

10. According to Ibn Taymiyah, for example, "the Prophet . . . proscribed sale and purchase—generically lawful acts—until the seller knows the market price, i.e. the fair price, and the customer is familiar with the goods. . . . For in sale we must look for consent and consent follows knowledge. . . . If it becomes apparent that the article is misrepresented or defective it is as if the seller had described it in one way and it turned out to be quite the opposite. So he may or may not consent. If he does so, well and good, but if not he is entitled to rescind the sale." Ahmad ibn Abd al-Halim Ibn Taymiyah, *Public Duties in Islam: The Institution of the Hisba*, trans. Muhtar Holland (Leicester: Islamic Foundation, 1982), 57.

11. Kristen Stilt and Roy Mottahedeh, "Public and Private as Viewed through the Work of the Muhtasib," *Social Research* 70:3 (2003): 741–42.

12. Several "book of sales" (*kitab al-bay'*) volumes in *fiqh* compilations and the detailed nature of the legal opinions on declaration of price during the purchase illustrate the theological complexity of market practices. For example, see Ömer Nasuhi Bilmen, *Hukuk-ı İslamiyye ve İstilahat-ı Fikhiyye Kamusu*, 8 vols. (Istanbul: Ravza, 2013), 6:14–23. A "fair price" is established through honest appraisal and consensus of the buyer and the seller on the value of a commodity, see Diya' al-Din Muhammad ibn Muhammad [Ibn al-Ukhuwah], *The Ma'alim Al-Qurba fi Ahkam Al-Hisba of Diya' Al-Din Muhammad Ibn Muhammad Al-Qurashi Al-Shafi'i Known as Ibn Al-Ukhuwwa: Edited, with Abstract of Contents, Glossary and Indices* (London: Cambridge University Press, 1938), 23–4; Ibn Taymiyah, *Public Duties*, 29–31. Political authorities' involvement with this process led to a variety of opinions. Sixteenth-century Ottoman officials calculated a "fair estimate of the sale value of commodities" in important cities based

The two most important mechanisms of control over market activity were proper inspection of economic activity at the markets (which is one of the two related meanings of the Arabic term *hisba*) and determination of a price ceiling by state officials (*narh*). *Hisba* generally refers to the duty that is incumbent on every Muslim to "command the right and forbid the wrong." As the official specifically commissioned to oversee the market activity, a *muhtasib* would play a role in determining the *narh* but could not do so alone. In the Ottoman Empire, the *kadı* would establish the *narh* through consultation with craftsmen and the *muhtasib*.[13] The *kadı* and *muhtasib* worked in tandem and their relationship had a bearing on commercial activities.

The institution of *hisba* does not appear to be simply a continuation of pre-Islamic practices. Cahen points out that the *hisba* could be considered "the successor of the *agoranomos* of the Hellenistic cities: his duties were broadly similar and the Arabic expression can be seen as a translation of the Greek term." But he notes that sources make no reference to an *agoranomos* for about 300 years prior to the Arab conquests and no reason to assume that the Arabic predecessor to the office of market inspector, *sahib al-suq* could have appeared "without inspiration from outside." [14] Cook points out two isolated traditions in the late pre-Islamic era that used the term *muhtasib* for individuals in Mecca who were charged with the official task of "commanding right and forbidding wrong," yet he adds that the meaning of the phrase should be considered different than the terms "right" and "wrong" (*ma'ruf* and *munkar*).[15] While evidence suggests that the use of these terms in the Quran parallel their usage in pre-Islamic Arabia, the order of "commanding" and "forbidding" them seems to be a "Quranic innovation."[16]

---

on a principle of "sufficient profits." A notion that was "never theoretically elaborated on in either official documents like *kannuname*s or narrative sources," according to Cemal Kafadar, "When Coins Turned into Drops of Dew and Bankers Became Robbers of Shadows: The Boundaries of Ottoman Economic Imagination at the End of the Sixteenth Century" (PhD diss., McGill University, 1986), 126, 130. The Hanafi scholar Ibn Qayyim al-Jawziyya (d.1350) argued that the *muhtasib* "should allow the merchants to make a uniform level of profit but not allow them to increase their prices to increase that profit" in cases when the merchants refuse to sell their goods (for which there is established need) citing low prices, see Adam Sabra, "'Prices Are in God's Hands': The Theory and Practice of Price Control in the Medieval Islamic World," in *Poverty and Charity in Middle Eastern Contexts*, ed. Michael David Bonner, et al. (Albany: State University of New York Press, 2003), 83.

13. Mübahat S. Kütükoğlu, "Narkh," *Encyclopaedia of Islam*, 2nd ed., ed. P. Bearman, et al. (Leiden: Brill, 2012) [Herafer cited as *EI²*].

14. C. Cahen, M. Talbi, and R. Mantran, "Hisba," in *EI²*.

15. Michael Cook, *Commanding Right and Forbidding Wrong in Islamic Thought* (New York: Cambridge University Press, 2000), 564–66.

16. Ibid., 569.

Pre-Ottoman Islamic *hisba* manuals seem to be in agreement that *muhtasibs* should not set prices under normal conditions.[17] In "the earliest source on the subject [of *hisba*]" Yahya ibn Umar (d. 901), relates that Malik ibn Anas forbade the practice of fixing prices on the grounds that it is "unjust" (*zulm*).[18] Although Hanafi scholars considered setting prices in a properly functioning market as *makruh* and other schools of law considered it *haram*,[19] in the sixteenth-century Ottoman Empire, "systematic government intervention in price rates" was considered the norm. Historians in the sixteenth century did not question the validity of the practice even though it is not necessarily sanctioned by Islamic tradition. In fact, Kafadar notes that in condoning price controls the Ottomans not only sidestepped "liberal tendency of the classical jurists" such as Shayzari (d. 1193) and Ibn al-Ukhuwa (d. 1329), but also "went further than other [Islamic states as they] systematized and codified [such controls] through secular legislation" in the aftermath of the conquest of Constantinople to establish a "strict control over the bazaar among other realms of economic activity."[20] Ottomans' use of *narh*, however, had some backing in *fiqh*. Sabra notes that while Shafi scholars opposed price fixing, predominantly Malikis, and post-fourteenth-century Hanbali and Hanafis scholars, commonly tolerated price ceilings, particularly in times of scarcity "in the interests of the common people (*fi masalih al-'amma*)."[21] While it would be interesting to see how Ottoman administrators and jurists justified widespread use of price ceilings through *fiqh*, such an exploration is beyond the scope of this article. Whether justified or not, use of *narh* from the middle of the fifteenth through the eighteenth centuries made Ottoman intervention into markets a consistent administrative reality.

Markets served as a testing ground for Ottoman rulers. On the one hand, the ruler appointed the *muhtasib* to regulate the marketplace.[22] (Despite that, the *muhtasib*'s authority extended over the ruler. They were expected to "frequent the audiences of princes and governors and command them to show clem-

---

17. Abd al-Rahman ibn Nasr Shayzari, *The Book of the Islamic Market Inspector: Nihayat Al-Rutba fi Talab Al-Hisba (the Utmost Authority in the Pursuit of Hisba)*, trans. R. P. Buckley (New York: Oxford University Press, 1999), 37; [Ibn al-Ukhuwah], *The Ma'alim*, 21; Ibn Taymiyah, *Public Duties*, 35.

18. Ahmad bin Che Yaacob, "The Development of the Theory of the Institution of Hisbah in Medieval Islam" (PhD diss., The University of Edinburgh, 1996), 87.

19. Cengiz Kallek, "Narh," *Islam Ansiklopedisi* (Istanbul: Türkiye Diyanet Vakfı 2006).

20. Kafadar, "When Coins," 114–16.

21. Sabra, "Prices Are in God's Hands," 76–83.

22. [Ibn al-Ukhuwah], *The Ma'alim*, 4. "The Hisba is one of the institutions of the spiritual order—directed in the prime of Islam by the heads of the community themselves.... The head of the community is invested with the only right of appointing to the office." R. P. Buckley notes that "Prophet Mohammed is said to have appointed the first persons with jurisdiction over the market," see Shayzari, *Islamic Market Inspector*, 3.

ency towards the people subject to them and to remind them of the traditions of the Prophet.")[23] On the other hand, particularly in the post-Mehmed II era, the viziers were to pay utmost attention to the setting of prices, and not relegate responsibility to the *kadıs* or to the *muhtasibs*.[24] Markets served as one of the important public places where the Ottoman rulers did "command the good and forbid the evil"[25] and intervened with the relations between different socioeconomic institutions, such as guilds and waqfs.[26] When the administration set the official price it replaced a rate that would otherwise be determined by religiously enforced rituals of honest declaration of value and need. In the Ottoman Empire, the marketplace and its associated exchange processes presented a moral framework for the sultan's relationship with the subject populace that was an extension of a more complex equation involving justice and oppression.

Justice, Balance and Equality

For Ibn Taymiyah there is a peculiar relationship between justice, oppression and wisdom. "The root of all that is knowledge," he notes, "for there is no other way to learn of justice and [oppression (*zulm*)]. The whole of religion is knowledge and justice, and the opposite is [oppression] and ignorance."[27] Ottoman advice literature and chronicles placed the rulers' relationship with the subject population along a similar moral axis between wisdom and oppression. Like other rulers, the Ottoman sultan was expected to rule over his subjects with "justice," a responsibility defined in the context of a particular perception of society and how its members, including the ruler, interact with each other.[28] Ergene points out that justice alone, however, could not account for the legitimacy of the whole system, which what based on a balance of a variety of different, related, factors.[29] Accord-

---

23. [Ibn al-Ukhuwah], *The Ma'alim*, 87.

24. Ömer Lütfi Barkan, "XV. Asrın Sonunda Bazı Büyük Şehirlerde Eşya ve Yiyecek Fiyatlarının Tesbit ve Teftişi Hususlarını Tanzim Eden Kanunlar I," *Tarih Vesikaları Dergisi* 1:5 (1942): 326–27.

25. While this was a task shared by all Muslims, Islamic scholars attributed "'three modes' to three groups in society: the rulers are to perform it with the hand, the scholars with the tongue, and the common people with the heart." Cook, *Commanding Right*, 583. The first mode of this task was incumbent on the Ottoman Sultans, see İbrahim Erdoğdu, "Osmanlı İktisadi Düzeninde İhtisab Müessesesi ve Muhtesiblik Üzerine Bir Deneme," *OTAM* 11 (2000): 124.

26. Kafadar, "When Coins," 122.

27. Ibn Taymiyah, *Public Duties*, 125.

28. Halil İnalcık, "Osmanlı Hukuk Sisteminde Adaletin Üstünlüğü," in *Adalet Kitabı*, ed. Halil İnalcık, Bülent Arı, and Selim Aslantaş (Ankara: Kadim Yayınları, 2012), 144.

29. "[B]y its very definition, justice was expected to govern only a portion of what the 'circle of equity' was thought to encompass, that is, the relationship between the sovereign ruler and the taxpaying *reaya*. According to various definitions of the circle of equity, the system could not function without other separate (albeit interdependent) variables, including the sharia,

ing to Fatih Ermiş, Naima (d.1716), arguably the first official Ottoman historian,[30] held that society is divided into four "pillars" that interacted with each other like the four humors.

> Scholars are like blood because they provide the society with necessary information for their livelihood. The peasants are black bile because they provide money, through production of surplus, for the state treasury, which he considered as the stomach of the body. The merchants, the yellow bile that controls digestion and excretion, contribute to stable exchange and transactions leading to increase in social wealth under normal conditions. However if they were oppressed by the government, or were greedy, socio-economic balance would be adversely affected. The last component, bureaucracy—which makes the subjects obey the ruler—is like phlegm: they are necessary for the body, but damaging when they are in excess.[31]

Naima's efforts are reflective of the historiography of the Ottoman Empire. There are "no known historical accounts of Ottoman exploits by the Ottomans before the fifteenth century."[32] The initial surge in Ottoman "historiographic output" began in the fifteenth century, and in the century after the conquest of Constantinople, a series of ideological and institutional changes happened (including the widespread use of *narh*), paralleling the rise to prominence of the Ottoman state and the Bektashiyya Sufi order. Thus, for the Ottoman Empire it became necessary to produce "a historical vision of themselves that confirmed, explained, and legitimized that supremacy."[33] Kafadar points out that chronicles written in the fifteenth century included layers of different narratives, and were not necessarily organized around a single core like an onion. Instead, they brought together parallel or even contradictory narratives (like the bulbs of a garlic)[34] brought together under the historical circumstances of the time. This is characteristic not only of fifteenth-century chronicles, but also of legal treatises and advice literature of later periods discussed briefly here. Without dissecting the layers of these chronicles, we still can recognize their hetroglossia as facilitat-

---

the capacity of kingship, military power and wealth." Boğaç A. Ergene, "On Ottoman Justice: Interpretations in Conflict (1600–1800)," *Islamic Law and Society* 8:1 (2001): 58.

30. Born in Aleppo in 1655, Naima rose through the ranks of the Ottoman bureaucracy to become a figure who is often considered "as the first Ottoman official historian" although this appears to be an ad hoc position created so that he can complete the Ottoman history draft written by another scholar. Christine Woodhead, "Na'ima," *EI²*.

31. Fatih Ermiş, "Ottoman Economic Thinking before the 19th Century" (Ph.D. diss., Universität Erfurt, 2011), 69–72.

32. Cemal Kafadar, *Between Two Worlds: The Construction of the Ottoman State* (Berkeley: University of California Press, 1995), 93.

33. Ibid., 98.

34. In discussing narrative as an onion Kafadar borrows "[Rudi Paul] Lindner's alimentary imagery" and expands it by adding garlic: ibid., 116.

ing discussion around certain themes in a somewhat continuous manner from the twelfth to the nineteenth centuries.[35]

In his *History*, Naima borrows from a variety of other scholars. These included Kınalızade Ali Efendi (d.1572), an Ottoman legal scholar, the judge of Damascus and Istanbul, and eventually, the chief judge for Anatolia.[36] Kınalızade also described society as a human body in balance:

> An ideal Sultan is like a professional physician and the *reaya* are like the body. A physician should know the illnesses, their symptoms and their cures. Similarly, a sultan should have information about the health of the country—which consists of being at the level of equilibrium—and the illnesses—deviations from the equilibrium and corruption—and should know the remedies for retaining the level of equilibrium after some deviations from it. And this is only partial knowledge of the medicine of ruling. In addition to this, the ruler should put his knowledge into practice with his enthusiasm, maintain this equilibrium and avoid deviations from it so that he can be called an ideal sultan and a wise caliph. [37]

This balance is related to the four virtues: wisdom (*hikmet*), chastity (*iffet*), courage (*şeca'at*), and justice (*adalet*). For Kınalızade, each virtue, except justice, has two extremes and each interacts with the other to establish a vague mixture in perfect balance. Justice emerges from this mixture and "this form includes all of the virtues in a perfect way . . . The golden mean of practical power is justice. It does not have [two extremes]. However it has an opposite, which is [oppression]."[38]

Ermiş traces the definitions of justice in Kınalızade (and Adam Smith who also sees justice as a cardinal virtue) back to Aristotle.[39] While, Ergene notes that "Kınalızade's synthesis of an Aristotelian understanding of government and the fundamental principles of Islam may justifiably be considered unprecedented in post-16th-century Ottoman political thought."[40] Kınalızade based his argument on a wide array of thinkers from the Muslim world as well,[41] including

---

35. M. M. Bakhtin, *The Dialogic Imagination: Four Essays*, trans. Michael Holquist and Caryl Emerson (Austin: University of Texas Press, 1981), 333.
36. Mehmed Çavuşoğlu, "Kınalızade," *EI*².
37. Quoted in Ermiş, "Ottoman Economic Thinking," 79. Naima and Kınalızade do not agree fully on the matching of the parts of society with humors, but both considered society as different groups that needed to be managed in a "just" fashion.
38. Ibid., 86–7.
39. Ibid., 87.
40. Ergene, "On Ottoman Justice," 86.
41. Kınalızade Ali Efendi, *Ahlak-ı Ala'i*, (Istanbul: Tercüman, 1974[?]), 18; Ermiş, "Ottoman Economic Thinking," 85. Fleischer notes that "Kınalızade's discussion of rational and revealed law is a Muslim jurist's interpretation of Platonic political philosophy. As such, it bears many resemblances to the analysis of Ibn Khaldun." Cornell Fleischer, "Royal Authority, Dynastic

al-Ghazali (an "outstanding theologian, jurist, original thinker, mystic and religious reformer" from the twelfth century), Nasir al-Din al-Tusi (d.1274) ("the most important and influential Shi'i scholar in the fields of mathematics, geometry, astronomy, philosophy and theology"), Djalal al-Din al-Dawani (d.1502) (who wrote a "modernized and popularized" version of al-Tusi's moral treatise), and Husayn Kashifi (a Persian scholar known as a member of the Nakhshibandi Sufi order and an Imami Shi'i at the same time and whose 1495 book on ethics was translated to Turkish for the seventeenth-century Ottoman Sultan Ahmed I).[42] Characterizing justice as a virtue that serves as a gauge for political power that can only exist in a sensitive balance between interconnected forces had been a part of the Mediterranean world's legal/political literature since the twelfth century. That is also why for scholars, such as Ibn Taymiyah, justness and religious wisdom would be required characteristics for a Muslim ruler.[43] As the translation of Kashifi's work in the seventeenth century, and Naima's incorporation of Kınalızade would suggest, the chain of scholars does not stop in the sixteenth century either.

While in this tradition justice is represented by a delicate balance between several forces, justice itself has its own opposition—oppression (*zulm*). Ermiş relates Kınalızade's and Naima's discussions of oppression to Ibn Khaldun and his "circle of justice."[44] For all three, the idea of justice is closely connected with the ruler, who is responsible for balancing the interests of different societal groups. Oppression, therefore, is the product of the ruler's inability to maintain a balance, to treat all groups equally. Ergene emphasizes the importance of holy law in the definition of "equality":

> Political justice had nothing to do with the benevolence of the ruler or the state, but depended upon the acknowledgment of the authority of the holy law and the eminence of the hierarchical social order. The emphasis on the sharia was instrumental in enabling dissidents (and those fortunate members of the ruling elite who were able to appropriate state power) to approach the sultan as equals under the laws of God.[45]

Cyclism, and 'Ibn Khaldunism' in 16th Century Ottoman Letters," *Journal of Asian & African Studies* 18:3/4 (1983): 202.

42. W. Montgomery Watt, "Al-Ghazali"; H. Daiber and F.J. Ragep, "Al-Tusi, Nasir Al-Din"; Ann K.S. Lambton, "Al-Dawani"; Gholam Hosein Yousofi, "Kashifi," *EI*².

43. For Taymiyah "all governmental institutions are interconnected in such a way that the duty of each individual institution cannot be strictly defined." M. Izzi Dien, *The Theory and the Practice of Market Law in Medieval Islam: A Study of Kitab Nisab Al-Ihtisab of Umar b. Muhammad Al-Sunami (Fl. 7th-8th/13th-14th Century)* (Warminster: E.J.W. Gibb Memorial Trust, 1997), 33.

44. Ermiş, "Ottoman Economic Thinking," 90–1.

45. Ergene, "On Ottoman Justice," 86.

The rulers' meddling with the economy, through *muhtasib* or *narh*, therefore, ran the risk of upsetting the sensitive societal balance.

Oppression and Economy

Another key element shaping understandings of market intervention was the perceived relationship between oppression and economic inefficiency. Ermiş notes that for Ibn Khaldun the right to property is at the center of this relationship:

> It should be known that attacks on people's property remove the incentive to acquire any property.... When attacks (on property) are extensive and general, extending to all means of making a livelihood, business inactivity, too, becomes (general), because the general extent (of such attacks upon property) means a general destruction of the incentive (to do business).... When people no longer do business in order to make a living, and when they cease all gainful activity, the business of civilization slumps and everything decays.[46]

Thus, the ruler's governing focus is on balancing segments of the population. Justice is the natural equilibrium desired in one's body and in the social structuration. Oppression, *zulm*, is a sign of disequilibrium and governing without a proper balance of the other three primary virtues: wisdom, chastity, and courage. *Zulm* "refers to any acts of illegal taxation, unruly violence, bribery, or corrupt governance that would necessitate the punishment of those official and unofficial power-holders in the provinces who were responsible for them."[47]

The Arabic word *zulm* (ظلم) means "'putting a thing in a place not its own' ... i.e., displacement. In the moral sphere, it denotes acting in such a way as to transgress the proper limit and encroach upon the right of some other person."[48] The use of this term to refer to abuse of power, particularly in relation to property, underscores the tenuous nature of the balance and the limits on the sovereign. The ruler is not supposed to take from certain groups to give to others, as this would constitute attack on property rights. Instead, a just sovereign is to make sure that no group—neither the buyers nor the sellers—has an unfair advantage over the other.

Institutions of Balance: Provisioning, Prices and Markets

Kınalızade and Naima understood humans as naturally inclined towards evil, echoing the twelfth-century scholar Abu'l-Nacib al-Shayzari.[49] Naima praised Shayzari's work, summarized some of his arguments for the introduction of his

---

46. Ermiş, "Ottoman Economic Thinking," 91.
47. Ergene, "On Ottoman Justice," 59.
48. Roswitha Badry, "Zulm," *EI*².
49. Ermiş, "Ottoman Economic Thinking," 51.

History, and noted that Kınalızade translated and used him as well.⁵⁰ It is "the evil tendency of the individual" that necessitates the creation of government, which Naima defines as "a specific form of human socialization." The art of governance is a calculated intervention to prevent "evil" from happening. According to Kınalızade, "evil" happens because "everybody has some desires and wants to satisfy these desires no matter the price . . . when an object is demanded by two people . . . this results in conflict, sedition and disorder."⁵¹

This framework is similar to the idea of a "natural order" along the lines of Quesnay's *Tableau économique*. In his discussion of the myth of natural order, Harcourt notes that Quesnay's particular idea is traceable to the early eighteenth-century, to Mandeville's bees or even to an earlier period. He notes that Schumpeter, "traced the notion back to the Scholastics—the theologians of the fourteenth and fifteenth centuries."⁵² Unlike the earlier works, Quesnay's *Tableau* signified a turning point as it "helped shape a vision of the economic sphere as an autonomous, self-adjusting, and self-regulated system that could achieve a natural equilibrium spontaneously and produce increased wealth."⁵³ Harcourt relates the transformation of the relationship between the "belief in market orderliness" and the "expansion of the penal sphere" during the eighteenth and nineteenth centuries (in France) to Quesnay who published his *Tableau* first in 1758–59 in the midst of debates about the reach and necessity of *police des grains*.⁵⁴

Debates, in France and elsewhere, focused on a familiar theme: finding a balance on how much to interfere.⁵⁵ In the Ottoman Empire, there were concerns on the one hand about grain provisioning and on the other—in Ibn Khaldun's terms—about business inactivity due to attacks on property. In fact, concerns about provisioning and prices were not limited to grain. Uzun notes that similar concerns were relevant for Istanbul's sheep supply throughout the eighteenth century,⁵⁶ and Naima discussed problems with price ceiling (*narh*) policies at the

---

50. Abd al-Rahman ibn Nasr Shayzari, *Nehcü's-Süluk fi Siyaseti'l-Müluk*, trans. Efendi Nahifi Mehmed (Istanbul: Tercüman, 1974), 8.
51. Quoted in Ermiş, "Ottoman Economic Thinking," 52.
52. Bernard E. Harcourt, *The Illusion of Free Markets: Punishment and the Myth of Natural Order* (Cambridge: Harvard University Press, 2011), 28–9.
53. Ibid., 29.
54. Ibid., 34.
55. Several governments in Europe were debating how to remove restrictions on their grain trade to establish a "free" domestic market. Seven Ağır, "From Welfare to Wealth: Ottoman and Castilian Grain Trade Policies in a Time of Change" (PhD diss., Princeton University, 2009), 180; *idem*, "The Evolution of Grain Policy Beyond Europe: Ottoman Grain Administration in the Late Eighteenth Century," Working Paper No: 999 (New Haven: Yale Economic Growth Center, 2011), 5.
56. Ahmet Uzun, *İstanbul'un İaşesinde Devletin Rolü: Ondalık Ağnam Uygulaması, 1783–1857* (Ankara: Türk Tarih Kurumu, 2006), 13–6, 36.

beginning of the eighteenth century.[57] Naima (who was among the first Ottoman interpreters of Ibn Khaldun) was also trying "to solve the financial, political, and social problems which had plagued the Ottoman Empire since the late sixteenth century."[58] Naima's enthusiastic reception of Ibn Khaldun's work was due to the latter's "formulation of a descriptive theory of social organization which was already, in prescriptive form, part of the common intellectual stock of the age."[59]

Naima certainly was not the first or the only Ottoman scholar to question the necessity of price ceilings—which were abolished in the nineteenth century. Criticisms about price ceilings had been circulating since the mid-sixteenth century.[60] The basis for objections to widespread use of *narh*, though, changed over time. For the medieval Islamic scholars, administrative intervention into market activity was inadmissible on religious grounds: it interfered with the honest declaration of the value of property being exchanged. For Ahmed Cevdet Pasha (the nineteenth-century Ottoman politician, jurist, and historian, who contributed greatly to the transformation of Ottoman law), *narh* resulted in an artificial increase in the prices of commodities such as coal.[61] In praising the abolishment of the practice in the nineteenth century, Ahmed Cevdet cited a well-known hadith in which Muhammad refused to fix the increasing prices in Medina stating that "it is God who decides prices."[62] Ibn Taymiyah (d.1328) discussed the very same hadith in the context of the notion of "just price" and noted that one should not interfere with properly functioning markets.[63] He did consider fixing a "just price" permissible if circumstances prevented its establishment through the declaration process (e.g., when sellers use monopoly power to raise prices or there is a need for commodities due to unusual shortage). According to Taymiyah, in such instances, "the fixing of price is not absolutely unlawful. . . . If a man needs another's food, then this other is obliged to provide it for a fair price."[64] For Taymiyah, intervention was a necessary means to thwart the dangers posed to the societal balance by the wicked nature of human beings.[65]

---

57. Ağır, "From Welfare," 96,100; Ermiş, "Ottoman Economic Thinking," 138.
58. Fleischer, "Royal Authority, Dynastic Cyclism, and 'Ibn Khaldunism' in 16th Century Ottoman Letters," 200.
59. Ibid., 202.
60. Ahmed Güner Sayar, *Osmanlı İktisat Düşüncesinin Çağdaşlaşması: Klasik Dönem'den II. Abdülhamid'e*, 4th ed. (Istanbul: Otuken Nesriyat, 2009), 80.
61. Ahmet Cevdet, *Tezakir* (Ankara: Türk Tarih Kurumu, 1953), 2:47.
62. Sayar, *Osmanlı İktisat Düşüncesinin Çağdaşlaşması*, 82.
63. Ibn Taymiyah, *Public Duties*, 35; Ağır, "From Welfare," 41-2; Ermiş, "Ottoman Economic Thinking," 134.
64. Ibn Taymiyah, *Public Duties*, 54-5. For a thorough discussion of this, see Ağır, "From Welfare," 26-42.
65. Ibid., 97-9.

As a Hanbali scholar, Taymiyah was not always very popular in the Ottoman Empire where the Hanafi School of law dominated the official religious establishment. Still, the most commonly used Hanafi *fiqh* books in Ottoman madrasas promoted a similar perspective on the necessity of interventionism,[66] and Ibn Taymiyah's popularity increased in the seventeenth and eighteenth centuries.[67] By the nineteenth century, however, perspectives on *narh* had changed. And as Ağır aptly points out, institutional transformation began in the eighteenth century and the Ottoman experience with price mechanisms had European parallels.[68]

Considerations regarding when the "market price" might be considered "just" have their own history. While for medieval Islamic scholars this was associated with the Islamic regulations regarding sales, it appears to have changed for later scholars. In the history of Western political thought, the elite conceptions of "justness" of the market price evolved as well and did so in close relation with the rise of political economy from the eighteenth century onwards. During his 1978–79 lectures Foucault noted that "the market, in the very general sense of the word, as it operated in the Middle Ages, and in the 16th and 17th centuries, was, in a word, essentially a site of justice . . . a place where what had to appear in exchange and be formulated in the price was justice."[69] This changed in the eighteenth century as the market began to be perceived as the space for a natural spontaneous order. This change, which also led to the rise of political economy as a discipline, happened because "the relationship between population and resources [could] no longer be managed through an exhaustive regulatory and coercive system that would strive to increase the population by increasing resources."[70] The particular understanding of the market functioned as a normative statement: The market may not be in order but it "ought" to be, it is a site of social interaction with rules that should resemble those of nature.[71]

In this line of thinking, conviction in the natural order of the market necessitates a reconceptualization of the government's role. The perceived spontaneity

66. Ibid., 49–50; Sabra, "Prices Are in God's Hands," 80–1.
67. Ağır, "From Welfare," 50–1.
68. Ağır, "From Welfare," 196–203.
69. Michel Foucault, *The Birth of Biopolitics: Lectures at the Collège De France, 1978–79*, ed. Michel Senellart, trans. Graham Burchell (New York: Palgrave Macmillan, 2008), 30.
70. Michel Foucault, *Security, Territory, Population: Lectures at the Collège De France, 1977–78*, ed. Michel Senellart, trans. Graham Burchell (New York: Palgrave Macmillan, 2007), 366. Cf.: "The intellectual instrument, the type of calculation or form of rationality that made possible the self-limitation of governmental reason was not the law . . . starting from the middle of the 18th century . . . it is political economy": *The Birth of Biopolitics*, 13.
71. Harcourt notes that Quesnay, a well-established surgeon, spent "several intense days and nights [with Adam Smith] at the sickbed of Smith's charge, the Duke of Buccleugh" in 1766 and that his insistence to let a patient's fever take its natural course might have cost the Duke his life; Harcourt, *The Illusion of Free Markets*, 81 and 90.

of the market makes it impossible and unnecessary to interfere with it—at least at the theoretical level. This has two implications. First, the nature of governing changes. The logic of governing is not left in the hands of a cameralist state. Rather, we see a shift from government to governance that entails relinquishing a big part of our life and freedoms ("everything that goes beyond the realm of the negotiation of measurable values") to the law and the state.[72] Schecter points out that this is because of the priority that legality gained over legitimacy.[73] As a characteristic feature of liberalism, we consider practices and institutions that are legal as legitimate. The second implication is that the market becomes "a site of veridiction" as it assumes the function of "a privileged site of experiment in which one can pinpoint the effect of excessive governmentality and take their measure."[74] That is, the market becomes the ruler that one uses to measure how much one should govern—just enough to bring all the humors to that delicate state of balance. A similar intellectual turn appears to have happened in the Ottoman Empire. Findley points out that Ottoman intellectuals in the nineteenth century encountered a variety of different intellectual currents. As a result of these discussions among eighteenth-century intellectuals on concepts such as Ibn Khaldun's "circle of justice" did not disappear, but rather merged with these new currents, gaining a new character.[75] The shift was reflected on the institutional transformation of the empire.

An example of this change is the provisioning mechanism. To guarantee provisioning of its urban populace and the army the Ottoman government relied on a variety of institutions and means: price controls, monitored guild structures, monopsonistic purchases through a quota-based requisitioning system, and a special redistributive network for the armed forces.[76] By the end of eighteenth century, demographic pressure and interruptions in trade networks had strained the capital's grain supply and ended Ottoman self-sufficiency.[77] A commission charged with identifying systemic inefficiencies cited general corruption, marked by requisitioning agents' abuse of power and smuggling as significant systemic problems. In 1793, the official price policy was abolished and a Central Grain Administration was founded to prevent irregularities by supervising a system in

---

72. Alain Supiot, *Homo Juridicus: On the Anthropological Function of the Law* (New York: Verso, 2007), 50–1 and 167.

73. Darrow Schecter, *Beyond Hegemony: Towards a New Philosophy of Political Legitimacy* (Manchester: Manchester University Press, 2005), 13.

74. Foucault, *The Birth of Biopolitics*, 320.

75. Carter V. Findley, "Osmanlı Siyasal Düşüncesinde Devlet ve Hukuk: İnsan Hakları mı, Hukuk Devleti mi?" in *Tanzimat: Değişim Sürecinde Osmanlı İmparatorluğu*, ed. Halil İnalcık and Mehmed Seyitdanlıoğlu (Istanbul: Türkiye İş Bankası, 2008).

76. Uzun, *İstanbul'un İaşesinde Devletin Rolü*, 3.

77. Ağır, "The Evolution of Grain Policy," 12.

which private merchants provided grain for Istanbul.[78] A similar trend can be observed in the provisioning of sheep and mutton for Istanbul. By the end of the eighteenth century Istanbul was negotiating the price with producers' representatives in a competitive manner, and by the mid-nineteenth century the system was abolished all together "because of the requisitioning agents' corruption."[79] In 1854, the office of the *muhtasib* was abolished as the Ottoman Empire relegated market supervision to newly established provincial councils.

Nineteenth Century Implications: Security and Information

Provisioning was not the only sphere in which Ottoman administrators, like administrators in other states, shifted towards a view of economic reality that presumed economies operate most effectively when unhindered and unobstructed. Examples multiplied as nineteenth-century governments focused more on observing how the economy and society functioned, calculating the state's needs and resources, supplying necessary professional cadres, and eliminating threats to the natural functioning of markets posed by dangerous individuals or groups who smuggle, hide information, or pose a danger. Foucault and Harcourt noted this connection between "natural" life, "danger," policing, and economy.[80]

Consider the case of customs. Over the course of the nineteenth century, through different regulations state control on the commercial flow of goods within the empire was eased. Finally, in 1843, internal customs were abolished—just a year after the Ministry of Commerce came under the authority of the Customs Administration. In the mid-1800s, the government's perception of the function of customs seems to have changed. Sarkiz Karakoç's comprehensive list of Ottoman laws and codes lists twenty-seven imperial "decrees" pertaining to customs, beginning in 1742 and continuing until the first "regulation" regarding the customhouses' operation in 1859.[81] Most of these decrees granted exemptions to certain groups. After 1859, however, we see a particular emphasis on "smuggling" as a criminal act. A second regulation in 1859, explained what to do with unclaimed property at the customs, and a third one discussed the criminal culpability of those who assist in smuggling. In the following two decades, the Porte issued seven regulations focusing on smuggling as a crime. Eliminating customs and criminalizing smuggling might appear contradictory. What constituted "crime" in these regulations was not avoiding tariffs, but concealing information about commercial activity that ought to be measured.

78. Ibid., 28; Ağır, "From Welfare," 115.
79. Uzun, *İstanbul'un İaşesinde Devletin Rolü*, 29–30, 115.
80. Foucault, *Security, Territory, Population*, 6–18; idem, *The Birth of Biopolitics*, 66–70; Harcourt, *The Illusion of Free Markets*, 16–22.
81. Sarkis Karakoç, *Külliyât-ı Kavânîn Kavânîn ve Nizâmât ve Ferâmîn ve Berevât ve Irâdât-ı Seniyye ile Muâhedât ve Umûma Ait Mukâvelâti Muhtevidir* (Ankara: Türk Tarih Kurumu, 2006).

Provincial administration became significant in this process of creating knowledge. The new Ottoman bureaucracy—geared towards functionalism and professionalization—involved with the politics of local administration created this political knowledge and made the government possible.[82] Members of the government and local elites were not the sole actors in this creative process, and relied on informants—the people who they counted and whose wealth they measured.

Of course, there were those who did not want to participate fully in the creation of political knowledge. On 1 December 1838, the official newspaper, *Takvim-i Vekayi*, reported the story of a Mehmed Ali, who attempted to conceal one of his dwellings from the surveyor: "With the divine wisdom of God, may his name be exalted," the house of Mehmed Ali was burned down while he and his household had to run out "stark naked to save their lives. . . . As there had not been a precedent of fire in the district up until [then]" the event served as a "means of warning" to the others. Despite such "divine warnings," however, some subjects of the empire insisted on not complying with the demands of an inquisitive state at all times.

Concealing information and armed resistance were among the ways people responded to the transformation of the Ottoman Empire. Such non-compliant social agents constituted a "criminal threat" to order. Others were more compliant. After all, the local populace and bureaucrats were a part of this change as well, and being a part of the transformation was beneficial to the compliant groups' strategies. The information that these groups provided constituted the Ottoman "political arithmetic."[83] The base for this arithmetic (what outlined its possibilities and limitations) was a belief in the spontaneity and naturalness of market mechanisms. It is through that conviction that good government is defined as a limited government. The government "exists to serve its subjects' well-being, and should be held to account if it can be shown to have injured them."[84] What emerges from regulations and institutional change in the nineteenth-century Ottoman imperial and local government is an attempt to legitimize governance through incorporating local agents into a judicio-administrative sphere designed to protect the proper functioning of market mechanisms through the collection of information, identification of market related problems, and devising of strategies to solve such problems.

Government "is a problematizing activity: it poses the obligations of rulers in terms of the problems they seek to address. The ideals of government are in-

---

82. The significant relationship between keeping statistics and being modern was emphasized by the Ottoman state in the introduction to the 1879 regulation for the Bureau of Statistics: Prime Ministry Ottoman Archives (BOA) DUİT 37–2/18 (1).
83. This phase is drawn from Foucault, *The Birth of Biopolitics*.
84. Katherine Henry, *Liberalism and the Culture of Security: The Nineteenth-Century Rhetoric of Reform* (Tuscaloosa: University of Alabama Press, 2011), 16.

trinsically linked to the problems around which it circulates, the failings it seeks to rectify, the ills it seeks to cure."[85] In the second half of the nineteenth century, theft, particularly cattle theft attributed to Circassian refugees flooding the empire quickly became a "failing" or an "illness" that the Ottoman government had to cure.[86] In 1876, the office of the sub-governor in Vidin circulated a detailed regulation aiming to prevent this particular problem by introducing offices to monitor all inhabitants and imposing strict regulations on how refugees could travel.[87] Such governmental scrutiny was justified by the threat theft posed to the economy and civil society.

The regulation required election of a council of elders composed of the village headmen, the village imam (*ex officio*) and six "reliable" members. If there was an already existing council, then the "trustworthy" members could continue to serve. The members were to acquire brand new personal identification seals for official correspondence and to keep these in one box that would be opened only in the presence of the entire council. Following the election of the rest, *all* village inhabitants were to take a public oath to not steal or let others steal and to report those who thieve—a higher level bureaucrat was to serve as witness in this communal oath ceremony.

This regulation proposed to impose severe limitations on refugees' (and others') freedom. Its primary goal was to prevent theft committed by Circassians. The council also was to pay attention to thieves disguised as Circassians. Should the council suspect thievery committed by non-refugees, they were to report to

---

85. Nikolas Rose and Peter Miller, "Political Power Beyond the State: Problematics of Government," *British Journal of Sociology* 43:2 (1992): 181.

86. These refugees were fleeing Russian expansion into the Caucasus. Quataert gives an estimate of 3.8 million Muslims emigrating from areas of Russian imperial expansion in the Crimea, the Caucasus, and Central Asia between 1783 and 1913: Donald Quataert, "The Age of Reforms, 1812–1914," in *An Economic and Social History of the Ottoman Empire*, ed. Halil İnalcık, et al. (Cambridge: Cambridge University Press, 1997), 792–95. The overwhelming majority of these refugees was destined for the Ottoman Empire. "The thievery of Circassians" was a common trope all across the empire. A war correspondent for the *Daily News*, noted, from Zevin—in modern day Azerbaijan—how their reputation followed their exile throughout the Ottoman lands from the Balkans to the eastern Ottoman-Russian battlefront in Erzurum: "these Circassians are steadily earning for themselves here the same unenviable reputation for violence and thievery which they enjoyed in Servia. Go where you will, your ears are filled with tales of their depredations." Archibald Forbes and Januarius Aloysius Macgahan, *The War Correspondence of the "Daily News," 1877, with a Connecting Narrative Forming a Continuous History of the War between Russia and Turkey*, 3rd ed. (London: Macmillan and Co., 1878), 113.

87. Bulgarian National Library, Oriental Section [NBKM], 26/12101. A recent study estimated 140,000–150,000 "Muslim refugees" came to the Danube province including the Vidin County during 1860s. The population of the province in 1868 was around two million: Milen V. Petrov, "Tanzimat for the Countryside: Midhat Paşa and the Vilayet of Danube, 1864–1868" (PhD diss., Princeton University, 2006), 352 and 360.

the higher authorities. There were limits on Circassians' right to bear arms: *only* the "trustworthy" refugees were allowed to carry weapons *as long as* they were travelling to a different town and *only* with a permit that was *exclusively* issued for that trip. To travel, the refugees needed permits from these councils (bearing the official seals and summarizing the details of the trip). Undocumented refugee travelers were to be arrested and interrogated. If they were to sell cattle at another town, detailed descriptions of the animals would have to be included in these permits. Circassians caught travelling with cattle, but without a permit, were to be treated as thieves.

Such limitations on liberty were considered necessary in facing the dangers posed by theft and the tensions between the refugees and natives. Whether or not the refugees were responsible for these tensions and the resulting dangerous environment, the problematization of this "danger" constituted a sufficient reason for the government's involvement. As such, this particular document exemplifies how "the game of freedom and security [was] at the very heart of... governmental reason."[88] Within this framework, biopolitics functions as a technology to maintain the proper processes of production and exchange.[89] While liberalism, the ideology forming the basis for such strategies, helped establish the limits on how much to govern by exchanging freedom for security. Governing became a necessity to make sure that things happened according to the natural mechanics of behavior, exchange, and economic life. A constant threat of derailment became the *raison d'être* for technologies of government.

Eyalet Meclisi in Context

The regulation of 1849 helped establish a new era in provincial governance and paved the way to the 1864 regulation by consolidating under the authority of a single consultative body, the new *eyalet meclisi*, the application and supervision of various tasks, from tax collection to adjudication, that were hitherto conduct-

---

88. Foucault, *The Birth of Biopolitics*, 65.

89. Foucault defines biopolitics as "the attempt, starting from the eighteenth century, to rationalize the problems posed to governmental practice by phenomena characteristic of a set of living beings forming a population: health, hygiene, birthrate, life expectancy, race...": ibid., 317. Although some scholars (Thomas Lemke, *Biopolitics: An Advanced Introduction* [New York: New York University Press, 2011], 34) noted that Foucault's use of "biopolitics" may not always have been "consistent," his lectures devoted to the topic provide a consistent and connected group of meanings, for this particular technology of government. Biopolitics, through the way that it operates, reaffirms the validity of a liberalist system where governing is a necessity defined and limited by the effort to avoid obstacles to market operations which are inseparable from the well-being of civil society. For the liberal critique, the belief that the economy "obeyed and had to obey 'natural,' that is to say, spontaneous mechanisms" gave a particular role for the market: "that of a 'test', of a privileged site of experiment in which one can pinpoint the effect of excessive governmentality and take their measure," Foucault, *The Birth of Biopolitics*, 31 and 320.

ed by assorted individual agents.[90] These councils were essential components of a system of governance designed to counter the constant threat of derailment. They were introduced in conjunction with the gradual transformation of the provincial fiscal, military, and judiciary infrastructure.

At the fiscal level, appointment of *muhassıls* to collect taxes, together with the founding of the *muhasıllık* councils in 1840, took away an important fiscal responsibility from provincial governors. While part of the provincial administrative structure, the *muhassıls* directly answered to the imperial administration.[91] In 1842, the provincial treasurer, the *defterdar* (who also reported to the imperial treasury), became responsible for tax collection.[92]

The nineteenth-century provincial reorganization of the empire was, in part, a consequence of military reforms.[93] This is reflected in the relationship between administrative and military ranks. A *kaymakam* was a lieutenant-colonel in the *Asakir-i Mansure-i Muhammediyye* Army, (established in 1826) and a district general; since the beginning of the 1840s, military personnel chaired the provincial councils, which had fiscal responsibility.[94] After 1849, however, the new councils came to supervise the new military structure.

The 1864 provincial regulation said little about military structure. The 1849 regulation, however, outlined a close connection between the new councils and the military. It explicitly pointed out that the provincial council members were responsible for supervising the discharge and replacement of soldiers at the provincial level (Article 13) and in particular for assisting in the recruitment process for the recently established *redif* soldiers.[95] In addition, the council supervised the public security forces (*zabtiye*), and the administrative staff at the lower divisions of administrative levels (counties, districts, etc.) (Articles 18 and 16, respectively).

---

90. Musa Çadırcı, "Osmanlı Döneminde Yerel Meclisler," *Çağdaş Yerel Yönetimler* 2:5 (1993): 5.

91. Musa Çadırcı, *Ülke Yönetimi*, 262; Abdüllatif Şener, *Tanzimat Dönemi Osmanlı Vergi Sistemi* (Istanbul: İşaret, 1990), 39.

92. Serkan Ağar, "Geçmişten Bugüne Mahalli İdare," *TBB Dergisi* 19/73 (2007): 415.

93. Musa Çadırcı, *Tanzimat Sürecinde Türkiye: Askerlik*, ed. Tülay Ercoşkun (Ankara: İmge Kitabevi, 2008), 39.

94. Reşat Kaynar, *Mustafa Reşid Paşa ve Tanzimat*, 2nd ed. (Ankara: Türk Tarih Kurumu, 1985), 238; ibid.

95. This new army was established in 1834. Virginia H. Aksan, *Ottoman Wars 1700–1870: An Empire Besieged* (Harlow: Longman/Pearson, 2007), 376–91. Aksan translates *Asakir-i Redife-i Mansure* as "Victorious Reserve Soldiers." Çadırcı adds that these soldiers behaved more like regular provincial personnel, who trained and served in three-month rotation to meet the military needs of the provinces. Çadırcı, *Askerlik*, 36–7. These forces were mostly infantry (*piyade*). Ahmet Uzun, "1257/1841 Tarihli Bir Belgeye Göre Osmanlı Devleti'nde Mevcut Olan Askeri Birlikler ve Bunlara Yapılan Harcamaların Türü ve Miktarları," *C.Ü. Sosyal Bilimler Dergisi* 25:2 (2001): 236.

At the judicial level, these councils overlapped with the reorganization of the *shariʿ* judiciary and the extensive reforms of 1855.[96] A significant proportion of the articles were devoted to legal matters (thirteen out of sixty-eight), such as delineation of the council's jurisdiction and proper judiciary procedure. (In contrast, the *muhasıllık* councils had limited legal authority.)[97] While the judge would oversee the "*sharʿi* and *hukuki* cases that typically were adjudicated at the *mahkeme*"—e.g., debtor-creditor cases, civil disputes or *terekes*—the council was the designated platform for "[1] issues that could not be resolved at the court or [2] serious matters, in particular homicide and road banditry or [3] other cases that needed to be adjudicated *nizaman* and *kanunen* . . . and [4] issues that cannot be resolved at the county governorships."[98] The complementary pattern outlined in this article between *sharʿi/hukuki* and the *nizami/kanuni* is reflective of the *Nizamiye* court system in the nineteenth century. These councils, as Rubin suggests, served as the immediate predecessors to the *Nizamiye* courts established by the 1864 regulation.[99] As an official court, the council was also responsible for vetting adjudicatory witnesses (Article 50), and corresponding with the Bab-ı Ali should a dispute require an *irade* (Article 51).

The Structure and Duties of the Council

The 1849 regulation was a part of these larger fiscal, military, and judiciary transformations. What made the new provincial council unique was its ability to combine the changing aspects of governance in one institutional body as well as its composition. There were three groups of members: the *ex officio* executive, judiciary and fiscal staff—the governor, the judge (*hakim* or *naib*), and the chief finance officer (*defterdar*); the appointed members—a council head, a member of the *ʿulama* and two clerks; and confessional/communal representatives—the *mufti*, four Muslim notables, and one non-Muslim member for each community (Article 6). Unanimity or a majority of the members' approval was necessary for

---

96. For more on this change, which was essential to the new *Nizamiye* courts, see Jun Akiba, "From Kadi to Naib: Reorganization of the Ottoman Sharia Judiciary in the Tanzimat Period," in *Frontiers of Ottoman Studies: State, Province, and the West*, ed. Colin Imber and Keiko Kiyotaki (London: I.B. Tauris, 2005).

97. Ortaylı, *Tanzimat Devrinde Osmanlı Mahalli İdareleri*, 35.

98. Article 49. The counties and the districts had similar councils (Article 62), "significant" cases would be promoted upward. "Significant" is not explained in this regulation; however, in 1864 the boundaries of authority were explained in more detail.

99. Avi Rubin, *Ottoman Nizamiye Courts: Law and Modernity* (New York: Palgrave Macmillan, 2011), 24. These councils were challenging the judicial monopoly of the *sharʿi* courts—not working against them. The provincial commercial courts (established 1847), according to Rubin, served a similar function as well: ibid., 8, 26.

all decisions, while members could indicate their dissent with a note around their seals (serving as their signatures).[100]

The regulation differentiates between the standing members (*aʿza-yı daimi*)—everyone except the *ex officio* staff and the *mufti*—and the others. The former were to meet for business all days except Friday and the *ex officio* members would join them for "important issues" two days a week.[101] The former were responsible for the transfer of official documents when the *ex officio* members changed office (Article 15), but no such safekeeping was necessary when the standing members changed office. Appointing an independent council head was:

> Largely different from the earlier practice in which the provincial governor acted as the president of the council. Apparently, the state intended to check the balance of power between the governor and the local notables by appointing a third party that was under the direct control of the center.[102]

The first thirteen of sixty-eight articles (nineteen percent) detail the composition and responsibilities of the councils. Among these, the council was charged with explaining and disseminating the reforms and new regulations to the populace and supervising the application of the *Tanzimat* reforms. The remaining articles (the majority) focus on the procedures. In contrast, the first twenty-eight articles of the 1864 regulation (thirty-six percent), explain the councils' structure through references to earlier regulations and the remaining articles focus on the tasks of the lower-level provincial councils and the election of the local notables.[103]

The regulation outlines the council's regulatory functions associated with the modern state governing practices. The members were to supervise the issuing/use of travel permits (*mürur tezkeresi*), and quarantines (Articles 20 and 24, respectively). Members also were required to inspect prison log books (*jurnal*) to ensure full provisioning of the inmates' necessities and proper separation of the convicts according to their crimes (Article 19). Furthermore, the council was to supervise the functioning of the new schools, which were essential for "the improvement of humanity through sciences" (Article 42). Torture was clearly condemned and the council was held responsible for its prevention.[104]

---

100. "Meclis azalarının icab-i me'muriyetleri" *Mecmuʿa-yı Kavanin* (*Düstur*) (Istanbul: Takvimhane-i ʿAmire 1851), 12; *Düstur-ı Atik 1*, 484.

101. Article 7. Thus, local notables were the majority mostly.

102. Akiba, "The Local Councils," 182.

103. *Düstur: I. Tertib* (Istanbul: Matbaʿa-yı ʿAmire, 1872), 1:608–24. The 1864 regulation introduced a different election process for notables. For the earlier process used in these councils, see Ortaylı, *Tanzimat Devrinde Osmanlı Mahalli İdareleri*, 20–1.

104. No torture or undue pressure was to be applied to anybody (Article 3), including those who came to the councils to be heard (Article 10), the suspects (Articles 56, 57), confessed criminals (Article 59) and the incarcerated prisoners (Article 41). On the link between torture

The Council and the Markets

The council was the fiscal epicenter of provincial administration: it supervised the apportionment, collection or auctioning of taxes at all levels of the province. Its responsibilities, however, went beyond that. Councils were responsible for maintaining the ideal environment for the production and exchange of goods and, to a degree, for the availability and circulation of capital. In a sense, the council was to maintain the presumed "spontaneity" or "naturalness" of the economy. It had to identify and eliminate the "conditions in and around peoples' homes, vineyards, orchards, [etc.] that were detrimental to production" (Article 45). It had the authority to spend up to 2,000 *guruş* to maintain public buildings, roads and bridges; and could spend up to twice that amount for emergency repair—if it explained the need in a report to Istanbul (Article 35). It took over the tasks of the *muhtasib*, making sure that new construction of homes and shops followed the building code (issued in 1849), and that the marketplace functioned in a clean and orderly manner without the use of forced labor (Article 48).[105] Council members had to ensure that necessities were sold at equitable prices, with proper scales and measures, that government offices respected the market prices when purchasing (Article 21), and that everyone observed the regulation on contracts (issued in 1848) when selling or leasing real property (Article 22).[106]

These councils also regulated access to real and financial capital. In accordance with the regulation on title deeds (issued in 1847), the council was responsible for "holding public auctions for the buying and selling of vacated and empty lands at an appropriate price and for encouraging those who do not have a property certificate [*temessük*] to obtain one."[107] The councils were to prevent relatives, legal guardians, or judges from wasting an orphan's property and to identify *shar'i* methods of making profit or loaning it with interest (Article 52). This was before the establishment of the Authority for the Supervision of Orphan Properties (*Emvâl-i Eytâm Nezâreti*) by the end of 1851, which, as Agmon argues, openly interfered with wealth transfer in the family.[108] Here it was justified as a way to prevent waste of wealth. Article 43 emphasized farmers' and artisans' losses due to improper *selem* contracts and required the councils to ensure the conformity of such contracts with existing regulations (issued in 1843).[109]

---

and the secular order, see Talal Asad, *Formations of the Secular: Christianity, Islam, Modernity* (Stanford: Stanford University Press, 2003), 100–24.

105. Article 47. This regulation is in *Mecmu'a-yı Kavanin*, 48.
106. No reference was given to Hanafi *fiqh* books.
107. Article 46. This regulation is in *Mecmu'a-yı Kavanin*, 42.
108. See Iris Agmon, *Family and Court: Legal Culture and Modernity in Late Ottoman Palestine* (Syracuse: Syracuse University Press, 2006), 148–51.
109. *Selem* is a sale contract for goods that are unavailable at the moment of purchase (such as fruit that has not matured and been picked yet) but will be delivered at the end of a specified period.

Councils and Legitimacy

The 1849 regulation is important for understanding how law was legitimized in the Ottoman Empire at the central and provincial level. These councils were important because, (1) unlike the *muhasıllık* councils, they controlled a wider array of functions; and (2) they involved local notables in these functions. They increased local notables' involvement with governance. For example, in 1844, the Ministry of Agriculture began appointing provincial agriculture directors to improve agricultural and artisanal production. In 1849, this ministry came under the authority of the Ministry of Public Works and the provincial directors came under the new councils' supervision (Article 44). In 1851, a regulation required these directors to appoint representatives from the local notables to explore ways to increase efficiency in agricultural and artisanal production in cooperation with provincial councils.[110]

At the imperial level, legitimization of law was done through the use of a variety of tactics that did not necessarily alienate *fiqh* from the legal process and that presented the codification attempts as a "compilation and not a departure" from earlier legislation.[111] As is clear from even this brief summary, the regulation was imbued with references to other recently issued contemporary regulations.

At the local level, notables in these councils were instrumental in legitimizing law through deliberations on "justice" as part of Ottoman governance. As the standing members of these administrative/legal councils, the Muslim and non-Muslim members contributed to the explanation and legitimization of the new codes through their direct political involvement. The 1849 regulation increased the potential for the local notables' routine involvement in various aspects of government. Their political involvement increased with the promulgation of the 1864 regulation.

Consider, for example, the 1850 uprising in Vidin. Most recently, Atilla Aytekin noted that land use and taxation were at the center of the uprising: "In Vidin . . . a cultivating class who depended on land for livelihood and a non-cultivating class for whom land was the major source of income came together in a setting where agricultural productivity was low, capital and investment scarce, and possibilities for technological innovation limited."[112] Aytekin's assertions about agricultural productivity and capital investment may be debatable, howev-

---

110. *Mecmu'a-yı Kavanin*, 6.
111. This is one of the central claims of İslamoğlu on the nature of *Mecelle*. Huricihan İslamoğlu, "Intractable Elusiveness of Ottoman Law or Law as the Focus of the Modern Predicament of Ottoman Society," Workshop on Global History of International Law, Interlaken, 19–23 Jan. 2011. It also applies to nineteenth-century codices like the *Mecmua-yı Kavanin* that included the 1849 regulation.
112. E. Attila Aytekin, "Peasant Protest in the Late Ottoman Empire: Moral Economy, Revolt, and the Tanzimat Reforms," *International Review of Social History* 57:2 (2012): 200.

er, his observations regarding the oppositional tone are interesting.[113] The peasants were complaining about oppression and "adopted [a] language of reform, justice, and equality."[114] A British consular agent who sent a report regarding the uprising echoes this as well: "The arbitrary and tyrannical conduct of the Turks generally towards the Bulgarian Christians and the cruelties and injustice practiced by them on an industrious and inoffensive peasantry" was listed as the first reason for the uprising.[115]

In January 1851, Vidin's governor forwarded a note from various land-owners attached to a report from the provincial council.[116] The proprietors, *gospodars*, who gave up their land in return for government bonds with regular annual payments, were expressing their gratitude to the government.[117] The signatures at the end of the council's report indicate that some of the non-Muslim members of the council were related to the some prominent members of the post-1864 councils in Vidin.[118] The continued involvement of the local elite in provincial councils before and after the 1864 reforms is not surprising, recent studies point at the prominence of provincial notables involved in the politics of local administration. Their involvement with matters of justice, politics, and economy was not coincidental. The nineteenth-century Ottoman Empire witnessed a proliferation of debates about these concepts. The dispute over land use and tax justice in Vidin lasted several years, and many peasants and some notables were killed in the violence of the uprising. The council remained deeply involved in the ongoing debates and the eventual resolution of the matter. Some of their reports indicate that these councils served as a platform for the *gospodars* and the peasants to negotiate over an equitable distribution of land and the tax burden.[119] These

---

113. In *The Balkan Economies, 1800–1914: Evolution without Development* (New York: Cambridge University Press, 1997), Michael Palairet claims that the economy of the region was developing. The provincial yearbooks indicate that capital in the agricultural credit funds and orphanage funds increased during 1860s and 70s as well.

114. Aytekin, "Peasant Protest," 227.

115. FO 195/296, 04.09.1850, from Bennett to Neale.

116. BOA IDH 13733.

117. "In rural Vidin, a feudal land regime called *gospodarlık*, based on a complex set of relations of exploitation, including corvee, and legal and social obstacles to land ownership by Christian cultivators, was in effect." Aytekin, "Peasant Protest," 197.

118. Iovan Ganzovyanov, one of the council members in this document, is the father of Sevastaki Iovanov Ganzovyanov, a chorbadji in late 1850s and a prominent member of the post-1864 provincial administration in Vidin. The younger Ganzovyanov was also the brother-in-law of Nikolço Hadjiangelov (another member of the council in 1851. See Milena Christova Stefanova, *Kniga Za Bulgarskite Chorbadzii* (Sofia: Univ. Izdat. Sv. Kliment Ohridski, 1998), 152; cf. Genadi Vulchev, *Vidinskite Rodove* (Vidin: n.p., 2001), 1:60.

119. BOA IMVL 8007 or IMVL 7683 reveal how the council was involved in trying to collect unpaid taxes by the villagers and oversee the payment of shares to the *gospodars* in return for the bonds they held.

debates overlapped with a shift in the eighteenth to nineteenth centuries in perceptions of the state's primary function and how the economy operates in which markets and the "spontaneous nature" of the economic order became linked with perceptions of justice.

Conclusion

Al-Shayzari lived during the twelfth century, but his advice book on the methods of government was incorporated into the works by Kınalızade in the sixteenth century and by Naima in the eighteenth and was printed three times in 1841, 1855, and 1869.[120] Books by Ibn Khaldun, Kınalızade, and Naima had a similar surge in popularity in the nineteenth century while the Ottoman state made substantial attempts to change the traditional self-sufficient farming structure towards a market-oriented agricultural economy.[121] While the perspective on these issues did not remain the same over the centuries, it is clear that a literature on sovereign power and proper government remained in circulation. The renewed interest in these authors, changing imperial fiscal policies in the course of the eighteenth century, and debates about boundaries of government practices indicate a particular articulation of the limits of government in the Ottoman Empire. Contemporaries did not necessarily explain this through the works of scholars such as Quesnay or Adam Smith (although there were translations and discussions of those works). There appears to be a connection—similar to what Harcourt observes in France—between the focus (and legislation) on market related crimes and the development of a liberal economic narrative that considers markets as a site of veridiction. When Cevdet Pasha referred to the hadith on the Prophet Muhammad's ostensibly noninterventionist approach to the markets he was, I would argue, deliberately conflating a line of reasoning in which market *procedures* are *legitimate* as long as people declare the price/value of their goods and needs honestly with another line of reasoning that treated markets as legitimate places of veridiction where spontaneous dealings are *legitimate* as long as they are *legal*.[122] To explore this reconceptualization of the economy and the role of lawmaking in this process requires a more detailed reading of works by scholars like Kınalızade or Naima, and an analysis of the changing nature of regulations on market related activity in the eighteenth and nineteenth centuries. Recent studies on the eighteenth century indicate an Ottoman transformation similar to the European

120. Shayzari, *Nehcü's-Süluk*, 9.
121. Deniz T. Kilinçoğlu, "The Political Economy of Ottoman Modernity: Ottoman Economic Thought During the Reign of Abdülhamid II (1876–1909)" (PhD diss., Princeton University, 2012), 26.
122. The distinction between procedures being legitimate because of their inherent nature as opposed to a process of legitimation through a procedural adherence to legality was essential in the design of the panels that included the articles constituting this special issue. For more on this distinction, see Schecter, *Beyond Hegemony*.

one: the rise of centralized policing of the markets framed by a faith in a natural order leading to more liberal economic policies in the nineteenth century.

Ottoman codification attempts in the nineteenth century were a part of this larger transformation. The offices and institutions created with these reforms helped create a necessary framework for Ottoman governance characterized by the creation of a particular "triangle formed by government, population and political economy."[123] Political economy assumed its role in this triangle because liberal philosophy presumed that the economy "obeyed and had to obey 'natural,' . . . spontaneous mechanisms."[124] It envisioned a particular role for the market: "that of a 'test', of a privileged site of experiment in which one can pinpoint the effect of excessive governmentality and take their measure."[125] Thus, while political economy required governance to manage the population through biopolitics, the "natural order of the market" became the gauge to measure excessive intervention. The provincial councils created by the 1849 decree were not only instruments for incorporating the local notables into administration, but also a part of this larger transformation in the understanding of governance and legitimacy which began before the 1839 Gülhane decree.

M. SAFA SARAÇOĞLU is an Associate Professor in the Department of History at Bloomsburg University, Bloomsburg, PA.

---

123. This relationship constitutes the main theme of Foucault's lectures at the Collège de France in 1977–78, and serves as an introduction to the lectures of the following year devoted to "the birth of Biopolitics." When he introduces the notion of "governmentality," Foucault emphasizes the centrality of political economy for the art of governing: Foucault, *Security, Territory, Population*, 87–114.

124. *The Birth of Biopolitics*, 31.

125. Ibid., 320.

5 Reorganization of the Sharia Courts of Egypt

How Legal Modernization Set Back Women's Rights in the Nineteenth Century[1]

Kenneth M. Cuno

Historians have tended to neglect the reorganization of the Sharia courts in the nineteenth-century Ottoman Empire and its autonomous Egyptian province, both as a process that was part of the Tanzimat-era restructuring of the legal system and in terms of its social consequences. Standard if somewhat dated accounts have emphasized the drafting of new codes of law that emulated the French codes in form and often in content, the establishment of new courts to administer those codes, and the subsequent rise of the modern legal profession.[2] Recent social-historical studies addressing developments in the judicial system of nineteenth-century Egypt have mainly focused on the application of criminal law, in which the Sharia courts played a minor role.[3] While valuable, those studies have not challenged the assumption in the older literature that the restriction of the jurisdiction of the Sharia courts to family matters as a consequence of the issuance of codes of criminal, commercial, civil, and property law reduced their importance. That literature equated legal "modernization" or "reform"[4]

---

1. I am grateful for the comments of two anonymous reviewers for *JOTSA*. This essay draws on material in my book, *Modernizing Marriage: Family, Ideology, and Law in Nineteenth- and Early Twentieth-Century Egypt* (Syracuse: Syracuse University Press, 2015).

2. For Egypt e.g., see Latifa Muhammad Salim, *Al-Nizam al-Qada'i al-Misri al-Hadith 1875–1914* (Cairo: Markaz al-Dirasat al-Siyasiyya wa al-Istratijiyya bi-l-Ahram, 1984); and Farhat J. Ziadeh, *Lawyers, The Rule of Law & Liberalism in Modern Egypt* (Stanford: Hoover Institution, 1968), 24–43.

3. E.g., see Khaled Fahmy, "The Police and the People in Nineteenth-Century Egypt," *Die Welt des Islams* 39:3 (1999): 340–77; Rudolph Peters, "Administrators and Magistrates: The Development of a Secular Judiciary in Egypt, 1842–1871," *Die Welt des Islams* 39:3 (1999): 378–97; Liat Kozma, *Policing Egyptian Women: Sex, Law, and Medicine in Khedival Egypt* (Syracuse: Syracuse University Press, 2011).

4. I usually prefer "legal reorganization" to those terms, since the process involved the reorganization of the legal systems of semi-colonized states in emulation of European models in

with codification. But the codification of Muslim family law did not begin until the twentieth century, and so it was assumed that until then "the one area that remained essentially untouched" by modern change "was family law."[5]

Generations of scholars have studied the adoption of European civil law in the Turkish republic and the codification of Muslim family law in other Ottoman successor states. The Ottoman Law of Family Rights (OLFR, 1917) was the first code derived from Muslim family law. In Egypt, which by then was no longer part of the Ottoman Empire, the codification of family law began in the 1920s. Unlike the OLFR, which was a comprehensive family law, the Egyptian approach was piecemeal. Law No. 25 of 1920 dealt mainly with the problem of husbands who failed to fulfill their legal obligation to financially support or maintain their wives. Law No. 56 of 1923 set a minimum age of marriage for both sexes. Law No. 25 of 1929 reformed the law of divorce, restricting the ability of men to pronounce divorce capriciously and expanding the ability of women to petition a judge for a divorce for cause. In the standard view the OLFR and the Egyptian laws of the 1920s marked the beginning of modern change in family law and hence of legal modernization in the Sharia court system.

Ottomanist historians have begun to overturn this orthodoxy by demonstrating, first, the continued importance of the Sharia courts in social life in this period, and, second, how new procedural rules changed the way that the law was applied. New measures beginning in the 1850s established a provincial judicial hierarchy with an appeals process, regulated the terms of service of judges, and fixed legal fees. A school for Sharia court judges opened in 1855, and a few years later the Ministry of Şeyhülislam took control of appointments, ending the practice of judges selling lower positions.[6] Throughout the reorganized judicial system a greater emphasis was placed on the use of legal documents as evidence, and necessarily their proper drafting. Regulations concerning the drafting of

---

the nineteenth and early twentieth centuries, a process that paralleled the imposition of European legal systems in colonized societies. On this, see Richard S. Horowitz, "International Law and State Transformation in China, Siam, and the Ottoman Empire during the Nineteenth Century," *Journal of World History* 15:4 (2005): 445–86.

5. On the supposed reduced importance of the Sharia courts, see Judith Tucker, *Women in Nineteenth-Century Egypt* (Cambridge: Cambridge University Press, 1985), 12–3, 15. Quotation from John Esposito, *Islam: the Straight Path*, 4th ed. (Oxford: Oxford University Press, 2011), 172; also, see John Esposito with Natana J. DelongBas, *Women in Muslim Family Law*, 2nd ed. (Syracuse: Syracuse University Press, 2001), 48. Two more recent works that use of Sharia Court records to examine changing family dynamics are Ron Shaham, *Family and the Courts in Modern Egypt* (Leiden: Brill, 1997) and Hanan Kholoussy, *For Better, For Worse: The Marriage Crisis That Made Egypt* (Stanford: Stanford University Press, 2010). However, both focus on the early twentieth century, leaving the nineteenth century unexamined.

6. Iris Agmon, *Family and Court: Legal Culture and Modernity in Late Ottoman Palestine* (Syracuse: Syracuse University Press, 2006), 69–70; Jun Akiba, "A New School for Qadis: Education of the Sharia Judges in the Later Ottoman Empire," *Turcica* 35 (2003): 125–63.

Sharia court protocols were issued in the 1870s, and the curriculum of the school for Sharia court judges emphasized the drafting of documents.[7] Iris Agmon, in her study of the Sharia courts in late Ottoman Palestine, noted that the volume of court cases increased in the second half of the nineteenth century, which is indicative of the growing importance of the courts in documenting as well as adjudicating the affairs of people. She also challenged the idea of a static family law, pointing to the new court procedures as indirectly effecting change and the creation of a government body to supervise the properties of orphans as a more direct intrusion. Changes such as these in the application of family law went unnoticed by historians, she wrote, because they were "introduced as . . . administrative instructions" and not as substantive changes in or codifications of the Sharia.[8]

The reorganization of the Sharia court system in Egypt followed a similar path, though with some differences. Beginning in the mid-nineteenth century a series of laws reorganized the Sharia courts, introducing a hierarchical structure, detailing the qualifications of their personnel, setting fees, and defining procedures. Like their Ottoman counterparts, the Egyptian procedural laws have not been understood as representing a phase of legal modernization in the Sharia court system, because they did not involve the codification of the Sharia itself. I argue that they comprised a preliminary phase of modernization and that the second phase began in the 1920s with codification.

In Egyptian historiography the family law codes of the 1920s are important for a second reason, as reforms that improved the lives of women. These laws enabled married women to collect arrears of maintenance from their husband more easily and to free themselves from marriage on the grounds of non-support, desertion, the husband's disappearance or imprisonment, and marital difficulties resulting in harm. It also enhanced their security in the marital relationship by not permitting men to exercise their right of unilateral divorce (*talaq*, or repudiation) conditionally, in anger, or while inebriated, and by requiring that a triple pronouncement of repudiation be done at intervals. The minimum marriage age (sixteen for women, eighteen for men) promoted consent in marriage, since in Muslim family law women and men were considered to have achieved adulthood at the age of fifteen at the latest, and adults could be married off only with their express consent.[9]

---

7. Agmon, *Family and Court*, 54, 88, 102; Akiba, "A New School for Qadis," 143–48.
8. Ibid., 55, 147.
9. The text of Law No. 25 of 1920 and its explanatory memorandum are in Ibrahim Ahmad Abd Allah, *Majmuʿa alAwamir wa alManshurat wa alQawanin alMutaʿalliqa biLaʾihat Tartib alMahakim alSharʿiyya (alQanun Nimra 31 Sanat 1910) min Sanat 1910 ila Sanat 1926*, 2nd ed. (Tanta: alMatbaʿa alAhliyya alKubra, 1926), 166–79, and a discussion of Law No. 56 of 1923 occurs on 188–89. The text of Law No. 25 of 1929 and its explanatory memorandum are in

Third, the family codes of the 1920s were innovative in method. Their drafters enhanced the position of women by incorporating aspects of Maliki jurisprudence into a law based primarily on Hanafi jurisprudence. The selection (*takhayyur*) of rules from the different schools of jurisprudence to achieve a desired result had been advocated by the late Grand Mufti Muhammad Abduh (1899–1905) and his followers. Hence the family codes of the 1920s fit nicely into the progressive meta-narrative of modern Egyptian history. They were landmarks in family law reform, women's rights, and Islamic modernism.

This article, which begins with a description of the pre-modern Sharia Court system in Ottoman Egypt, argues that the principal legal disadvantages of married women that the legislation of the 1920s ameliorated were not features of a "traditional" Islamic system, as the modernist meta-narrative implies. Rather, those disadvantages were a consequence of the procedural changes introduced in the Sharia court system during the nineteenth century. The legislation of the 1920s restored to married women most of the legal options that their great-grandmothers had enjoyed.

Prior to its reorganization the Sharia court system in many Ottoman provinces was characterized by a kind of pluralism, in the sense that jurists from one or more of the schools of jurisprudence, in addition to judges from the officially patronized Hanafi school, were available to litigants and those seeking notarization of their affairs. In the courts of Ottoman Cairo there were deputy judges of the Shafi'i, Maliki, and Hanbali schools. The old system permitted "forum shopping," in which one could approach a jurist from the school of jurisprudence that was most amenable to the desired outcome. Although the doctrine of each school of jurisprudence was relatively rigid, forum shopping allowed for a degree of flexibility in the application of the law. By the middle of the nineteenth century, however, this flexibility was lost. As part of the reorganization of the Sharia court system, judges were instructed to apply only Hanafi jurisprudence in their rulings. In Egypt the change was effective perhaps as early as the mid-1830s, and it is evident in the fatwas issued by the Grand Mufti Muhammad al-Abbasi al-Mahdi (served 1847–97) at mid-century.[10] The rule restricting judges to Hanafi jurisprudence was inscribed subsequently in the procedural laws of 1856, 1880, and 1897. The Hanafi school made it more difficult for women to collect arrears of maintenance from their husbands than the other schools of jurisprudence; and unlike the other schools it severely restricted the ability of women to seek a judicial divorce or annulment for a cause. Thus the procedural laws dealt a setback to

---

Ibrahim Ahmad Muhammad, *Majmu'a Qawanin alAhwal alShakhsiyya* (Alexandria: Al-Dar al-Misriyya li-l-Tiba'a wa al-Nashr, 1956?), 18–36.

10. On al-Abbasi and his fatwa collection, see Rudolph Peters, "Muhammad al-Abbasi al-Mahdi (d. 1897), Grand Mufti of Egypt, and his al-Fatawa al-Mahdiyya," *Islamic Law and Society* 1:1 (1994): 66–82.

the rights of married women in Egypt by eliminating their ability to forum shop in the judicial system.

Judicial reorganization in the provinces under direct imperial rule also put an end to the system of forum shopping, but the government softened the harshness of Hanafism by permitting women to petition for annulments according to Shafi'i and Maliki jurisprudence in cases of non-support and desertion. The OLFR included those exceptions and also enabled women to divorce a husband who had gone missing for four years.[11] It is not clear why Hanafi jurisprudence was applied more strictly in the Sharia court system of Egypt than in the rest of the Ottoman Empire. It is evident that while in both systems the intent was to establish a unified family law in application, the imperial authorities alone recognized the need to incorporate elements of non-Hanafi jurisprudence so as to offer relief to women in difficult marriages. The Ottoman example and the memory of the old system of forum shopping was probably what inspired Abduh to advocate *takhayyur* as a remedy for the difficulties faced by married women in Egypt.[12] The legislation of 1920 and 1929 was to a large extent a response to his advocacy, and it improved the situation of women by incorporating elements of Maliki jurisprudence.

The Egyptian procedural laws were also similar to their Ottoman counterparts in putting gradually more emphasis on the use of notarized documents in establishing legal evidence. By the end of the century the Sharia courts required documentary evidence in matters involving marriage and divorce, and the courts themselves were a principal forum for issuing documents. Consequently there was a decline in legal informality as more people contracted marriages and documented divorces formally—that is, before an officer of the court—and necessarily in conformity with the letter of the law. As in late Ottoman Palestine, in late Ottoman Egypt the Sharia courts were busier than ever.

Pluralism and Forum Shopping

Multiple forms of legal pluralism existed within the pre-modern Ottoman Empire. Jews and Christians were subject to their own religious laws, and foreigners to their own national laws, under the Capitulations. A third type of pluralism—Islamic legal pluralism—existed in the Ottoman Sharia court system. The chief judges in the major towns, appointed from Istanbul, were Hanafis and graduates

---

11. J.N.D. Anderson, "Recent Developments in Shar'ia Law II," *The Muslim World* 41:1 (1951): 37; Text of the OLFR in Arabic, Qarar Huquq al-A'ila, in Bassam Abd al-Wahhab al-Jabi, *Al-Majalla: Majallat al-Ahkam al-Adiliyya; ma'ha Qarar Huquq al-A'ila fi al-Nikah al-Madani wa al-Talaq* (Limassol: Dar Ibn Hazm, 2004), 538, Arts. 126, 127.

12. E.g., see his fatwa of 3 Aug. 1900 in Muhammad Abduh, *Al-A'mal al-Kamila li-l-Imam Muhammad Abduh*, ed. Muhammad Amara, 6 vols. (Beirut: AlMu'assasa alArabiyya lilDirasat wa alNashr, 1972), 2:653–59. Abduh himself was an adherent of the Maliki school.

of the imperial madrasas in the central part of the empire (with some exceptions in the eighteenth century). But in districts where the population included adherents of the other schools of jurisprudence, deputy judges (*na'ibs*) from those schools were also appointed. Thus, Shafi'i deputies were appointed in some Anatolian provinces and in all of the provinces of Greater Syria and Iraq, and Maliki deputies were appointed in the North African provinces.[13] All four schools of jurisprudence were represented in the courts of Ottoman Cairo, a legacy of the appointment of co-equal judges from the four schools during the Mamluk Sultanate (1250–1517).[14]

Although there are large areas of agreement between the Sunni schools of jurisprudence they differed in the historical development of their method for deriving normative rules from the Qur'an and Sunna, and hence their rules differed to some degree. The accompanying table shows some of the salient differences between the schools that appeared in a sample of handbooks on marriage written in Ottoman Egypt, all of them published in the nineteenth century. Some of these handbooks were comparative works—that is, comparing the doctrines of the juridical schools—since legal pluralism persisted in the Sharia courts though the first third of the century. I do not claim that the table represents immutable doctrines. Juridical opinions varied over time and place within schools as well as between them, and so I have drawn on Ottoman Egyptian works for the preferred opinions of that place and time.

Each school of jurisprudence offered women favorable options in some areas and restrictions in others. For example, Hanafi jurists were the only ones to allow an adult woman to marry without the involvement of her guardian, but once she was married they would not permit her to seek an annulment for non-support, desertion, or abuse, nor would they declare a husband gone missing deceased within a reasonable period so that she could re-marry. On the other hand, Shafi'i and Maliki judges would grant women annulments on the aforesaid grounds and declare a missing man deceased after four years, but they absolutely required a woman to be married off by a qualified guardian. The latter also accounted unpaid maintenance as a debt against the husband from the day he ceased to

---

13. "Mahkama," Part 2, "The Ottoman Empire." Halil Inalcik, "i. The earlier centuries." *Encyclopaedia of Islam*, 2nd ed. (Brill Online); Wael B. Hallaq, *Shari'a: Theory, Practice, Transformations* (Cambridge: Cambridge University Press, 2009), 216–17; Knut Vikør, *Between God and the Sultan: A History of Islamic Law* (Oxford: Oxford University Press, 2005), 209, 217; Alan Christelow, *Muslim Law Courts and the French Colonial State in Algeria* (Princeton: Princeton University Press, 1985), 86.

14. Nelly Hanna, "The Administration of Courts in Ottoman Cairo," in *The State and its Servants: Administration in Egypt from Ottoman Times to the Present*, ed. Nelly Hanna (Cairo: American University in Cairo Press, 1995), 45; Yossef Rapoport, "Legal Diversity in the Age of *Taqlid*: The Four Chief *Qadis* under the Mamluks," *Islamic Law and Society* 10:2 (2003): 210–28.

provide it, while the Hanafis required the rate to be set formally before a debt could accumulate. During marriage negotiations women (or their guardians) often insisted upon certain stipulations to offset the marital authority of their husband-to-be. The most popular stipulation was that the husband would not marry a second wife nor acquire a slave concubine, and other common stipulations concerned where the wife would reside, her ability to work, and her ability to visit friends and relatives and receive visitors. As the table illustrates, each of the four schools recognized stipulations of that sort, using different legal devices.

One of the fatwas of the Palestinian *mufti* Khayr al-Din al-Ramli (d. 1671) illustrates how women forum shopped between the schools to their advantage. The question involved a woman who had gone to a Shafi'i deputy judge to have her marriage annulled on the ground that her husband deserted her without support, and the Hanafi chief judge had executed the decision of his Shafi'i colleague. Then the woman re-married on her own, without a guardian, making use of the Hanafi rule. Asked whether such maneuvering between the juridical schools was permissible, al-Ramli responded that under the circumstances she could marry in accord with either the Shafi'i or Hanafi rules, since the earlier decision had been made by a Shafi'i and executed by a Hanafi.[15] Al-Ramli was one of the Hanafi authorities cited most often by the Egyptian Grand Mufti al-Abbasi.

According to Judith Tucker, Syrian women obtained annulments in similar circumstances from Shafi'i or Hanbali judges, and in Cairo, James Baldwin found that women preferred Maliki and Hanbali judges for annulments.[16] Nor was forum shopping unique to the Ottoman Empire and that era. In his answer al-Ramli cited a similar case decided by al-Marghinani, who lived in Central Asia in the twelfth century. Muslim women in India forum-shopped between the Hanafi and Shafi'i schools to obtain annulments and to re-marry on their own, and forum shopping for these and other purposes between the legal schools was also practiced in the East Indies, Malaya, Yemen, East Africa, and West Africa.[17]

In Egypt in 1849 the Grand Mufti al-Abbasi considered a case in which a woman was abandoned by her husband for four years without support, and she re-married after receiving an annulment from the judge in her village. Al-Abbasi responded that, legally, she was still married to her first husband, saying that a judge was not permitted "to divorce a missing man for non-payment of mainte-

---

15. Khayr alDin b. Ahmad al-Ramli, *AlFatawa alKhayriyya liNaf' alBarriyya*, 2 vols., 2nd ed. (Beirut: Dar alMa'rifa lilTiba'a wa alNashr, 1974), 1:76.

16. Judith Tucker, *In the House of the Law: Gender and Islamic Law in Ottoman Syria and Palestine* (Berkeley: University of California Press, 1998), 83; James E. Baldwin, "Islamic Law in an Ottoman Context: Resolving Disputes in Late 17th / Early 18thcentury Cairo" (PhD diss., New York University, 2010), 138–39.

17. Al-Ramli, *AlFatawa alKhayriyya*, 1:76; A.A. Fyzee, *Outlines of Muhammadan Law*, 3rd ed. (London: Oxford University Press, 1964), 75–6; Seymour Vesey-Fitzgerald, *Muhammadan Law: An Abridgment According to its Various Schools* (Oxford: Oxford University Press, 1931), 18.

Table 1. Marriage and Divorce in the Four Sunni Schools of Jurisprudence in Ottoman Egypt: Some Differences

	Hanafi	Shafi'i	Maliki	Hanbali
Unpaid maintenance is a debt owed the wife	After the rate is formally set	Automatically	Automatically	Automatically
A wife may seek an annulment for non-support, desertion or abuse	No	Yes	Yes	
A missing husband may be declared deceased	After he would be 90 or older	After four years	After four years	
Marriage guardian	Necessary for minors; not for adult men and women	Necessary for minors and adult women	Necessary for minors and adult women	Necessary for minors and adult women
Stipulations in a marriage agreement may be included	In a conditional or delegated divorce	In a conditional divorce	In a separate legal agreement	In the marriage contract itself

Sources: Muhammad b. Umar al-Nawawi, *Sharh Uqud al-Lujayn fi Bayan Huquq al-Zawjayn*, 2nd ed. (Cairo: al-Matba'a al-Wahbiyya, 1296/1879); Abd al-Majid Ali al-Hanafi b. Shaykh Ali Ismail al-Idwi, *Matla' al-Badrayn fima Yata'allaq bi-l-Zawjayn* (Cairo: n.p., 1278/1862); Hasan al-Idwi al-Hamzawi, *Ahkam Uqud al-Nikah* (Bulaq: al-Matba'a al-Amiriyya, 1276/1859); Ahmad b. Umar al-Dayrabi, *Kitab Gayat al-Maqsud li-Man Yata'ati al-Uqud* (Cairo: Matba'a al-Wahbiyya, 1880).

nance under any circumstances, even if the judge sees that as proper according to his [own] school of jurisprudence, because of the ruler's prohibition of that."[18] Cases such as this one indicate that in Egypt non-Hanafi judges were accustomed to applying the rules of their own schools of jurisprudence, including the annulment of marriages for desertion and non-support, until recently. But the policy of Hanafism was in force by mid-century, albeit with some confusion at the village level.

The Procedural Reforms and the End of Pluralism

In 1835 the Viceroy Muhammad Ali created the position of Grand Mufti (*Mufti al-Diyar al-Misriyya*) and a few years later he restricted the right to issue fatwas on matters of public policy to officially appointed *muftis*, all of whom were

18. Muhammad al-Abbasi al-Mahdi, *Al-Fatawa al-Mahdiyya fi al-Waqa'i' al-Misriyya*, 7 vols. (Cairo: al-Matba'a al-Azhariyya, 1883–86), 1:162, 13 al-Qa'da 1265/12 Oct. 1849. Hereafter this source is cited as FM.

Hanafis.[19] A decade later the policy of Hanafization was reflected in the fatwas of al-Abbasi, as we have seen. The procedural law of 1856 specified that Sharia court decisions be made according to "the sound opinions (*al-aqwal al-sahiha*)" of the Hanafi school,[20] meaning that only the accepted, mainstream opinions should be applied, and not any dissenting or minority views. The procedural law of 1880 reiterated the instruction to judges to rule in accord with "the predominant view" (*arjah al-aqwal*) in the Hanafi school,[21] and the 1897 law instructed them to rule "in accord with the established doctrine of the school" (*hasab al-muqarrar fi al-madhhab*), it being unnecessary to state that "the school" was the Hanafi school of jurisprudence.[22] Under Muhammad Ali's successors only Hanafi jurists were appointed as Sharia court judges. At the end of the century, in his report on the reform of the Sharia courts, the Grand Mufti Abduh complained that this resulted in the appointment of some poorly qualified judges, and he proposed expanding the pool of potential judges by considering ulama from the other schools of jurisprudence for appointment.[23]

The Hanafization of the Sharia court system had a significant impact on family life due to the progressively enhanced role of the Sharia courts in documenting and litigating family affairs. Until the mid-nineteenth century documents played a subsidiary role as evidence to the testimony of notary-witnesses. But the procedural laws emphasized documentation. The law of 1856 instructed the courts to issue official copies of proceedings and transactions to the persons involved, and so long as their documents and the court records matched no subsequent challenge to those proceedings and transactions would be heard.[24] The law of 1880 stated that a notarized document would not fail to be accepted as valid in court.[25] That included the records kept and the documents issued by marriage registrars or *ma'dhun*s, who were provided for in the 1856 law (though the term was used first in 1880). Their duties included ascertaining the eligibility of women to marry—that they were unmarried and free of a waiting period—in addition to recording marriage contracts, along with the names and patronymics

---

19. Juan Cole, *Colonialism and Revolution in the Middle East: Social and Cultural Origins of Egypt's 'Urabi Movement* (Princeton: Princeton University Press, 1992), 37.
20. *La'ihat al-Qudat*, 28 Rabi' II 1273/26 Dec. 1856, Art. 2. Text in Filib Jallad, *Qamus al-Idara wa al-Qada'*, 4 vols. (Alexandria, 1890–92), 4:129–32.
21. *La'ihat al-Mahakim al-Shar'iyya*, 9 Rajab 1297/17 June 1880, Art. 10. Text in Jallad, *Qamus*, 4:145–56.
22. *La'ihat Tartib al-Mahakim al-Shar'iyya wa al-Ijra'at al-Muta'alliqa bi-ha*, 27 May 1897, Art. 16. Text in *Majmu'at al-Awamir al-'Ulya wa al-Dikritat al-Sadira fi Sanat 1897* (Bulaq, 1898), 155–75.
23. Muhammad Abduh, *Taqrir Fadilat Mufti alDiyar alMisriyya alUstadh alShaykh Muhammad Abduh fi Islah alMahakim alShar'iyya* (Cairo: Matba'at al-Manar, 1900), 15.
24. *La'ihat al-Qudat*, Art. 9.
25. *La'ihat al-Mahakim al-Shar'iyya*, Arts. 13 and 14.

of the spouses, their guardians, and the witnesses, the amount of the dower paid and the delayed portion due. The *ma'dhun*s kept separate registers for divorces. The 1897 law went a step farther, stating that no posthumous claim of marriage or divorce would be heard by a court unless it was supported by proper documents.[26] This in effect required the civil registration of marriages and divorces in order to protect one's rights in the event of disputes over issues such as financial maintenance, child support, the prompt or delayed dower, or inheritance, to mention the most common sources of litigation. Marriages and divorces done informally—that is, extra-judicially—could be formalized by bringing witnesses to a court and requesting the judge to issue a document.

The following sections discuss in detail how Hanafization put married women at a disadvantage in cases in which the husband failed to support his wife or deserted her, and when he was absent or missing.

Non-support and Desertion

Each of the schools of jurisprudence held married men responsible for supporting their wives by providing them with financial maintenance (*nafaqa*), clothing (*kiswa*), and an appropriate domicile (*maskan shar'i*). After paying the advance portion of the marriage dower, a man's fulfillment of these financial obligations entitled him to his wife's submission and obedience. Maintenance was not theoretical: it was accounted in monetary terms, according to the economic status of the couple, and there are multiple examples of that in the fatwas and court records.

A woman who was not obedient to her husband risked the loss of maintenance. The main form of disobedience discussed in the juridical literature and that which appeared exclusively in fatwas and court cases consisted of a wife leaving the marital domicile without the consent of her husband. Examples include women who went out without permission to visit their friends or relations, and women who went out of the house daily to work. It was commonplace for women to leave the marital home over some grievance and to stay with their parents or another close relative. These acts of disobedience relieved the husband of his obligation to maintain his wife financially, as long as the disobedience lasted. If a woman refused to return to her husband he could petition a judge for an order of obedience (*hukm al-ta'a*) ordering her to return. If she persisted in refusing, he could ask the judge to declare her disobedient and undeserving of maintenance.

When the husband failed to provide maintenance to a legally obedient wife it automatically became a collectable debt according to the Shafi'i, Maliki, and Hanbali schools, but not in the Hanafi school, which required the rate of maintenance to be determined formally before any arrears would be counted against

---

26. *La'ihat Tartib al-Mahakim al-Shar'iyya*, Art. 31.

the wayward husband. Maintenance could be determined by a judicial decree or agreed to between husband and wife.[27] The difficulty of collecting arrears of maintenance was mitigated further in the Maliki, Shafiʻi, and Hanbali schools, each of which allowed women to petition a judge to annul their marriages on the ground of a husband's non-support, his desertion, or his disappearance. Here too, the Hanafi school was much less permissive, permitting annulment only on the ground of a husband's impotence. Thus the requirement that Sharia court judges apply only Hanafi law disadvantaged married women by making it more difficult for them to recover unpaid maintenance, and it deprived them of the remedy of annulment on the ground of non-support or desertion, which was the option chosen by the woman in al-Ramli's fatwa.

The fatwas of al-Abbasi and court cases from this period illustrate the difficulties that women had in this new legal environment. For example, men who traveled were legally obligated to maintain their wives and children while absent. Some left money and/or provisions with their wives or appointed a legal agent to see that their wives received the amounts they were due. But other men left without making any such arrangements, or stayed away longer than anticipated,[28] so that the money or provisions they left were exhausted, leaving their wives without support. This posed a dilemma for respectable women with limited means due to their obligation of obedience, which required them to remain in the marital home even if their husbands were away. Women who went out to work without their husbands' permission became "disobedient" and undeserving of maintenance, regardless of whether their husbands were present.[29] Deserted wives who moved in with a relative also became "disobedient."[30] Some women supported themselves and their children from their own resources or by borrowing, but they could not recover the arrears of maintenance from their husbands without a prior determination of it.[31] Many women who were left without support went to court to set the amount of maintenance they were due,[32] but that only enabled them to sue their husbands if and when they returned. Those who delayed a month or more before petitioning lost the right to claim the arrears for those days.[33]

---

27. Muhammad Amin b. Umar, known as Ibn Abdin, *Radd alMuhtar ala alDurr alMukhtar Sharh Tanwir alAbsar*, 5 vols., 3rd ed. (Bulaq: al-Matbaʻa al-Amiriyya, 190508), 2:676. FM 1:400, 30 al-Hijja 1267/27 Oct. 1851; 408, 13 Rabiʻ I 1269/25 Dec. 1852; 431–32, 30 al-Qaʻda 1276/20 June 1859; 442, 13 al-Qaʻda 1283/19 Mar. 1866.

28. FM 1:384–85, 14 al-Hijja 1265/31 Oct. 1849.

29. Ibn Abdin, *Radd al-Muhtar*, 2:665; FM 1:416, 30 Shawwal 1270/26 July 1854.

30. FM 1:399, 1 al-Hijja 1267/27 Sept. 1851.

31. FM 1:391, 9 al-Qaʻda 1266/16 Sept. 1850; 398–99, 11 al-Qaʻda 1267/7 Sept. 1851.

32. E.g. FM 1:423, 18 al-Hijja 1272/21 Aug. 1856; 426, 15 al-Qaʻda 1273/7 July 857; 436, 29 Rajab 1279/20 Jan. 1863; 447–48, 8 Jumada I 1288/26 July 1871.

33. FM 1:418, 10 Rabiʻ II 1271/31 Dec. 1854.

The most prudent strategy was for a woman to secure a formal determination of the maintenance she and her children were due while her husband was still present and her marriage intact. Though al-Abbasi's fatwas are not statistically representative of all cases he considered, in the chapter on maintenance there were many more examples of "pre-emptive" lawsuits of this sort than post-desertion suits. In a number of these cases it was stated that the woman requested a judge to set the amount of her maintenance after she and her husband had quarreled.[34] Similarly, in my analysis of a register of legal proceedings from the Sharia court of al-Daqahliyya in 1899, by far the most common type of lawsuit was brought by women in ongoing marriages to establish the maintenance they and their children were due from their husbands.[35]

The proliferation of this type of legal action in the second half of the nineteenth century is due not only to the "Hanafization" of the law, but to the steadily enhanced role of the Sharia court in notarizing documents and thus in the protection of married women's rights. The 1897 law made documentation mandatory for all claims regarding marriage and divorce. Thus while Hanafization made it more difficult for married women to collect arrears of maintenance, these lawsuits show their savvy response to the changing legal environment.

Most of the couples in these cases were from the middle income and status range. The men were mainly artisans and tradesmen, along with a handful of waged workers and professionals. The daily maintenance assigned to their wives was in the range of one to two piasters. These women may have been constrained from working outside their homes by fear of scandal and loss of status as much as by their obligation of obedience. The paucity of suits by working-class women might be attributed to their employment more often as market vendors, domestic servants, bathhouse attendants, and so on. This made them less dependent on their husbands' support than women of the middle stratum, and if they took their husbands to court a judge was likely to deny them maintenance, since by working outside the home they could be deemed "disobedient." Upper class women appeared rarely in these cases. Presumably they had resources of their own and could rely on their natal families, if necessary.

After a formal determination of the maintenance a woman was due, and if her husband failed to provide it, she could demand that he be imprisoned or that his wages or property be garnished, but that was an arduous and an expensive

---

34. In the chapter on maintenance (*nafaqa*) there are some twenty-seven cases mentioning pre-emptive judgments or agreements setting the amount of maintenance due compared to handfuls of post-desertion cases. Quarrels: FM 1:405, 19 Shawwal 1268/7 Aug. 1852; 410, 7 Sha'ban 1269/16 May 1853; 419, 16 Jumada II 1271/6 Mar. 1855.

35. See Kenneth M. Cuno, "Disobedient Wives and Neglectful Husbands: Marital Relations and the First Phase of Reform of Family Law in Egypt," in *Family, Gender and Law in a Globalizing Middle East and South Asia*, ed. Kenneth M. Cuno and Manisha Desai (Syracuse: Syracuse University Press, 2009), 3–18.

process. No more than a fourth of a civil servants' salary could be garnished, and men under threat of garnishment of their wages and property resorted to legal maneuvers and deceptions to evade it. Abduh identified the non-enforcement of Sharia court decisions, including court orders to pay maintenance, as a serious problem in his report on the Sharia courts.[36] His concerns and those of other elite men to enforce the payment of maintenance expressed gendered notions of women's abilities and character. They regarded normative women as dependent on a male provider for maintenance, and their calls for more effective enforcement of maintenance payments included the expressed fear that women left destitute would resort to immoral activity to support themselves and their children.

Absent and Missing Husbands.

Closely related to the problem of non-payment of maintenance was that of the absent (*gha'ib*) or missing (*mafqud*) husband. This too was a standard topic of discussion in the books of jurisprudence, and numerous examples are preserved in al-Abbasi's fatwas, which, along with internal government documents, testifies that it was a continuing source of concern. Hanafi jurists did not permit women who were abandoned or whose husbands went missing to seek an annulment, and they presumed a missing man to be alive into his nineties.[37]

However, a judicial practice (*amal*) had developed some time earlier in the Hanafi school that offered relief to women with long-absent or missing husbands. Hanafi judges would accept the testimony of these women that they had heard by word of mouth that their husband had either died or divorced them. These women were permitted to re-marry, after completing their waiting periods, on the basis of such hearsay evidence.[38] Başak Tuğ found this practice in eighteenth-century Anatolia, and it also appears in al-Abbasi's fatwas from nineteenth-century Egypt. Every one of al-Abbasi's fatwas concerned a woman who re-married after claiming that her husband had divorced her or died while away, and whose

---

36. National Archives of Egypt, Majlis alNuzzar walWuzara, File no. 0075016689. Copy of the proposal of his Excellency Ibrahim Afandi al-Jarim . . . requesting transfer to the Sharia Court judge of the power of imprisonment in matters of maintenance and the empowerment of the Sharia Courts to enforce their rulings, 17 April 1910; and Abduh, *Taqrir*, 37, 67–8, 71. On garnishing a government employee's salary: Decree of 26 Feb. 1890, *Majmu'at alAwamir al'Ulya wa alDikritat* (Cairo: alMatba'at alAhliyya, 1890), 52–3.

37. FM 1:58, 20 Sha'ban 1271/8 May 1855; 1:153, 8 Safar 1265/4 Jan. 1849; and 1:162, 13 al-Qa'da 1265/12 Oct. 1849.

38. This device was also resorted to in the Sharia courts by Christian women, whose marriages were indissoluble in canon law. See Başak Tuğ, "Politics of Honor: The Institutional and Social Frontiers of 'Illicit' Sex in Mid-Eighteenth-Century Ottoman Anatolia" (PhD diss., New York University, 2009), 352–58.

original husband took her to court after returning.³⁹ Military conscription and the engagement of Egyptian troops in foreign wars in the nineteenth century probably made the problem of missing husbands more widespread than in earlier times. Two cases were recorded in the Sharia court registers of al-Mansura in 1857, involving village women married to soldiers who left with the Egyptian force sent to the Crimea in 1853. Roughly two years later in one case, and a year and a half later in the other, the women claimed to have received word of the death of their husband, and then remarried. When their husbands returned and brought the matter to court, the judge ruled the original marriages were still in effect and the second marriages invalid. But the women were not subject to a penalty since they were found to have acted sincerely on the basis of erroneous information.⁴⁰ There is no way of knowing how many women made use of this legal device. But so long as the Sharia courts were restricted to Hanafi jurisprudence, a widow was better off than the wife of a missing man.

The difficulties caused by situations such as these were the subject of an unsigned essay in 1889 in the newspaper *al-Adab*, edited by Ali Yusuf, who later edited the popular newspaper *al-Mu'ayyad* (1889–1915). The essay referred specifically to the problem of the wives of soldiers who had gone missing in the Crimean War and the subsequent wars in Ethiopia and Sudan.⁴¹ The problem was that the Hanafi school was "the one in force in our country today by a decision of the government," and the author pleaded with the ruler to allow Shafi'i and Maliki judges to apply their doctrines in cases of missing husbands. This essay, which was published a decade before Abduh's report on the reform of the Sharia courts, shows that there was public awareness and discussion of the difficulties caused by the policy of strict Hanafism in the Sharia courts. It also shows that the memory of the old judicial system, which permitted forum shopping, was alive. The author (likely Ali Yusuf himself) also anticipated the gendered arguments of Abduh and others on the enforcement of maintenance payments by framing the issue of the impoverishment of the wives of missing soldiers in terms of the moral hazard that posed. Citing a well-known misogynist hadith, the author stated that women are deficient in intellect and faith, and hence the wives of missing soldiers might be driven by necessity to dispose of "the cloak of honor and chastity."⁴²

39. FM 1:17, 16 Rabi' II 1265/12 May 1849; 1:35, 24 al-Qa'da 1267/20 Sept. 1851; 1:36, 9 Muharram 1268/4 Nov. 1851; 1:40, 5 Rajab 1268/26 Apr. 1852; 1:42, 3 al-Qa'da 1268/20 Aug. 1852; 1:44, 5 Muharram 1269/20 Oct. 1852; and 1:49, 16 Sha'ban 1269/26 May 1853.

40. See Kenneth M. Cuno, "Women with Missing Husbands: Marriage in Nineteenth Century Egypt," in *Objectivity and Subjectivity in the Historiography of Egypt: In Honour of Nelly Hanna*, ed. Nasser Ahmed Ibrahim (Cairo: General Egyptian Book Organization, 2012), 156–70.

41. "Zawjat al-Mafqud bi-Hukm al-Shari'a al-Islamiyya al-Ghara'," *Al-Adab*, 3rd year, no. 61, 16 Feb. 1889, 201–02.

42. Ibid., 202.

Conclusion

In 1900 the Grand Mufti Muhammad Abduh took up a question sent to him by the Ministry of Justice concerning the injury suffered by some married women who were deprived of maintenance due to the imprisonment of their husbands, and in answering he expanded the question to cover two related situations that have been discussed in the foregoing.[43] In addition to women with incarcerated husbands, others were deprived of maintenance by husbands who were unable or unwilling to do so, and still others by husbands who were absent for a long periods or who went missing without adequate provision for the wife's support. Then he raised a related issue, saying that he had received reports of women who were so miserable in their marriages that they committed apostasy or threatened to do so in order to free themselves.[44] His solution, as was mentioned earlier, was to permit the women to be divorced from their husbands in accordance with Maliki jurisprudence. Otherwise, he warned, the destitution of women would lead to immorality, and damage to the family, the faith, and the nation.

This male reformist discourse constructed women as dependents and lacking the ability and skills to support themselves if not supported by a male provider. It also invoked the image of desperate, impoverished women resorting to immoral activity in an effort to spur legal reforms of the sort that were incorporated in the laws of 1920 and 1929. To the extent that these reforms were motivated by concern for the integrity of the family and the preservation of morality, they do not fit as neatly into a narrative of progressive enlightenment and reform as in the standard accounts of modern Egyptian history. Moreover, neglect of the reorganization of the Sharia court system in the nineteenth century has left the impression that the codification of Muslim family law in the 1920s was an innovative step towards the "emancipation" of women. But in reality these codes restored most of the options married women had lost three generations earlier. Muslim women in history (and in the present) have tended to be viewed dichotomously, as both victims and agents. As the nineteenth-century procedural laws reshaped the legal terrain, married women faced new disadvantages, but they also adapted to the situation with savvy strategies. They raised lawsuits to establish a record of the maintenance they and their children were due. Those whose husbands went missing cited hearsay (perhaps fraudulently at times) to convince a judge that their husbands had divorced them or perished, so that they could re-marry.

---

43. Fatwa of 3 Aug. 1900 in Abduh, *Al-A'mal al-Kamila*, 2:653–59.

44. Marriage was indissoluble in the Coptic Church, and has become so again, and so Coptic women have resorted to conversion to Islam to automatically divorce themselves from their husbands, and men have converted so as to be able to divorce their wives: e.g., see Edward Wakin, *A Lonely Minority: the Modern Story of Egypt's Copts* (New York: William Morrow & Co., 1963), 83–7. However, the context suggests that Abduh was referring to Muslim women who may have been trying to provoke their husbands to divorce them.

Legal historians have emphasized the innovativeness of the method of selection (*takhayyur*) of rules from the different schools of jurisprudence to achieve the desired result, which was advocated by Abduh and put into practice in the legislation of the 1920s. But these accounts have overlooked the point that, nearly a century earlier and before the beginning of modern judicial "reform," women were able to achieve the same result by forum shopping. It is likely that the memory of the old system, which permitted forum shopping, and which persisted into the late nineteenth century as we have seen, inspired Abduh and other modernists to advocate the use of *takhayyur* in drafting modern family law codes. Egyptian family law in the twentieth and twenty-first century is modern in the sense that it is comprised in a uniform code. But some of the flexibility of the old system has been recovered by incorporating the most desirable rules from the various schools of jurisprudence into that code.

KENNETH M. CUNO is an Associate Professor in the Department of History at the University of Illinois at Urbana-Champaign.

6 Regulating Land Rights in Late Nineteenth-Century Salt

The Limits of Legal Pluralism in Ottoman Property Law

Nora Barakat

THIS ARTICLE EXAMINES the relationship between different district-level decision-making bodies in the late nineteenth-century Ottoman context. Using Sharia court records and property registers produced in the rural Syrian district of Salt as well as investigations from the district that reached Istanbul, I explore the roles and personnel of various courts and bureaucratic offices involved in allocating rights to landed property and settling disputes over land. With this examination, I aim to add nuance to characterizations of the late Ottoman legal system as pluralistic. These descriptions have emphasized Ottoman litigants' abilities to choose between multiple state-sanctioned legal forums with overlapping duties, especially Sharia and *Nizamiye* courts, to obtain the most beneficial ruling.[1] I argue that in the realm of property law, litigants had different goals when approaching the various courts and bureaucratic agencies governing land relations in Salt and their cases had different possible outcomes. Investigating the discrete roles of these government agencies and courts in different areas of late Ottoman law and governance is crucial for a deeper understanding of litigants' experience of the late Ottoman legal environment.

Historians have mainly borrowed the concept of legal pluralism, in what Sally Merry termed the "social science" sense, from anthropologists.[2] When early twentieth-century anthropologists encountered people in colonized societies utilizing the legal systems of the colonial state alongside "indigenous" legal systems, which anthropologists of that era generally interpreted as pure and autonomous, they labeled such situations legally pluralistic. Later in the twentieth

---

1. Avi Rubin, *Ottoman Nizamiye Courts: Law and Modernity* (New York: Palgrave Macmillan, 2011), Chapter 2; Iris Agmon, *Family and Court: Legal Culture and Modernity in Late Ottoman Palestine* (Syracuse: Syracuse University Press, 2006), 74; Ido Shahar, "Legal Pluralism and the Study of Shari'a Courts," *Islamic Law and Society* 15:1 (2008): 112–41.
2. Sally Engle Merry, "Legal Pluralism," *Law & Society Review* 22:5 (1988): 871.

century, the concept came to include non-colonized locales, with the definition of "legal system" encompassing non-state normative orders, both institutionalized orders like university codes and informal orders like family rules.[3]

In the context of Ottoman studies, historians have used the concept of legal pluralism to re-conceptualize the relationship between Sharia courts, the main state-sanctioned judicial forum available to provincial Ottomans before the late nineteenth century, and the *Nizamiye* courts established throughout the empire in the 1870s and 1880s. While earlier scholars had argued that *Nizamiye* courts' gradual usurpation of Sharia court duties in the late nineteenth century marked a process of secularization,[4] more recently scholars have asserted that the Sharia and *Nizamiye* courts were actually part of a single legal system and played complementary rather than antagonistic "religious" vs. "secular" roles. Avi Rubin, for example, has asserted that while the *Nizamiye* courts did take over some of the functions that had previously been under the Sharia court's purview, central jurists saw Sharia courts and Sharia-based legal doctrine as central aspects of Ottoman sovereignty and had no intention of sidelining them.[5]

Rubin and others have also noted that many Ottoman litigants continued to use Sharia courts extensively, and in multiple areas of law, even after the establishment of *Nizamiye* courts at the various levels of provincial administration. He argued that although central jurists issued numerous directives in the late nineteenth century refining the details of the separate spheres of authority of the Sharia and *Nizamiye* courts, numerous "grey areas" remained that afforded litigants multiple opportunities to choose their preferred legal forum.[6] Iris Agmon, investigating the legal environment of late nineteenth-century Jaffa and Haifa after the establishment of *Nizamiye* courts, argued that the Sharia court maintained an "open door attitude" especially at the lower levels of government, allowing litigants to take their legal business where they pleased. The establishment of *Nizamiye* courts, therefore, provided further options in terms of where to take legal business, i.e., the opportunity to forum shop.[7]

This focus on the litigant experience and forum shopping led Ido Shahar to argue for a new concept of state-sanctioned legal pluralism. Rather than focusing on the prevalence of non-state normative orders to gauge the pluralistic nature of

---

3. Ibid., 873; Also, see John Griffiths, "What Is Legal Pluralism?" *Journal of Legal Pluralism and Unofficial Law* 24 (1986): 1; For a dissenting view, see Brian Z. Tamanaha, "The Folly of the 'Social Scientific' Concept of Legal Pluralism," *Journal of Law and Society* 20:2 (1993): 192–217.

4. For an example of these narratives, see Niyazi Berkes, *The Development of Secularism in Turkey* (London: C. Hurst & Co. Publishers, 1998); For a comprehensive overview of this literature, see Rubin, *Ottoman Nizamiye Courts*, Introduction.

5. Rubin, *Ottoman Nizamiye Courts*, 77.

6. Ibid., 63–5.

7. Agmon, *Family and Court*, 74.

a legal environment, he proposed that legal systems could be described as pluralistic depending on the level of choice they afford their litigants regarding where to take their business.[8] In his extensive review of the *Nizamiye* court system, Avi Rubin used this concept of state-sanctioned legal pluralism to discuss examples of forum shopping between Sharia courts, *Nizamiye* courts and administrative councils.[9] Legal pluralism in the late Ottoman case, therefore, has come to signify forum shopping among state-sanctioned legal venues, rather than the contested relationship between the state-sanctioned legal system and other types of non-state normative orders.

My investigation of the legal system governing property relations in Salt yields three main observations pertinent to the discussion of legal pluralism, and specifically the litigant experience of forum shopping, among Ottoman historians. First, forum shopping in the late Ottoman context had different parameters and possibilities depending on the area of law. Scholars have noted that the *Nizamiye* courts assumed authority for criminal cases in the late nineteenth century, but this seems to be true for certain areas of civil law as well. In the realm of property law, and especially with regard to transactions and disputes involving agricultural land, legally sanctioned forum shopping was very limited in Salt.

Second, while Sharia court judges rejected cases dealing directly with rights to agricultural land, they did rule on civil cases that involved land indirectly. Litigants often used the Sharia court to make claims on debt with unregistered agricultural land as collateral, and the Sharia court would issue rulings ordering the borrower to pay the creditor back without mentioning the mortgage. This meant that the Sharia court provided a forum for litigants to obtain a ruling that recorded the existence of such mortgages, which were otherwise illegal because the land was unregistered. In this way, the Sharia court supported, and preserved for historians, the existence of an extra-state land market in which transactions were conducted outside the purview of the district land administration. Legal pluralism in Salt, at least in the realm of property law, therefore, resembled anthropologists' descriptions of extra-state normative orders that challenged the hegemony of the state-sanctioned legal system. However, litigants' use of the Sharia court, itself a state-sanctioned legal forum, to obtain record of these mortgages illustrates the way such extra-state normative orders were themselves intertwined with the vocabulary and legitimation mechanisms of the state system.[10]

Finally, the roles of the Sharia and *Nizamiye* courts in regulating control over land must be understood alongside not only the activities of bureaucratic offices, but also district and provincial administrative councils. In Salt, these councils had a more prominent role in settling large-scale disputes over agricul-

8. Shahar, "Legal Pluralism and the Study of Shari'a Courts," 125.
9. Rubin, *Ottoman Nizamiye Courts*, 61–2.
10. Tamanaha, "The Folly of the 'Social Scientific' Concept of Legal Pluralism," 211.

tural land than the courts. The administrative council's ongoing role in settling property disputes points to struggles within the bureaucracy over which agencies and bodies would have the power to allocate rights to increasingly valuable land. Litigants were able to take advantage of these struggles by petitioning the agencies they thought might support their specific rights to land, but their attempts were not state-sanctioned forum shopping. Further, these attempts occurred in the context of an expanding bureaucracy with new opportunities for notables in towns and cities as well as rural community leaders to participate in administering and deciding disputes over rights to land.[11] This bureaucratic expansion meant that litigants interacted with Ottoman governing agencies more intensively, especially in rural areas. The knowledge and connections forged through this expansion were crucial to litigants' attempts to defend their land rights by manipulating the complex and rapidly changing system.

Background: The Legal/Administrative Scene in Hamidian Salt

The district of Salt is an appropriate choice for analyzing how late Hamidian bureaucratic agencies and courts worked together, or sometimes at odds, to regulate land control for two main reasons. The first has to do with the accessibility of sources. The region of the Ottoman Empire that became Jordan in the twentieth century is one of the few with surviving land registers from the late nineteenth and early twentieth centuries that recorded ownership and transactions of land in the terms of the 1858 Land Code and are accessible to scholars.[12] Second, the Salt region was composed largely of state-owned agricultural (*miri*) land that fell under the Land Code's provisions in the late nineteenth century.

Thanks to a few important studies, we also have a fairly extensive idea of the region's social history in the late Ottoman period, the various social groups with interests in the district's land and the stakes of that interest. Raouf Abujaber chronicled not only the region's environmental features and dominant agricultural practices, but also stories of specific agriculturalists, including newcomers from Palestine, immigrant refugees and nomadic leaders heading plantation farms in the late nineteenth century.[13] Eugene Rogan's work illuminated not only the contours of Ottoman governance in Salt, but also extensive details of the

---

11. On the expansion of the Ottoman bureaucracy in the late nineteenth century and the related struggles especially in relation to property, see Huri İslamoğlu, "Politics of Administering Property: Law and Statistics in the Nineteenth-Century Ottoman Empire," in *Constituting Modernity: Private Property in the East and West*, ed. Huri İslamoğlu (London: I.B. Tauris, 2004), 277–79.

12. For a detailed study of such land registers for the district of Ajlun to Salt's north, see Martha Mundy and Richard Saumarez Smith, *Governing Property, Making the Modern State: Law, Administration and Production in Ottoman Syria* (London: I.B. Tauris, 2007).

13. Raouf Sa'd Abujaber, *Pioneers Over Jordan: The Frontiers of Settlement in Transjordan, 1850–1914* (London: I.B. Tauris, 1993).

district's population and property and credit relations.[14] In the realm of Salt's history, this article builds on Rogan's work on the implementation of the Land Code in particular to detail the relationship between different Ottoman legal and administrative institutions governing property relations and the way local litigants used the district's legal system. However, it also seeks to use Salt as a case study to bring out broader themes in the Hamidian legal environment especially as it pertained to agricultural land.[15]

In the organizational structure of the late Tanzimat period, the southeastern region of the province of Syria surrounding the town of Salt became a district along the detailed lines of the 1864 Provincial Administration Regulation in the late 1860s.[16] Previously, Salt had been governed indirectly, mainly through agreements with leaders of various pastoral nomadic groups who were involved in provisioning and protecting the Damascus Hajj route, which ran through the district.[17] When the Syrian provincial government created a district around Salt in 1867 and 1869 along the lines of the Provincial Administration Regulations, it was attached to the county (*liva/sancak*) of Balqa, which straddled the Jordan River and had its center in Nablus.[18]

While reliable population statistics for the later nineteenth century have not been uncovered,[19] the local population included cultivators and merchants settled in the town of Salt itself and the villages in its environs as well as groups that the Ottoman government referred to as nomadic.[20] Because of its high level of mobility, the population of the Salt district had been in some state of flux throughout the Ottoman period. Starting in the 1860s, groups of agricultural

14. Eugene Rogan, *Frontiers of the State in the Late Ottoman Empire: Transjordan, 1850–1921* (Cambridge: Cambridge University Press, 2000).
15. In particular, I conceptualize legal and administrative reform in the Salt region in the late nineteenth century as typical of other rural regions where Ottoman rule became more intensive in the late nineteenth century rather than as the incorporation of a formerly autonomous "frontier."
16. For more on the administrative system set out by the 1864 and 1871 Provincial Administration Regulations, see M. Safa Saraçoğlu, "Letters From Vidin: A Study of Ottoman Governmentality and Ottoman Politics of Administration, 1864–1877" (PhD diss., The Ohio State University, 2007), 101–08; For an account of the contested process of forming the Salt district, see Rogan, *Frontiers of the State*, 49–51.
17. For the importance of the Hajj route to the Ottoman administration of the region before the 1860s, see Hind Abū al-Shaʿr, *Tārīkh Sharqī Al-Urdun Fī Al-ʿahd Al-ʿUthmānī, 922H–1337 H/1516M–1918 M* (Amman: Ministry of Culture, 2010).
18. *Salname-i Vilayet-i Suriye* (Damascus: Matbaʿa-i Vilayet-i Suriye, 1285/1868–69), 1:59.
19. For available population estimates for Salt, see Rogan, *Frontiers of the State*, 162–65.
20. The Ottoman bureaucracy used a number of terms to refer to people practicing pastoral nomadism in the Arab regions. The term *aşiret*, commonly translated as tribe, served as an administrative category for purposes of identification and taxation and was used all over the empire. In the Arab provinces, bureaucrats also sometimes used the words *bedevi* to refer to Bedouin or "urban" to refer to Arab nomads.

investors, merchants, and their families and employees came to the district looking for fertile land and business opportunities mainly from urban centers in Palestine to the west and the Damascus region to the north. Because of their relative wealth, shared language, and commercial ties with Salt's existing inhabitants, as well as their previous experience with direct Ottoman rule in more urban settings, the members of this group would become the main local representatives of Ottoman governance in the elaborating administrative system in Salt beginning in the 1870s.[21] In the 1880s, the central and Syrian governments also began resettling refugees of the Ottoman-Russian wars, especially Circassians, around Salt. Salt was chosen as a settlement site in part because of the perception that the district enjoyed a wealth of highly fertile and unused, or "empty," land.[22]

In the late nineteenth century, this perception translated into the legal categorization of large swaths of the district's land as *mahlul*, or unused or deserted state land. In the developing exclusive ownership-based terms of the 1858 Land Code, the provincial land administration had the legal authority to sell this land to interested private bidders or to allocate it for public purposes.[23] These purposes included settling the aforementioned refugees with the expectation that they would cultivate the purportedly unused land and pay taxes, as well as allocating land for various development projects, the most important in the Salt region being the building of the Hijaz Railway along the pilgrimage route.[24]

The problem in Salt that would quickly become apparent was that even if parts of the district were not continuously cultivated, which in Ottoman legal terms meant they could be claimed as *mahlul* by the land administration, they were hardly unused or "empty."[25] Groups living both inside and outside of the town's boundaries laid claim to these lands mainly for purposes of grazing their

---

21. For a profile of this community, see Rogan, *Frontiers of the State*, Ch. 4; Abujaber, *Pioneers Over Jordan*.

22. For discussion and debate among Ottoman land officials around the classification of lands in Syria, including Salt, as *mahlul* and suitable for refugee settlement, see BOA.BEO 238/17824, 1 M 1311/15 July 1893; BOA.DH.MKT 217/23, 12 N 1311/13 February 1894; BOA.BEO 1023/76697, 19 Ca 1315/16 October 1897.

23. For detailed analyses of the 1858 Land Code, see Mundy and Smith, *Governing Property, Making the Modern State*; Huri İslamoğlu, "Property as a Contested Domain: A Reevaluation of the Ottoman Land Code of 1858," in *New Perspectives on Property and Land in the Middle East*, ed. Roger Owen (Cambridge: Harvard University Press, 2000).

24. Rogan, *Frontiers of the State*, 65–6.

25. For an account of a similar problem in Northwestern Anatolia and the problematic nature of the categories of the Land Code in reference to actual rural agricultural practice, see Yücel Terzibaşoğlu, "Landlords, Nomads and Refugees: Struggles over Land and Population Movements in North-Western Anatolia, 1877–1914" (PhD diss., Birkbeck College, University of London, 2003), 64–8.

herds, but also increasingly for agriculture.[26] When refugees settled in the Salt region with state sanction and claimed the agricultural land the government allocated to them, conflict ensued that often became violent. At the same time, prominent merchants in Salt attempted to secure control over agricultural products and sometimes over agricultural land itself, elaborating a network of mortgage-based debt that also highlighted issues of land control.[27]

The stakes of legal disputes over land in Salt were therefore very high, just as they were all over the Empire in the late nineteenth century. As the Ottoman administrative and judicial apparatus in the district expanded and became more complex, its main preoccupation soon became addressing the various claims over land whose control and ownership was thrown into question by the terms of the 1858 Land Code. Tracing the development of the government agencies involved with granting exclusive legal control over state land is possible through a reading of the provincial yearbooks of Syria (*Suriye salnameleri*), in which Salt appears as a district in most volumes. Litigants faced these agencies and courts and their complex division of labor as they attempted to maintain control over as much land as possible, and pay the lowest possible taxes, at the turn of the century. At the same time, some litigants became members of these courts and councils and worked closely with bureaucratic agencies to allocate rights to land themselves.

As multiple scholars have noted, the Provincial Administration Regulations envisioned governance by council. In Salt, the first governing council, which combined administrative and judicial functions (*meclis-i idare ve dawa*), appears in the provincial yearbook of 1870.[28] This district-level council was the successor of an institution established in the 1840s in the empire's provincial cities: the "great council," whose wide-ranging administrative and judicial responsibilities were outlined in an 1849 directive. In that directive, the council was envisioned as being intimately involved in the slow and uneven process of transferring the rights of tax farmers over agricultural lands in the empire to the central bureau-

---

26. Beyond the practice of cultivators from the town of Salt to travel to fields in their control outside the town to farm these lands, there is evidence that groups classified as pastoral nomads were also increasingly involved in agriculture in the region during the second half of the nineteenth century. For example, see Lars Wåhlin, "How Long Has Land Been Privately Held in Northern Al-Balqa', Jordan?," *Geografiska Annaler. Series B, Human Geography* 76:1 (1994): 33–49.

27. Eugene Rogan, "Moneylending and Capital Flows from Nablus, Damascus and Jerusalem to Qada' al-Salt in the Last Decades of Ottoman Rule," in *The Syrian Land in the 18th and 19th Century: The Common and the Specific in the Historical Experience*, ed. Thomas Philipp (Berlin: Franz Steiner, 1992), 239–60.

28. In *Salname-i Vilayet-i Suriye* Vol. 2 from 1286/1869–1870, this council is simply referred to as *meclis*; in the *salname* from the following year it is called "*meclis-i idare ve dawa.*" *Salname-i Vilayet-i Suriye*, 1288/1871–1872, 3:46.

cracy and its agents in the provinces.²⁹ Significantly, the council was also to issue decisions regarding the legal status of land, especially with regard to which lands were to be considered unused (*mahlul*) or legally available for repurposing by the state.³⁰

In the 1860s and in subsequent legislation, as the system of separate judicial and administrative arms of government was more fully elaborated, many duties of the great council deemed "judicial," especially in the criminal realm but also in terms of property disputes, were placed under the authority of the *Nizamiye* court system. At the same time, many of its "administrative" duties were taken over by various bureaucratic agencies like the imperial land administration (*Defter-i Hakkani*). By 1876, the combined administrative/judicial council in Salt had split into two separate entities, an administrative council chaired by the district governor, and a judicial council chaired by the same deputy judge (*naib*) who also chaired the Sharia court.³¹ This judicial council was the precursor to the *Nizamiye* court of first instance, which had authority over land disputes at the district level. Like most other district *Nizamiye* courts, the minutes for the Salt Court of First Instance have not survived. However, the surviving Sharia court records indicate that the court of first instance was the main forum for deciding small-scale land disputes between individuals and families in the late nineteenth century.

However, Sharia courts also had historical involvement in allocating control to agricultural land. Litigants in other districts had long taken disputes over privately owned property, such as houses, shops and urban plots, to local Sharia courts. There is also evidence that in the mid-nineteenth century wealthy individuals, mainly tax farmers, began illegally transacting in usufruct rights over *miri* land in Sharia courts in the same way that they previously had for *mülk* property.³² The situation in Salt was different because the first district Sharia court, at least for which records survive, was established in 1869, the year before the establishment of the first administrative and judicial council. The records of this court include three volumes of property transactions from the 1880s, before the establishment of a regular property administration in Salt, including sales and mortgages of agricultural (*miri*) land.

29. See the 1849 Provincial Administration Regulation (Eyalet Kanunnamesi), Article 27, on the administrative council's duties with regard to auctioning of taxation rights. *Mecmua-ı Kavanin (Düstur)* (Istanbul: Takvimhane-i Amire, 1851), 64. I would like to thank Safa Saraçoğlu for bringing this law to my attention and providing me with a copy.

30. Ibid., Article 46, p. 69.

31. *Salname-i Vilayet-i Suriye*, 1293/876–1877, 8:121.

32. Beshara Doumani, *Rediscovering Palestine: Merchants and Peasants in Jabal Nablus, 1700–1900* (Berkeley: University of California Press, 1995), 155–60; İslamoğlu, "Politics of Administering Property," 312 n. 22; Terzibaşoğlu, "Landlords, Nomads and Refugees," 73.

The earliest records of a property administration in Salt along the lines of the 1858 Land Code and 1859 Tapu Regulation are five volumes of initial land registrations (*yoklama*) among two of the main parties to later conflict over land, pastoral nomads and Circassian immigrants, dating from the late 1870s and early 1880s.[33] These volumes detail that the registrations were carried out in accordance with an order from the provincial governor's office in Syria and include signatures that provide an idea of the wide range of district authorities involved: the district governor, the deputy judge who chaired both the Sharia court and the judicial council, the district *mufti*, the financial director (*müdür mal*), the survey scribe (*tahrirat katibi*), two or three members of the district administrative council, the property administration official (*tapu katibi*) and his deputy.[34] After these initial registers, there is no sign of a regular property administration in Salt until the 1890s.[35]

Two tax volumes (*defter-i tahsilat*) from the 1890s followed by regular title registers (*defter-i hakkani*) that cover the remainder of the Ottoman period detail the process for land transactions in Salt. Beginning in January 1895, the tax registers show that individuals wishing to gain title to property would present a certificate (*ilmühaber*) attesting to their longstanding control over that land issued by the "headmen" (*muhtar*s) and elders' councils of their respective communities. In 1904, the district administrative council's involvement in this process also began to be listed, with individuals presenting documentation from both their local *muhtar*s and the district administrative council at each new initial registration of title to *miri* land.[36] At the end of each month the registers again include seals representing the myriad entities required to sanction these registrations and transactions as well as the collection of taxes based on them: at least one member of the administrative council, the financial director, the property administration official, the survey scribe, the *mufti* and the deputy judge, who as of 1892 was described as "deputy judge and president of the Salt Sales Commission."[37]

---

33. These volumes seem to have been lost or misplaced during the moving of the Salt property registers to the Amman Department of Lands and Surveys. I would like to thank Eugene Rogan for providing me with his personal copies. On the *yoklama* process, see Mundy and Smith, *Governing Property*, 70–3. For a more detailed account of these initial registers, see Eugene Rogan, "Incorporating the Periphery: The Ottoman Extension of Direct Rule over Southeastern Syria (Transjordan), 1867–1914" (PhD diss., Harvard University, 1991), Ch. 7.
34. See DLS *Salt Yoklama* Vol. 1.
35. See *Salname-i Vilayet-i Suriye* Vols. 8–25, 1293–1310/1876–1893.
36. Starting with DLS *Salt Defter-i Hakkani* Vol. 31, Eylül 1320/September 1904 *yoklama*, entry 22, p. 61. This does not mean that the administrative council was not involved on a transaction by transaction basis before this date, but this is when its involvement began to be routinely recorded.
37. DLS *Salt Defter-i Tahsilat* Vol. 18, Kanunusani 1307/January 1892 *daimi*, p. 20.

In terms of the personnel involved in these procedures, the government entities referred to as councils—first the administrative council and the judicial council/court of first instance and, after 1895, a municipal council (*meclis-i belediye*) and a board of education (*meclis-i maarif*)—included by law semi-elected members from the local population in Salt.[38] These semi-elected members were by and large from the town's small "notable" class—they were largely merchants and landowners, and by the turn of the century they exercised a firm hold on the district's administration.[39] While the governors, bureaucrats, and judges appointed from Istanbul tended to serve for short terms lasting for a maximum of three years, there were particular local notables whose service as semi-elected members of various government councils and sometimes in bureaucratic positions spanned the thirty years covered by the yearbooks for the province of Syria, and most of the local notables who served did so for more than one term.[40] Of the eighty men who rotated among the administrative council, the judicial council/court of first instance, the municipal council and board of education, eighty percent served more than one term, and forty-one percent served more than three terms. Therefore, although the councils and agencies local notables served on were legally subordinate to a district governor or deputy judge who was always from outside Salt, their local knowledge as well as their multiple terms of service must have afforded them extensive influence on the councils, and therefore in local government. In fact, they effectively took on bureaucratic positions themselves, becoming the foundation of local Ottoman government in Salt.[41]

The Sharia court registers also show that there was overlap between the personnel of the Sharia court and the town's numerous councils, especially the judicial council/court of first instance.[42] This overlap placed the Sharia court firmly within the sphere of authority of the local notable bureaucrats and shows the complementarity of the Sharia court and judicial council/court of first instance not only in terms of legally defined authority, but in terms of everyday workings

---

38. For details of the complex election process to these councils, see Johann Büssow, *Hamidian Palestine: Politics and Society in the District of Jerusalem, 1872–1908* (Leiden: Brill, 2011), 72–3; Saraçoğlu, "Letters from Vidin," 109–17.

39. Rogan, *Frontiers of the State*, 98.

40. *Salname-i Vilayet-i Suriye* Vols. 1–31, 1285–1317/1868–1900.

41. For other examples of the late Ottoman bureaucratization of local notables, see Mundy and Smith, *Governing Property*, 97–102. For the importance of councils in providing experience in representative government generally, see Jun Akiba, "The Local Councils as the Origin of Parliamentary Government in the Ottoman Empire," in *Development of Parliamentarism in the Modern Islamic World*, ed. Tsugitaka Sato (Tokyo: The Toyo Bunko, 2009), 176–204.

42. One example was Rihan Ağa, a resident of Salt from the Abu Halawa family in Jerusalem who was listed in the Syria *salname*s as the *mübaşir* of the court and was also a mainstay at the Sharia court, performing all sorts of witnessing functions. See SSCR Vol. 5 Record 28, 4 B 1315/29 November 1897; SSCR Vol. 3 Section 2 Record 9, 26 Ra 1306/30 November 1888; SSCR Vol. 3 Section 3 Record 19, 11 Ca 1308/23 December 1890.

and personnel. Since these judicial venues were physically in the same building,[43] it would have been easy for notable bureaucrats to move between them along with the deputy judge himself to perform the court's everyday functions. In fact, the continued presence of certain notables in the Sharia court and the fact that they were the same men serving on Salt's governing councils calls into question the idea that the deputy judge had any firmer hold on the workings of the Sharia court than he did on those of the *Nizamiye* court of first instance, where his influence was checked by the presence of elected local notable bureaucrats as well as professional personnel.[44]

The bureaucratic career of Musa Efendi Sha'ban, identified in Sharia court records as a Christian Ottoman from the people (*ahali*) of Salt, provides a window into the varied nature of merchant/landowner notable bureaucrats' work in the Salt government. Sha'ban's career as recorded in the provincial yearbooks spanned twenty-two years, from 1876 to 1898, and the Salt Sharia court records show that he continued to participate in the business of local government until at least 1904. Despite the institutional barriers to serving consecutive terms,[45] Sha'ban served eleven straight terms on the district administrative council between 1876 and 1887 and also served on the court of first instance in 1895 and 1896.[46] Sha'ban was also active in the Sharia court, providing services such as witnessing property transactions, identifying litigants, and giving witness testimony into the early twentieth century.[47] His career, while unique in his intensive participation on the administrative council, gives an impression of the extensive influence Salt's new bureaucratic class had over the business of local government.

The members of the councils did not include the people who were often the main parties to land conflicts: cultivators, nomads and immigrant refugees. However, the notable bureaucrats did not stand outside of these conflicts; their mercantile and landholding interests were closely intertwined with the patterns of production in the district and they were also sometimes in direct conflict with

---

43. Rogan, *Frontiers of the State*, 61.

44. For studies documenting the importance of the roles of notables in early modern Sharia courts, see Ronald C. Jennings, "Limitations of the Judicial Powers of the Kadi in 17th C. Ottoman Kayseri," *Studia Islamica* 50 (1979): 151–84. Hülya Cankabal, *Society and Politics in an Ottoman Town: Ayntab in the 17th Century* (Leiden: Brill, 2006), 123–34; Boğaç Ergene, *Local Court, Provincial Society and Justice in the Ottoman Empire: Legal Practice and Dispute Resolution in Çankırı and Kastamonu (1652–1744)* (Leiden: Brill, 2003), Ch. 4.

45. These had to do with the intricacies of the multi-tiered election system for the councils. For details, see Saraçoğlu, "Letters From Vidin," Ch. 3.

46. *Salname-i Vilayet-i Suriye* Vols. 8–30, 1293–1316/1876–1898. Sha'ban served a final term on the district administrative council in 1898.

47. For example, see SSCR Vol. 3 Section 1 Record 10, 6 Ra 1305/22 November 1887; SSCR Vol. 7 Section 1 Record 103, 18 Ra 1320/25 June 1902; SSCR Vol. 11 Record 151, 6 C 1322/18 August 1904.

producers, many of whom they contracted in mortgage-based debt arrangements. Musa Efendi Sha'ban, for example, initiated a claim in the Sharia court against Sulayman bin Furayj, identified as a member of the Wiraykat 'Adwan Bedouin group, for an unpaid debt of wheat in August 1902.[48] This claim registered his involvement in Salt's lucrative wheat market, a market controlled largely by merchants who provided cash capital to producers identified in the records as pastoral nomads and settled cultivators.[49]

The people in the latter two groups of producers were not wholly unrepresented in the late Ottoman government in Salt, including the procedures for gaining title to state land and the judicial processes for deciding disputes over that land. All of these processes involved, at the most immediate level, semi-elected leaders of specific administratively defined local communities as well as councils meant to represent those communities.[50] In Salt, these communities included quarters of the town (*mahalla*), villages in the town's environs (*qarya*) and nomadic groups or subsections of those groups (*ashira* or *firqa*) who were administratively attached to the Salt district and usually spent at least part of the year camping there. In order to register control over land at the property administration office, individuals presented certificates from the leaders of these administratively-defined communities (*mukhtar*s) attesting to their longstanding and unchallenged control and cultivation of that land.[51] These leaders were also mainstays at the Sharia court, providing testimony, verifying witnesses, and performing many of the same services otherwise controlled by the bureaucrat notable class discussed above. While their resources were more limited than those of the bureaucrat notable group and their participation in local government did not extend to the councils, these local leaders formed an important middling group who took on lower-level roles in the elaborating bureaucracy.

While he does not appear in the Ottoman provincial yearbooks, the career of Nahar al-Bakhit, described as a *mukhtar* of the Manasir section of the Abbad group of pastoral nomads in the Salt district, is noticeable in the registers of the district property administration office and in the Sharia court records. Al-Bakhit registered, along with three other members of the Manasir, the largest plot of land among the entire Abbad group in the first land registration carried out by the property administration in Salt in 1879.[52] This registration implied that Bakhit

---

48. SSCR Vol. 9 Record 39, 19 Ca 1320/24 August 1902.
49. Rogan, "Moneylending and Capital Flows."
50. The procedures for land transactions are laid out in the Land Title Regulation (*Tapu Nizamnamesi*) of 1859. For the role of the *mukhtar*, see Article 3. *Düstur: I. Tertib*, (Istanbul: Matbaa-yi Amire, 1289), 1:300.
51. For example, see Amman Department of Lands and Surveys (DLS) *Salt Defter-i Tahsilat* Vol. 18, p. 136, Entry 9, Ağustos 1311 *yoklama* (Salt Tax Register for August 1895).
52. In a 1915 census completed for the Salt district, the Manasir are listed in two separate groups, Manasir Wadi Sir and Manasir al-Arda (these refer to two different geographical areas

was a powerful member of the group in the late 1870s.[53] His personal participation in Salt's land market would continue throughout his life, and included sales to merchants and immigrants as well as purchases of land from other members of the Manasir.[54] In his capacity as *mukhtar* of the Manasir, Bakhit also performed numerous other duties, most notably providing witness testimony and acting as guarantor for loans Manasir individuals took from merchants and landowners. Most importantly, he certified individual Manasir members' control over land in both the Sharia court and the district property administration office and was closely involved with tax collection.[55]

Alongside notable bureaucrats, the group of low-level Ottoman bureaucrats that Nahar al-Bakhit represents created new and more intensive points of contact between the Ottoman administration and rural communities. As the courts and bureaucratic agencies involved in sanctioning control over land in Salt multiplied, local litigants' participation in government also increased, albeit at uneven levels. The complex relationship between these different entities was the background for forum shopping in the late nineteenth and early twentieth centuries.

Maintaining Control over Land in Hamidian Salt

The system for allocating control and settling disputes over agricultural land at the district level in Salt reflected the expansion of the Ottoman bureaucracy. Among the agencies and courts described above that were involved with governing land relations in Salt, there were two main ways duties overlapped as the system changed, opening theoretical opportunities for forum shopping: the Sharia court and the property administration office both recorded transactions in agricultural land, and the Sharia court and the *Nizamiye* court of first instance both ruled on disputes involving agricultural land. Before the institution of a regular property administration registering and taxing transactions in the 1890s, records from the 1880s show that individuals took transactions of *miri* land and other

---

in the Salt district). The populations of the two groups are listed as 619 and 254, respectively. See BOA.DH.EUM.4Şb.3/72, 27 Za 1333/6 October 1915. The land registration is in DLS Salt Yoklama Vol. 1, p. 18 entry 428, Teşrinisani 1295/October 1879. This entry was for 3,000 *dönüms* (about 680 acres).

53. For a breakdown of how many properties were registered by each group in the region, see Rogan, *Frontiers of the State*, 86.

54. See SSCR Vol. 2 Record 67, published in Muhammad 'Abd al-Qadir Khuraysat and Jurj Farid Tarif Dawud, *Sijill Mahkama Al-Salt Al-Shar'iyya, 1885–1888* (Amman: Ministry of Culture, 2007), 99 (4 Safar 1303/12 November 1885); DLS *Salt Defter-i Hakkani* Vol. 30, p. 182, entry 1, *daimi*, and p. 184 entry 1, *yoklama*, Haziran 1318/June 1902.

55. SSCR Vol. 2 Record 3, published in Ibid., 14 Dhu l-Qa'da 1302/25 August 1885. For Bakhit's involvement in taxation, see BOA.ŞD 2304/6, p. 92.

types of property to the Salt Sharia court.[56] Given the simple choice, litigants would understandably go to the Sharia court over the property administration office to carry out their transactions since no mention of taxes taken either at the time of transaction or annually was made in the Sharia court.

While the deputy judge and staff of the Sharia court may have maintained an "open door attitude" to people wishing to record property transactions in the 1880s before the establishment of a regularly working property administration in the district, these transactions do not seem to have carried any lasting legal weight with that administration from the 1890s going forward. The Salt property registers include no evidence that a *Shar'i* certificate (*hujja*) was accepted as documentary proof of control over land any more than an informal contract created between parties outside state sanctioned legal environments; rather, if an individual did not have a formal title deed for the property in question, he or she would have to start the initial registration process of obtaining certification from his or her community *muhtar*s and the district administrative council before being able to sell the land, and, most importantly, this individual would have to pay the taxes involved with registration.[57] This observation corresponds to the point that the property administration's main goal was registering state lands to individuals in order to pursue taxation—a *Shar'i* certificate, in this case, did not prove to the administration that an individual had paid any taxes on the land in question, and therefore was not relevant to proving longstanding control over land.

The central and provincial governments were by no means unaware of the threat to the integrity of the developing property administration, and therefore taxation, systems posed by the practice of registering land transactions in Sharia courts, issuing warnings to deputy judges to discontinue the practice.[58] In fact, the Sharia court staff in Salt seems to have stopped issuing such certificates for

---

56. SSCR Vols. 1–3 are dedicated to recording property transactions, including transfers of *miri* land. James Reilly also found such transfers of *miri* land dating from both before and after the Land Code in the Damascus Sharia court registers. He points out the important difference in language between sales of *mülk* property and transfers of *miri* land, to which the Salt registers also conform. James Reilly, "Shari'a Court Registers and Land Tenure Around Nineteenth Century Damascus," *Middle East Studies Association Bulletin* 21:2 (1987): 158–59.

57. As found by Reilly in the context of the Damascus hinterland, the Salt Sharia court did accept *tapu* deed as proof of control over *miri* land. However, the reverse does not seem to have been true. Ibid., 168.

58. In 1878 the Damascus Sharia judge issued a letter to the deputy judges in courts all over Syria asking them to stop conducting land transactions in the Sharia courts and emphasizing the necessity of completing such procedures in the land administration offices. The text of the letter appears in Jurj Farid Tarif Dawud, *Al-Salt Wa Jiwaruha* (Amman: Jordan Press Association, 1994), 47. Mundy and Smith cite an epistle of a Damascene jurist from 1867, who laments the regional practice of "incompetent" judges who "draw up invalid contracts according to fiqh in ignorance of their regulation by sultanic decree." See *Governing Property*, 48.

transfers of *miri* land, or indeed sales of any other property, after the property administration office began registering transactions itself in the 1890s, which makes sense considering the deputy judge's intimate involvement with the workings of the property administration office in his capacity as "Chair of the Salt Sales Commission."

What the existing Sharia court contracts from the 1880s point to, however, is the existence of an extra-state market in *miri* land that predated the implementation of the property administration in Salt,[59] and the intertwining of that market's workings with long-existing Sharia procedures for sanctioning transactions in *mülk* property. The continuing existence of this extra-state land market in Salt throughout the Hamidian period and beyond is evidenced by a number of Salt Sharia court claims on unpaid debt contracts with agricultural land as collateral dating from the early twentieth century. The 1858 Land Code legalized using title over *miri* land as collateral against debt, but the authority to sanction these transactions was firmly under the property administration. A related procedural office had the authority to force auction of mortgaged property to compensate creditors.[60] However, between 1902 and 1912, eleven claims of unpaid debt with collateral of *miri* land were initiated in the Salt Sharia court. In these claims, the lender specifically noted that the mortgages had been contracted "outside the *tapu* system," and in each case the lender obtained a *Shar'i* ruling warning the borrower to compensate the lender.[61]

While the Sharia court did accept the debt claims by warning the borrowers to compensate the lenders, it did not issue any kind of direct ruling about the mortgaged *miri* land in question. This was possible in the Sharia court setting because unlike in the *Nizamiye* courts, which looked into issues other than those directly addressed by the litigants through the office of the assistant public prosecutor,[62] *Shar'i* procedure dictated that the deputy judge rule only on the issue specified by the plaintiff, in this case the debt, with the landed collateral being something of a procedural aside. However, while they had no weight in terms of the property administration's mortgage procedures and its links to foreclosure

---

59. Rogan notes that a missionary in Karak to the south of Salt, where a regular land administration was not instituted until after the turn of the century, described land transactions carried out "in the native way," i.e., "by a paper signed and sealed by witnesses." Rogan, "Incorporating the Periphery," 323 n. 41.

60. The property registers from the district of Salt include the oversight of this office at least from the 1890s. For example, see DLS *Salt Defter-i Hakkani* Vol. 30. For the imperial debates around legalizing the forced auction of mortgaged *miri* land, see Mundy and Smith, *Governing Property*, 46–7.

61. For example, see SSCR Vol. 9, p. 81, Record 126, 14 B 1320/17 October 1902. The phrase most often used for "outside the *tapu* system" is *"khārij 'an da'irat al-tābū."*

62. For more on the role of the public prosecution, see Rubin, *Ottoman Nizamiye Courts*.

enforcement agencies, these *Shar'i* rulings did serve as written agreements between individuals that recorded the use of unregistered *miri* land as collateral.

After 1891, when a regularly functioning property administration seems to have been established in Salt, the deputy judge did not directly impinge on its sphere of authority in his capacity as judge of the Sharia court. In fact, in one case in July 1902, the deputy judge specifically referred a claim regarding rent of a garden to the civil section of the *Nizamiye* court of first instance after finding that the garden in question was classified as *miri* land, denying the plaintiff's claim and explaining to both parties that disputes involving *miri* land were not under the authority of the Sharia court.[63] This argument was also used by attorneys in property disputes in the early twentieth century, who argued that property at issue in plaintiff claims was *miri*, not *mülk*, and therefore the claims should be referred to the civil section of the court of first instance and the property administration officer should be present for the hearing even if the case involved inheritance.[64] While the 1902 case of the judge specifically ruling that a garden was *miri* and, therefore, not under his authority was exceptional, deputy judges in Salt consistently declined to rule on claims when one party argued that the case in question should be heard by the court of first instance, explaining that he could only issue a ruling when both parties to the case agreed to its hearing in the Sharia court.[65]

What then did Sharia court rulings on debt with unregistered *miri* land as collateral mean for the state-sanctioned property administration system? Some cases did bring up the potentially problematic aspects of the Sharia courts' implicit sanctioning of mortgages of unregistered *miri* land, seemingly compromising the integrity of the system for regulating property control or rendering it pluralistic. In one case, the plaintiff lender learned after independently contracting a mortgage agreement with the defendant debtor that the land in question was already mortgaged to the Agricultural Bank in Salt in the official property register.[66] In another, a plaintiff lender wished to register a debt with the Sharia court because the defendants had promised they would register landed collateral and mortgage with the *tapu* administration but had failed to do so. However, in both cases, the Sharia court followed its established procedures to warn the borrowers to pay the lenders back, remaining silent, at least on paper, about the land aspects. This practice indicates that at least in the realm of adjudicating and sanctioning rights over *miri* land, the Sharia court's policy in Salt was decidedly "closed

---

63. SSCR Vol. 9, pp. 7 and 9, Record 12, 3 R 1320/10 July 1902.
64. SSCR Vol. 13, p. 264, 4 R 1327/26 March 1909.
65. For example, see SSCR Vol. 16, p. 21, 3 Ca 1328/13 May 1910, and SSCR Vol. 16 pp. 117–19, n.d.
66. SSCR Vol. 19, p. 89, Record 209, 27 M 1331/6 January 1913.

door," with Sharia court personnel recognizing, and indeed actively participating in, the authority of the land administration in this realm.

The Sharia court cases involving mortgages of *miri* land point not to state-sanctioned legal pluralism, but to litigants' ongoing challenge to the hegemony of the new land administration. However, these and other cases show that the Sharia court, while it stayed out of cases directly involving *miri* land after the 1890s, hardly retreated from the civil realm in the late nineteenth century. In fact, the majority of the claims on which the court ruled involved unpaid debts resulting from contracts between merchants and producers. Litigants, therefore, took advantage of their ability to forum shop in the realm of contracts to obtain record of otherwise illegal mortgages of unregistered *miri* land. While more research is needed into the laws governing litigants' use of the Sharia court for contract-related cases and the enforcement outcomes they could expect from the court's rulings, these cases show that litigants used their opportunity to forum shop in one area of law to problematize the property administration's absolute authority in another.

Land Conflict and the Administrative Council in Salt

The available records regarding registrations and disputes over land in the Salt district depict a rather smoothly running system in which the main conflict was over unpaid debts and the main players were the Sharia court and the land administration, with hints of the *Nizamiye* court system's involvement. This impression, created in the absence of a minute-type archive of either district-level *Nizamiye* court cases or the district administrative council, is troubled by reports of investigations originating in Salt that reached Istanbul. These reports highlight two main themes: first, they show the central role not only of the *Nizamiye* court system but also of the administrative councils and governors at different levels of the provincial hierarchy in the process of land settlement; second, they show the essentially conflictual nature of land relations in the Salt district and highlight the challenges government agencies faced in attempting to regulate those relations.

The example presented here is one of a series of investigations of officials in Salt that reached central ministries in Istanbul, most of them relating to conflicts over land. Mehmet Ali Efendi was the district governor (*kaymakam*) in Salt from 1888 to 1893.[67] In early 1893, one group of cultivators and two separate groups of notable bureaucrats from Salt submitted petitions to the Ministry of Justice in Istanbul complaining about the district governor. The cultivators complained that he had forced them off of lands near the village of Amman in order to settle a newly arrived group of Circassian immigrants. The notable bureaucrats, who

---

67. Dawud, *Al-Salt Wa Jiwaruha*, 108.

included Musa Efendi Sha'ban introduced above, complained that the district governor had forced them off of the district administrative council even though they had received the majority vote.[68]

Upon request from the Ministry of Justice, the Interior Ministry called for the provincial governor's office in Damascus to undertake an investigation. The subsequent, lengthy report effectively absolved Mehmet Ali Efendi of any wrongdoing. According to the report, between 1889 and 1891,[69] Circassian refugees had been sent to the Salt district from Adana following orders from the Ministry of the Interior. The district governor allocated *miri* lands to the immigrants that included 12,000 *dönüms*[70] in the vicinity of the village of Amman, where an earlier group of Circassians had settled twelve years prior. At that time, a number of Salt residents made a claim that the land in question was actually in their control. The ensuing district-level investigation found that they did indeed enjoy rights to use the land and, in light of the increasing conflicts between the immigrants and the Saltis, the lands should be returned to the Saltis.

An investigator sent by the Damascus provincial government in 1891–1892[71] reported that the lands in question were a seven-hour journey from the town of Salt, and that between these lands and Salt there were also lands claimed by three pastoral nomadic groups. The investigation found that there were constant violent conflicts between the Saltis and the nomads as they passed over each others' lands on the way to the regions they respectively controlled. Upon seeing this report, the provincial administrative council, therefore, had suggested a trade, with the nomads awarded legal claim to the 12,000 *dönüms* near Amman, and the Salti cultivators getting a similar amount of land closer to the town of Salt. The investigation found that at the time, the Saltis had agreed to this trade, and a property official had been sent from the county center, which at that time was in Hawran, to legally complete the land allocations.

The provincial governor's report to the Interior Ministry added that the land that had been given to the Saltis in the trade was both more convenient for the Saltis and more fertile than what the nomads had gotten, and that the current complaints were the result of incitement by a few "simpleminded" individuals and did not imply any wrongdoing on the part of the district governor, Mehmet Ali Efendi. With regard to the complaint about the membership of the district administrative council, the report simply noted that appointments to the council were not the district governor's responsibility, but were rather under the author-

---

68. BOA.DH.MKT 25/24, Page 3, 7 § 1310/24 April 1893.
69. The report states that this investigation occurred "during the governorship of Asim Pasha," who was the governor of the province of Syria between 1889 and 1891.
70. About 2,700 acres.
71. During Osman Pasha's governorship of Syria, between 1891–1892.

ity of the county-level governor's office in Hawran. Therefore, the report found no reason to pursue legal investigations into Mehmet Ali Efendi's conduct.

While the file regarding Mehmet Ali Efendi's case leaves a number of questions unanswered, especially regarding the rights of the Circassian immigrants who were initially allocated the disputed land, it does illuminate the players involved in the process of attempting to resolve land conflicts legally. It shows the central role of provincial officials and specifically the provincial administrative council in addressing land conflicts in Salt. Even in the absence of an elaborated property administration based in Salt itself in the early 1890s, the Ottoman government and specifically its administrative institutions were closely involved in the process of land settlement, and were quick to send officials from the county-level property administration to legally conclude the administrative council's recommendations. While the district Sharia court may have been a forum for gaining some form of attestation to informal land agreements, it was not an alternative government-sanctioned forum for resolving land disputes with the same legal authority as the property administration.

This example also illustrates the importance of the administrative council at various levels of provincial government in resolving land disputes, even though its judicial power was legally limited.[72] District administrative councils retained an important role in sanctioning property registrations and transactions, and Musa Efendi Sha'ban's complaints are testimony to the power council members wielded in the district. These nuances are important to comprehend for a fuller understanding of litigant experience and litigant choice, as well as the late Ottoman legal system in general.

The fact that the Saltis chose to petition the Ministry of Justice rather than say, the provincial governor or the provincial administrative council he chaired, is also significant. This decision implies an attempt to bypass the local/provincial administrative apparatus of which Mehmet Ali Efendi was himself a part, as well as a perception that the judicial apparatus might provide a more favorable response to the petition. While more details of the case would be necessary to clarify this possibility, the Saltis' petition shows extensive local knowledge of a complex government apparatus with multiplying local agencies. Attempting to manipulate that apparatus by taking advantage of possible inconsistencies between its different arms, local litigants contested the elaborating legal and administrative apparatus in its own terms.

---

72. The 1864 Provincial Administration Regulation, which amended and clarified the duties of administrative councils at the district, county and provincial levels, specifically stated that administrative councils were not to interfere in judicial (*hukuki*) affairs. *Vilayet Nizamnamesi*, Article 14, in *Düstur: I. Tertib*, 1:610. In this vein Saraçoğlu's conception of a "judicio-administrative sphere" is helpful, because the line between judicial and administrative was being defined, in highly contested ways, at this time. Saraçoğlu, "Letters From Vidin," 97.

Conclusion

In Hamidian Syria, allocating rights to *miri* land in terms of the 1858 Land Code and adjudicating land disputes were perhaps the most important issues faced by the Ottoman government. By examining this process in the district of Salt, I have outlined the roles of the multiple government institutions involved: the district property administration (*tapu* office), the district Sharia court, the administrative council, the *Nizamiye* court of first instance and the network of community leaders (*mukhtars*). I have found that these district courts and agencies largely upheld the division of labor that imperial regulations specified for sanctioning transactions and deciding disputes over *miri* land. Specifically, by the 1890s when a district land administration and *Nizamiye* court apparatus were fully elaborated in Salt, the Sharia court no longer accepted either land transactions or disputes directly related to control over *miri* land.

However, the "closed-door" nature of the state-sanctioned legal system for regulating property in Salt does not imply that litigants had no opportunities to negotiate and struggle to maintain their land rights during the Hamidian period, or that the system was in no way pluralistic. Existing Sharia court records, while they may not illustrate a state-sanctioned pluralism in the realm of property law, do show the continuing existence of an extra-state market for *miri* land throughout the Hamidian period that specifically contested the government's attempt to allocate control over and tax every piece of that land. This finding implies that the Ottoman experience, at least in the realm of property law, shares some aspects with other legal situations labeled pluralistic by anthropologists. In these environments, the main pluralism occurs through practices entwined with but existing "outside," and often compromising the hegemony of, state sanction.

Finally, district and provincial administrative councils continued to play crucial roles alongside the courts in late Hamidian Salt, especially in deciding large-scale land disputes. Their activities illuminate the contestations involved as central jurists attempted to delineate separate judicial and administrative authorities. If litigants' attempts to take advantage of these contestations are to be interpreted as forum shopping, it was forum shopping that took advantage of the complexities and inner struggles of a rapidly changing system rather than an activity sanctioned by the ruling regime.

In this vein, provincial forum shopping occurred in a context of bureaucratic expansion in which litigants' relationship with Ottoman governance was changing more broadly. As the Ottoman bureaucracy and judicial system expanded and more provincial actors joined the ranks of Ottoman civil officials, litigants' day-to-day experience of Ottoman governance became more intensive. Litigants like Nahar al-Bakhit and Musa Efendi Sha'ban effectively joined the bureaucracy, gaining insider knowledge and social connections that would have been key to their ability to forum shop. However, their communities of pastoral nomads, cultivators and merchants also gained new connections and experience with the changing judicial and administrative systems through intensive processes of property registration, transaction, and taxation. These procedures were the context for litigants' attempts to use the system to maintain their control over land at the lowest possible cost. Sometimes, this meant avoiding the property regime altogether and contracting mortgage agreements "outside the *tapu* system." Understanding forum shopping within this larger context of contested bureaucratic expansion and the complex relationships between different legal and administrative agencies is crucial for a fuller examination of the late Ottoman litigant experience.

NORA BARAKAT is Assistant Professor in the Department of History at Qatar University.

7 The *Mecelle*, Sharia, and the Ottoman State

Fashioning and Refashioning of Islamic Law in the Nineteenth and Twentieth Centuries

Samy Ayoub

Introduction

Contemporary Islamic legal scholarship is preoccupied with the relationship between pre-modern articulations of Sharia and its modern formulations in the context of positive legislation and the nation-state. A key debate in the field is whether modern civil codes in Muslim majority countries and the codification of Sharia in the late nineteenth and early twentieth centuries are authentic representations of Islamic law or whether they are alien legal formulations authorized by the modern nation-state under heavy European influence. This article explores how the creation of the *Mecelle*, the first Islamic Civil Law code, in 1876 was justified by its drafters in terms of the indigenous legal genres within the Hanafi school. Thus, I address three central questions: (1) To what extent does the *Mecelle* embody Hanafi norms and doctrines? (2) What are the ways in which the *Mecelle* was justified as a legitimate Islamic legal code? (3) How does the *Mecelle* articulate new norms and doctrines in the name of the Hanafi tradition?

I argue that the *Mecelle* articles are particularly faithful to late Hanafi jurisprudential norms and doctrines. The legal tradition of the late Hanafis (*al-muta'akhkhirīn*)[1] of the early modern period serves as the legitimizing basis for the formation of the *Mecelle*, both in terms of its form and content. The *Mecelle* consistently adopts the opinions of the late Hanafis of the early modern period and their revisions of the *madhhab*. I provide examples based on the content of

---

1. Late Hanafism emerged ca. eleventh century CE. It developed into a fully-fledged tradition in the Mamluk period and early modern Ottoman Empire. Late Hanafi jurists declared their own distinct identities, opinions, and consensus in relation to earlier Hanafi opinions. See Abd al-Ḥayy al-Laknawi, *'Umdat al-Ri'aya 'ala sharḥ al-Wiqaya* (Beirut: Dar al-Kutub al-'Ilmiyya, 2009), 15–6.

Mecelle articles and corresponding references to them in the late Hanafi tradition.[2] The *Mecelle* perpetuates the role and authority of the Ottoman state in the Hanafi legal literature, which is reflected in references to sultanic orders and permissions.[3] I situate the *Mecelle*, as an Ottoman state project, within the late Hanafi tradition to show how the *Mecelle* was justified based on the internal and indigenous mechanisms of the Hanafi school itself. The drafters of the *Mecelle* insisted that it was inspired by the existing legal genre of legal maxims (*al-qawā'id al-fiqhiyya*) within the Hanafi school. References in the *Mecelle* and its commentaries specifically invoke the foundational work by Ibn Nujaym al-Hanafī al-Misrī (d. 970/1562–3), *al-Ashbāh wa al-Nazā'ir*, for justifying the legal form (i.e., pithily expressed principles) of the *Mecelle*. This work was very popular among Ottoman Hanafi jurists. For instance, Abū Sa'īd Muhammad b. Mustafā b. 'Uthmān al-Husaynī al-Khādimī (d. 1762) composed *Majāmi' al-Haqā'iq*, a work on legal theory (*usūl al-fiqh*), which incorporated Ibn Nujaym's legal maxims as a conclusion to his work. This does not mean that some of the *Mecelle* articles did not depart from both early and late Hanafi legal norms. Many articles of the *Mecelle* departed from these formulations, but these changes were perpetuated through justificatory techniques within the Hanafi tradition itself. Therefore, I maintain that what is important about the *Mecelle* is not only that it represents a faithful synthesis of late Hanafi jurisprudential norms, but also it articulates new social and legal norms of the late Ottoman Empire.

Furthermore, the key function of the *Mecelle* was to satisfy the need of the growing Ottoman bureaucracy to create a reference to the judiciary and other judicial councils, which lacked traditional Islamic legal training.[4] I observed that Syrian and Anatolian Hanafi scholars were the prime participants in the formation of the *Mecelle*.[5] There are two distinct features of the *Mecelle*: (1) the systematic nature of the project under Ottoman state supervision; (2) its function among the Ottoman legal regimes. This article proposes that the *Mecelle* should be understood in the context of the Ottoman modernization project in which it

---

2. See Appendix A. I give examples from three different chapters of the *Mecelle*, namely: Chapters on Deposit for Safe-Keeping (*al-Wadī'a*), Trusts and Trusteeship (*al-'Āriya*), and Gift Giving (*al-Hiba*).

3. Alī Haydar Efendī, *Durar al-Hukkām fī Sharh Majallat al-Ahkām*, (Cairo: Dār al-Jīl, 1991), 598. See the following *Mecelle* Articles 1152, 1272, 1276, 1280, 1281, 1287, 1801.

4. Recep Şentürk, "Intellectual Dependency: Late Ottoman Intellectuals between Fiqh and Social Science," *Die Welt des Islams* 47 (2007): 295. Şentürk argues that the Ottoman bureaucrats saw that the modern state structure was incompatible with the legal pluralism of the Ottoman Millet System in which religious communities were allowed to follow their legal traditions in litigation. Also, he argues that late Ottoman officials were attempting to create modern Islamic law out of the traditional structures of *fiqh*.

5. The Egyptian Hanafi scholars are excluded due to the political tension between the Porte and the almost-independent Egypt.

was a response generated from within the Islamic legal tradition to the *Tanzimat* and penetration of Western laws in Ottoman society.[6]

To support these arguments, I engage the discursive reasoning of the drafters of the *Mecelle* to affirm its faithful adoption of late Hanafi legal norms and doctrines. Therefore, I pay special attention to the report that accompanied the *Mecelle*, which serves as the rationale for its creation. I discuss how the function of the *Mecelle* is different from Hanafi jurisprudential works. I also examine one of the authoritative commentaries on the *Mecelle* to evaluate how it characterized the nature and role of the *Mecelle* within the Ottoman legal system. Moreover, I explore some case studies to demonstrate the underlying departures and doctrinal shifts from early and late Hanafi norms.

The *Mecelle*

The *Mecelle* (Ar. *Majalla*) is the first Ottoman attempt to codify Hanafi jurisprudence. The decision to draft the *Mecelle* resulted from a controversy over whether or not the Ottoman Empire should adopt the French civil code.[7] The Ottoman Council of Ministers decided to commission a work based on Islamic jurisprudence and entrusted this task to a commission under the supervision of Ahmet Cevdet Pasha (d. 1895)[8] who had been the leading advocate of this course of action.[9] The committee included 'Alā' al-Dīn Ibn Ibn 'Ābidīn (d. 1889), the late nineteenth-century Damascene Hanafi authority. The *Mecelle* was written and promulgated between 1869/70 and 1877. It contains 1,851 articles in sixteen volumes written in Ottoman Turkish.[10] It covers contracts, torts, legal liabilities, and some principles of civil procedure.[11] Officially, the *Mecelle* had jurisdiction throughout the Ottoman Empire, but in fact it was never effective in Egypt.[12] In his *İslam ve Osmanlı Hukukunda: Mecelle*, Osman Kaşıkçı argues that the

---

6. Şenturk, "Intellectual Dependency," 294.

7. Wael B. Hallaq, *Sharīʿa: Theory, Practice, and Transformation* (Cambridge: Cambridge University Press, 2009), 411.

8. Al-Ziriklī, *al-ʿAlām*, 1:108. Ahmet Cevdet b. Ismāʿīl b. Alī b. Ahmad Agha was a Turkish minister. He travelled to Istanbul and studied Arabic and sacred sciences. He also studied law and was appointed a judge for a brief time. Then, he was appointed the head of the Ministry of Justice.

9. C.V. Findley, "Medjelle." *Encyclopaedia of Islam*, 2nd ed. (Brill Online, 2013); Şenturk, "Intellectual Dependency," 298.

10. There is a tradition of Hanafi jurisprudence authored primarily in Ottoman Turkish. This is reflected in the Ottoman *fatāwā* collections, legal epistles, or complaints filed to the Ottoman *mufti*s in the imperial capital.

11. Findley, "Medjelle."

12. Talal Asad, *Formations of the Secular: Christianity, Islam, Modernity* (Stanford: Stanford University Press, 2003): 211.

Mecelle was primarily dependent upon the Hanafi school.[13] He stresses that the codification of the *Mecelle* was a response to Western legal hegemony.[14] Yet, he asserts that the Ottoman officials were influenced by Western debates on law.[15] The *Mecelle* was immediately translated into Arabic, Greek, and French under the title of "Ottoman Civil Law." It served as the civil code in the Ottoman Empire, and briefly in the Turkish Republic, from 1869 to 1926.[16]

The *Mecelle* articulates two central issues in the late Ottoman Empire: (1) how Islamic jurisprudence responded to legal modernity; (2) the process by which Islamic law was able to articulate new ideals and values. The drafters of the *Mecelle* saw its creation as a rejection of Western legal hegemony over commercial litigation within the Ottoman Empire.[17] The project of the *Mecelle* underscores the course of legal codification of Hanafi norms and doctrines in ways that provide insight into the process of legal development in the late nineteenth century. What I propose, then, is to understand the emergence of the *Mecelle*, not in terms of an epistemic break from pre-modern Islamic legal reasoning, but in terms of a continuation and transformation within the Hanafi legal tradition. The *Mecelle* cannot exist without dependence upon and articulation with previously existing norms and legal literature. The *Mecelle* did not appear *ex nihilo*, as a legal framework alien and opposed to the existing legal literature and legal order, but necessarily emerged out of an existing legal genre of *qawāʿid* and norms of late Hanafi tradition in a manner that made it an authentic representation of the legal tradition for the experts of the legal profession.[18]

This article explores how the late articulations of Hanafi jurisprudence point to both the continuous internal processes of doctrinal change within the *madhhab* and the indigenous legal paradigm upon which these changes were jus-

---

13. Osman Kaşıkçı's work is a key secondary source, which offers a detailed documentation of the process of the formation of the *Mecelle*. Kaşıkçı provides original documents in Ottoman Turkish which include the meeting minutes, reports, and the final proceedings of the *Mecelle* committee. He provides some insights into the role of Hanafi jurists and *fatāwā* literature in the formation of the *Mecelle*.

14. Osman Kaşıkçı, *İslam ve Osmanlı Hukukunda: Mecelle* (Istanbul: Osmanlı Araştırmaları Vakfı, 1997), 52–5.

15. Osman Kaşıkçı, *İslam ve Osmanlı Hukukunda*, 52–5.

16. Findley, "Medjelle."

17. *al-Majallah: wa-hiya tahtawī ʿalā al-qawānīn al-sharʿīyah wa-al-ahkām al-ʿadlīyah al-mutābiqah lil-kutub al-fiqhīyah*, 2nd ed. (Qustantīnīyah: al-Matbaʿah al-ʿUthmānīyah, 1887), 4–5.

18. The *Mecelle* incorporates Ibn Nujaym's *qawāʿid* from Article 2 to Article 100. These maxims pertain to the broad understanding of the Hanafi *fiqh* literature and its legal discourse. Murteza Bedir, "Fikih to Law: Secularization through Curriculum," *Islamic Law and Society* 11:3 (2004): 386. See Sobhi Mahmassani, *Falsafat al-Tashri fi al-Islam: The Philosophy of Jurisprudence in Islam*, trans. Farhat Ziadeh (Leiden: Brill, 1961 [1946]), 42–7. The argument in this article situates the *Mecelle* within the larger context of late Hanafi tradition.

tified. For, the *Mecelle* is not only a rich site for interrogating competing legal doctrines within the Hanafi school, but also it represents the backdrop against which the codification of the Hanafi school and the canonization of its doctrines were completed.

The *Mecelle* not only embodies the internal processes of legal change in the Hanafi school, but also it points to the legal, social, and economic changes within the late Ottoman Empire. These changes reflect the new emerging social, economic, cultural, and legal structures and orders. However, they were understood as a crisis of tradition not simply a crisis of adaptation to the new emergent social, political, cultural, and legal institutions. These transformations were generated both from within and outside the Muslim experience. From within, the social, economic, cultural, and political transformations of unprecedented magnitude put tremendous strain upon traditional legal institutions, legal values, and legal concepts. These societal changes deeply challenged the legal tradition as a whole, not merely a particular element in it.[19] From outside, European legal hegemony started to be felt at the heart of the empire through European control of the litigation of most of the commercial activities and disputations involving European citizens within the Empire. The Ottoman Empire responded to these challenges by transforming its laws through radical centralization and bureaucratization.

Secondary Literature

Ottoman legal change has been represented in some of the secondary literature mainly through the prism of westernization.[20] For example, Joseph Schacht describes the project of the *Mecelle* stating: "The experiment of the *Mejelle* was undertaken under the influence of European ideas, and it is, strictly speaking, not an Islamic but a secular code."[21] He argues, "Strict Islamic law is by its nature not suitable for codification because it possesses authoritative character only in so far as it is taught in the traditional way by one of the recognized schools."[22] Moreover, Schacht recognizes that the *Mecelle* contains "certain modifications of the

---

19. David Luban, *Legal Modernism* (Ann Arbor: University of Michigan Press, 1994), 28.

20. Avi Rubin, *Ottoman Nizamiye Courts: Law and Modernity* (New York: Palgrave MacMillan, 2011), 15; Şenturk, "Intellectual Dependency," 284; Dora Glidewell Nadolski, "Ottoman and Secular Civil Law," *International Journal of Middle East Studies* 8:4 (1977): 518; Shirine Hamadeh, "Ottoman Expressions of Early Modernity and the 'Inevitable' Question of Westernization," *The Journal of the Society of Architectural Historians* 63 (2004): 34; Avi Rubin, "Ottoman Judicial Change in the Age of Modernity: A Reappraisal," *History Compass* 7:1 (2009): 123.

21. Joseph Schacht, *An Introduction to Islamic Law* (New York: Oxford University Press, 1982), 92.

22. Ibid.

strict doctrine of Islamic law, particularly in the rules concerning evidence."[23] In addition, Bernard Lewis describes the efforts of the *Mecelle* committee as: "a digest rather than a code of *Şeriat* law of the Hanafi school ... one of the great achievements of Turkish jurisprudence."[24]

The *Encyclopaedia of Islam* introduces the *Mecelle* by stating, "it reflects Western influence mainly in its division into numbered books, sections and articles, as in European codes."[25] Some insist that the *Mecelle* is a deviation from the authoritative opinions of the school.[26] Following the same discourse, without providing any evidence, some scholars have argued that the *Mecelle* is merely a random selection of legal doctrines from different schools of law.[27] These positions consistently juxtapose the *Mecelle* with the Hanafi jurisprudence, arguing that it is a formalized legal project that was authorized by the state.[28] Wael Hallaq, for instance, argues: "The transposition of Islamic law from the fairly independent and informal terrain of the jurists to that of the highly formalized and centralized agency of the state found manifestation in the *Mecelle-ı Ahkām-ı Adliye*."[29] He points out that a committee headed by the Sharia jurist Ahmet Cevdet Pasha produced it. Yet, Hallaq paints a picture in which the *Mecelle* was a result of a struggle between forces of tradition and Westernization. Hallaq pinpoints that Ahmet Cevdet Pasha insisted that the law had to be "faithful to the cultural constitution of the Empire against the powerful Westernizer Ali Paşa who called for the adoption of the French Code of 1804 (known as the Code Napoleon)."[30] Hallaq contends, "One of the aims of the *Mecelle* was to provide, in the manner of a code, a clear and systematic statement of the law for the benefit of both the Sharia and Nizamiyye courts."[31] Erroneously, Hallaq claims that the opinions chosen did not necessarily reflect the authoritative doctrines in the Hanafi school. Moreover, he asserts that these doctrines were not exclusively

---

23. Ibid., 93. Schacht argues that the *Mecelle* requires all traditional qualifications of a witness and his evidence, but not the quality of being a Muslim (art. 1684). Schacht's observation is accurate in that the section on testimony and evidence in the *Mecelle* do not address the religion of the witnesses. The focus is primarily on the exactitude and justice of the witness as well as his/her reputation (art. 1705). The just person is defined in the same article as the one whose good deeds are dominant over his/her bad deeds.

24. Bernard Lewis, *The Emergence of Modern Turkey* (New York: Oxford University Press, 1968), 123.

25. Findley, "Medjelle."

26. Abdullahi Ahmed An-Na'im, "The Compatibility Dialectic: Mediating the Legitimate Coexistence of Islamic Law and State Law," *Modern Law Review* 73:1 (2010): 20; Hallaq, *Sharī'a*, 411.

27. An-Na'im, "The Compatibility Dialectic," 20.

28. Hallaq, *Sharī'a*, 411.

29. Ibid.

30. Ibid.

31. Ibid.

Hanafi, for some of them were imported from other schools after being generally approved by the later Hanafis.³² The *Mecelle*, for Hallaq, was "a last-ditch effort to salvage the *sharī'a* as a law in force, but it was also an attempted remedy applied to a problem that had originated as a remedy."³³

The main concern with Hallaq's narrative is its dismissal of the arguments made by the drafters of the *Mecelle* that it is an authentic Islamic legal genre. He reduces its significance to a mere experimental project to rescue Islamic law at the end of the Ottoman Empire. Also, he disregards the stated intention of the *Mecelle* drafters as well as their justification for its formulation to burgeoning Ottoman bureaucracy and to expedite juridical litigation and court proceedings. Likewise, Hallaq overlooks the fact that 'Alā' al-Dīn Ibn Ibn 'Ābidīn, the Damascene Hanafi authority, after his father Ibn 'Ābidīn, was a member of the committee that formulated the *Mecelle*. More seriously, Hallaq neither explains how the *Mecelle* deviates from the authoritative Hanafi opinions nor identifies which doctrines were borrowed from other schools of law. This narrative in the secondary literature fails to engage with the legal logic and discursive reasoning advanced by the drafters of the *Mecelle*. The *Mecelle*, as a systematic legal project, is modern in the sense that it responds to the emergent patterns of social, economic, and legal challenges of the mid-nineteenth century from within the Hanafi tradition. The drafters of the *Mecelle* never claimed that the codification of Hanafi jurisprudence was inspired by Western legal influence. The claim that the codification of Hanafi jurisprudence was a Western legal import is based on two assumptions: (1) Pre-modern Islamic law is alien to its modern articulations; (2) The dichotomy between the modern and the pre-modern is epistemic.

The *Mecelle* Report: Continuity of Late Hanafi Tradition

The front cover of the *Mecelle* declares that it contains the *shar'i* codes (*al-qawānīn al-shar'iyya*) and juridical rulings (*ahkām 'adliyya*) which, the *Mecelle* drafters maintain, are consistent with the authoritative manuals of Hanafi jurisprudence that were edited by a committee composed of established scholars and meticulous jurists. The *Mecelle*'s cover announces that the Sublime Porte approved the *Mecelle* and the imperial rescript established it as the canon, exemplar (*dastūr*) to be acted upon.³⁴ The *Mecelle* is commenced with the report that was filed to the late Ali Pasha, the Grand Vizier (*al-Sadr al-Azam*) on 1 Muharram 1286 (13 April 1869) justifying and situating the significance of its formation among the different legal regimes in the Ottoman Empire. The report was signed by the principal of the *Dīwān al-Ahkām al-'Adliyya*, Ahmet Cevdet Pasha; the inspector of the Imperial Endowments, al-Sayyid Khalīl; members of the *Shūra al-Dawla*, Sayf

32. Ibid.
33. Ibid., 412.
34. *Mecelle*, 1.

al-Dīn and Muhammad Amīn al-Jundī; and members of the *Dīwān al-Aḥkām al-ʿAdliyya*: al-Sayyid Ahmad Khulūsī and al-Sayyid Ahmad Hilmī; and a member of the Committee, ʿAlāʾ al-Dīn Ibn Ibn ʿĀbidīn. The filed report is dated 8 Dhūl Hijja 1285/10 March 1869.

The report asserts that Islamic jurisprudence is the locus of the matters related to everyday life. It explains that *fiqh* is divided into personal status (*munākahāt*), transactions (*muʿāmalāt*), and criminal punishments (*ʿuqūbāt*). These same three categories, the report insists, are the principles of laws of civilized nations and it declares that the category of transactions (*muʿāmalāt*), in this legal scheme, is called the Civil Law.[35] The report confirms that Islamic jurisprudential norms are adequate to address all commercial cases that might be tried in courts.[36] Aware of the legal developments and legal regimes in Europe, the report attributes the three legal categories (*munākahāt*, *muʿāmalāt*, and *ʿuqūbāt*) to both the Islamic and European systems. The report does not claim that the legal systems of Europe are models for the *Mecelle*. Instead, the report affirms that Islamic jurisprudence is sufficient to address any of the emerging commercial activities and disputations. The report states:

> The Sublime Porte has, historically and recently, enacted many laws similar to the Civil Law and although these laws are insufficient to explicate all commercial activities, the cases that fall under the commercial transactions from the science of *fiqh* (jurisprudence) is sufficient and satisfy the recurrent needs in this regard and [avoiding] what is observed of some problems occur in referring claims to *sharʿ* and *kanun*.[37]

Furthermore, to affirm the sovereignty of the Sharia, the report reiterates that Islamic jurisprudence is the authoritative reference of the principal origin of laws and the imperial legal regulations. It emphasizes that cases that are litigated according to the imperial statutory law (*nizam*) are decided based on Islamic law. The *Mecelle* emphasizes that European laws should not be a reference in any litigations within the Ottoman Empire because the imperial rescript did not enact these laws; therefore, they do not constitute a source of law in Ottoman state courts.[38]

Additionally, the report touches on a key problem facing the different judicial bodies that were created in the Ottoman Empire, namely, the lack of traditional Islamic legal training. The report establishes that the science of *fiqh* is a "sea without a shore" and the process of deducing the core principles of the cases to solve these problems is contingent upon scientific skill and legal craft, especially in the Hanafi school. The report explains that the *madhhab* has many

---

35. Ibid., 2.
36. Ibid.
37. Ibid., 3.
38. Ibid., 4.

independent legal scholars (*mujtahidūn*), yet they differ based on their generation and authoritativeness, adding to the plurality of the opinions [in the *madhhab*]. The report laments that the Hanafi school has not been standardized, in contrast to the Shafi'i school. In the Hanafi school, the report claims, the jurisprudential cases still suffer divergence and thus distinguishing the sound authoritative opinion among these divergent opinions and applying the new emergent cases based on them is extremely difficult.[39]

To justify changes to key Hanafi doctrines and norms in the *Mecelle*, the report relies on the concepts of custom, changes of time, and necessity, which are part and parcel of Hanafi legal reasoning.[40] This process confirms that the doctrinal shifts in the *Mecelle* were perpetuated from within the *madhhab* and were a continuation of an internal mechanism. In this context, the report emphasizes that changes of time affect changes in legal rulings of cases that are based on tradition (*ʿāda*) and customary practice (*ʿurf*).

The report provides the following case. According to early Hanafi jurists, if someone wanted to purchase a house, it would have been sufficient for the buyer to see one of its rooms to finalize the sale. However, late Hanafi jurists insisted that it was necessary for the buyer to see each room in the house individually. The report asserts that this shift of opinion is not based on the introduction of new evidence, but it rises from a change in tradition and custom pertaining to the matters of house construction. The report explicates that the old tradition in building houses used to have very similar rooms and styles, thus, to see one of the rooms would be considered a valid sight of all rooms in the house. In this age, however, the *Mecelle* report postulates that the established custom of the day stipulates that houses now have different rooms with different styles and spaces. Therefore, it is necessary to see every room at the time of purchase.[41] The new guiding principle that was formulated due to this change of custom is the attainment of a sufficient knowledge of the purchased item. The drafters insist, "The shift of legal ruling in this case is not enabled due to a change of a legal principle but rather a change for the legal ruling based on the change of circumstances of the time."[42]

---

39. Ibid.
40. The late Hanafi authority, Ibn ʿĀbidīn (d. 1836), wrote a famous treatise *Nashr al-ʿarf fī binaʾ baʿd al-ahkām ʿalā al-ʿurf* (*Disseminating Fragrance: On Building some Laws on Custom*) on the status of custom as a source of law which gained significant attention in the secondary literature. For examples of Ibn ʿĀbidīn's discussions of Cairene customs see Ibn ʿĀbidīn, *Radd al-Muhtārʿalā l-Durr al-mukhta* (Beirut: Dar al-Kutub al-ʿIlmiyya, 1994–1998), 3:131; 4:423, 521, 548; 5:189, 198, 516, 542. For examples of Ibn ʿĀbidīn's discussion of Damascene customs, see *Radd al-Muhtār*, 1:189, 197, 324; 2:99, 169; 3:131, 746; 4:186. For examples of his discussions of Anatolian customs, see *Radd al-Muhtār*, 1:325, 2:160, 3:608, 4:364, 395, 432, 435; 5:279, 420; 6:12.
41. *Mecelle*, 4.
42. Ibid.

The report asserts the importance of codification in the following manner. First, it points out that the exhaustion of the knowledge of all prior Hanafi *fatāwā* was already an extremely difficult task. The efforts of legal scholars could not encompass all the jurisprudential cases and accommodate all *intra-madhhabic* differences.[43] Second, the report introduces the importance of legal maxims in the process of legal reasoning and judicial proceedings. It explains that Ibn Nujaym gathered many of the jurisprudential canons and overarching legal principles under which the particular cases of jurisprudence are treated. The report insisted that Ibn Nujaym's work opened up a new window that would facilitate the knowledge of the particular cases in the school.[44] Third, the report claims, in our time, it is rare to find those who possess this deep *shar'i* knowledge in all fields, let alone that it is impossible to appoint members to the *Nizamiye* courts possessing the ability and skill to review manuals of jurisprudence at a time of need to solve emergent problems. Also, the report reveals that it has become difficult to find enough judges for the Sharia courts that already exist in the provinces of the empire.[45] For these reasons, the report justifies the necessity for the creation of the *Mecelle*. The *Mecelle* was considered an easy text to read, free from any legal disputation, and contained the most preponderant opinions in the Hanafi school. In other words, Ottoman state officials, judges, members of the new *Nizamiye* courts, and administrative employees can confidently rely upon the *Mecelle* in their legal determinations.[46] The drafters stress that in the process of formulating the *Mecelle* they were cognizant of the Hanafi *madhhab* doctrinal boundaries and its authoritative opinions:

> We were assigned, despite our weakness and inability, to be responsible for completion of this great project and good sign to satisfy the current commercial activities and transactions based on the jurisprudential canons fulfilling the needs of this age. Upon the Imperial will, we gathered in the *Diwān al-Ahkām* and took the initiative to organize the *Mecelle* containing the many cases and matters that are frequently recurrent and represent an urgent necessity from the jurisprudential commercial activities. They are gathered from the legal authentic opinions of the Hanafi scholars and they were divided into various chapters and were labeled "*al-Ahkām al-'adlīyya*".[47]

The report informs us that after the completion of the introduction and first book of the *Mecelle*, a copy of both were given to the Ottoman religious establishment (*mashyakhat al-Islām*), and other copies were sent out to authoritative

43. Ibid.
44. *Mecelle*, 5.
45. Ibid.
46. Ibid.
47. Şemseddin Sami, *Kamus-i Turkī* (Der-Saadet: Ikdam, 1899), 930. The Ottoman Turkish word '*adliyya* does not have a religious connotation.

scholars who possess sufficient skill and knowledge in the science of *fiqh*.⁴⁸ The reason for these scholarly screenings was to confirm both the legitimacy of this work as a representative of Islamic legal literature and the accuracy of its Hanafi content.

From *Fiqh* to *Mecelle:* Judicial and Religious Norms

Upon reading this report, it becomes clear that the *Mecelle* was created to fulfill a specific judicial function within the Ottoman bureaucracy. Also, it appears that the legal maxims and the books of *fatāwā* were essential in the formulation of the *Mecelle*. Most importantly, these works are the loci for the revised opinions and norms found in the late Hanafi tradition. The *Mecelle* was not meant to be a substitution of the process of legal reasoning, but it was thought of as a framework through which judges and state employees could reason about the filed cases.

One of the most important aspects of the *Mecelle* is that it signifies the creation of a legal genre that is solely dedicated to judicial reasoning and court procedures. It is through this understanding that we can grasp the treatment, function, and role of the codified Hanafi legal norms in a single project. While the *Mecelle* elaborates on the important function of *fiqh* to preserve human life, perpetuate civilization, and to protect social and moral order, it appears to also have an entirely different function. The *Mecelle* encapsulates the "judicial" (*qaḍā'ī*) aspect of *fiqh*.⁴⁹ In other words, the purely religious and ethical considerations are not the objective of the codification of the Hanafi legal doctrines.⁵⁰ The six categories that qualify human actions in the Hanafi *fiqh*—obligatory (*fard*), duty (*wājib*), prohibited (*ḥarām*), recommended (*mandūb*), reprehensible (*makrūh*), and permitted (*mubāḥ*)—are not incorporated into the process of legal reasoning in the judicial process.⁵¹ The main function of the *Mecelle* was to influence judicial reasoning and to expedite court proceedings. The categories of "recommended" and "reprehensible" are more intertwined with the *fatāwā* discourse. Most importantly, these ethical categories are designed to address the conscience of the believers (*diyāna*) and to promote piety and good behavior. Islamic legal practice already distinguishes between these two categories of legal classifications: judicial and moral/religious.⁵² Islamic law recognizes the fact that "the in-

---

48. *Mecelle*, 6.
49. Ibn 'Ābidīn, *Radd al-Muḥtār*, 5:365.
50. Late Hanafis discuss the differences between the role of the *muftī* and the judge. They insist that *fatwā* cannot be utilized by judges in all types of cases litigated before them. Ibn 'Ābidīn states that *muftīs* address the conscience of the believers (*diyāna*), while judges rule according to the *ẓāhir* (material consequences of one's actions). See Ibid.
51. The other Islamic legal schools identify only five categories for qualifying human actions. They combine the *fard* and *wājib* in one single category.
52. Baber Johansen, *Contingency in a Sacred Law: Legal and Ethical Norms in the Muslim Fiqh* (Leiden: Brill, 1998), 35–6. Talal Asad, *Formations of the Secular*, 246. Asad rightly argues

dividual may violate a religious duty without subjecting oneself to the sanction of the judicial prosecution."⁵³ The *Mecelle*, as a legal project, specifically addresses the needs of the judiciary and the new "secular" and Sharia court systems in the Ottoman Empire in the late nineteenth century. The intent of the drafters of the *Mecelle* was not to reproduce a *fiqhī* text, but to stipulate standardized criteria for judicial reasoning.

The *Mecelle* discusses the role and function of *fiqh* in society in Article One. Article One states that *fiqhī* issues are either related to the Hereafter, namely, *al-ʿibādāt* (ritual acts); or they are concerned with worldly affairs, namely, *munākahāt* (personal status), *muʿāmalāt* (transactions), and *ʿuqūbāt* (punishment).⁵⁴ The *Mecelle* asserts that since human beings—unlike animals, are civil by their nature—they are driven to live in communities and not on their own. Humans, therefore, need to cooperate and collaborate in order to preserve civilization.⁵⁵ However, because it is also in human nature to seek what s/he desires and would fight whomever competes with him/her to reach his/her goal, it is necessary to establish laws to maintain justice and order. In particular, this situation requires the establishment of laws in the matter of personal status, which is the *munākahāt* division of *fiqh*.⁵⁶ Also, human beings need laws to protect civilization—which is maintained by cooperation and collaboration—and these fall under the *muʿāmalāt* division of *fiqh*. Finally, human beings require laws of punishment to preserve the continuity of civilization in this ordered manner. These laws belong to the *ʿuqūbāt* division of *fiqh*.⁵⁷ Thus, it is through *fiqh* that the moral-social order is guaranteed and that civilization is maintained and sustained.

The *Mecelle*: Change and Continuity of Hanafi Legal Doctrines

The *Mecelle* enumerates few examples in which the opinions of the Hanafi school have shifted from its pre-modern articulations to reflect new legal and social norms. The justification for such changes varies among the cases provided. Murteza Bedir rightly argues, "All of the provisions formulated by the *Mecelle* Committee in the nineteenth century were more or less in conformity with the recognized opinions of the Hanafi school."⁵⁸ Yet, Bedir asserts that the formulation of the preferred opinions (*rājih*) that ended up in the *Mecelle* was driven by

---

that we should not identify the ethical dimension of *fiqh* in its relation to the law in terms of "disembodied conscience." I confirm Asad's thesis that the ethical/religious dimension of *fiqh* is "set doctrinally outside the jurisdiction of an earthly court of law. Muslim jurists simply regarded it to be legally inviolable."

53. Bedir, "Fikih to Law," 380.
54. *Mecelle*, 11.
55. Ibid.
56. Ibid., 12.
57. Ibid.
58. Bedir, "Fikih to Law," 388.

"new considerations." Bedir claims that the authors of the *Mecelle* articulated this new idea in the report that accompanied the *Mecelle*, stating, "*nasa erfak ve asrın maslahatına evfak*" or "that which is easiest for the people and the most suitable for contemporary needs."[59] Bedir contends that the drafters of the *Mecelle* "used this maxim as the sole justification for their singling out a particular opinion and promulgating it as the law on a given case."[60]

Bedir's assessment that the doctrinal shifts in the *Mecelle* were solely driven by people's needs requires attention. The *Mecelle* report gives us a unique glimpse into the logic and discursive reasoning of the deliberations within the *Mecelle* committee on this issue. The *Mecelle* shifts from the hierarchical authoritative positions of the Hanafi school to alternative positions within the same school based on *masālih al-nās* (people's interests), *taysīr muʿāmalāt al-nās* (facilitating people's transactions), *muraʿāt maslahat al-waqt* (taking into consideration the interests of the due time), and *muraʿāt al-ʿurf* (considering customs and tradition). Strictly speaking, these techniques are no different from premodern Hanafi jurisprudence. Also, the late Hanafi revisions of the early authentic opinions in the *madhhab* (*zāhir al-riwāya*) were carefully incorporated into the *Mecelle*. It is in this context only that we can make sense and appreciate the drafters' insistence:[61]

> Because we have not departed from the doctrinal boundaries of the Hanafi school, and since the greater part of those articles published in the *Mecelle* are consistent [essentially true in spirit] with the currently valid and observed opinions of the House of Religious Edicts (*fetva hane*), there is no need for a discussion about them. The opinions of certain key jurists of the Hanafi school are more suitable to the peoples [needs] and to the interest of this age and thus we have admitted them within the *Mecelle* [as well as the *madhhab*], and we give below our justification and reasons [report of the *mecelle*].[62]

The *Mecelle* drafters shifted some opinions of the school by utilizing the justificatory techniques and tools available for Hanafi jurists. For instance, in Articles 85 and 197, the *Mecelle* stipulates that the sale of non-existent things is void. However, the current situation, the *Mecelle* committee elaborates, is that things

---

59. Ibid.
60. Ibid.
61. Kuyucaklızade Mehmet Âtıf and Hoca Eminefendizade Ali Haydar, *Mecelle-yi Ahkâm-ı Adliye* (Istanbul, 1901), 6.
62. This specific paragraph does not appear in all the Arabic versions of the *Mecelle* to which I had access, despite the fact that it appears in the original Ottoman Turkish version of the *Mecelle*. It appears that the two English translations of the *Mecelle* that I consulted include this specific paragraph. They have depended upon original Turkish versions or Greek and French translations of the original Ottoman Turkish. See *Mecelle-i ahkâm-i adliye* (Istanbul: Matbaa-yi Osmaniye, 1882), 12. One of the most accurate English translations of the *Mecelle* is: *The Medjelle or the Ottoman Civil Law*, trans. W. E. Grigsby (London: Stevens and Sons Limited, 1895), viii.

الحاصل بوجه له ده مذهب حنفینك خارجنه
چیقلیوب مواد مندرجه سنك ا كثرى الحاله هذه
فتوا خانه ده معتبر و معمول به اولدیغی جهته له بونلر
حقنده بچه لزوم كورلمز فقط ینه فقهای حنفیه دن
بعض قول ائمه دنك اقوال معتبره سی ناسه ارفق
و مصلحت عصره اوفق اولق حسبیله اختیار اولنمش
ایدو کندن بونلرك مأخذ مقبوله و اسباب موجهه سی
روجه آتی بیان اولنور.

Mecelle-i ahkâm-i adliye (Istanbul: Matbaa-yi Osmaniye, 1882)

such as flowers, artichokes, vegetables, and fruit (representative crops that do not all grow at the same rate—some flowers will bloom before others; some fruit will ripen early, others later) are valid for sale even if only some of the expected yield is successfully grown. Since it is not possible for any crop to grow altogether at the same time, people agreed on the custom of contracting the sale of the entire potential yield—the existent and those expected to grow—in one commercial deal. The origin of the Hanafi support for this custom is Muhammad b. al-Hasan al-Shaybānī, who permitted this type of sale based on juristic preference (*istihsān*), and justified it by arguing that the existent should be considered the basis of the commercial transaction (*al-asl*) and the non-existent to follow it in its ruling. This opinion was the basis of the *fatwā* by the Bukhāran Shams al-A'imma al-Hulwānī (d. 1056), and Abū Bakr b. Fadl (d. 1118). The *Mecelle* drafters affirm that forcing people to give up one of their established customs is not possible. The priority is to consider their transactions to be valid; therefore, the drafters of the *Mecelle* chose Muhammad's opinion to preponderate in this case.[63]

Similarly, according to Abū Hanīfa, the person who is engaged in a manufacturing contract (*istisnā'*) has the right to withdraw from the contract; however, Abū Yūsuf argued that if the person found the manufactured product in accordance to the criteria that were stipulated and approved in the contract, he cannot withdraw from the contract. As a clear shift from Abu Hanīfa's position to Abū Yūsuf, the *Mecelle* asserts that due to the current situation "in our times," there are many factories where canons, ships, and the likes are produced through manufacturing contracts, thus, it became clear that giving the choice to the buyer alone to finalize or nullify the contract would result in violating substantial interests of one of the contracting parties. In this situation, it is incumbent to choose the opinion of Abū Yūsuf considering the interests of "our time," as it was declared in Article 392 of the *Mecelle*.[64]

63. *Mecelle*, 8.
64. Ibid., 9.

Commentaries on the Mecelle: Affirming Its Late Hanafi Character

Many authors were inspired by the *Mecelle* to write commentaries on it. These authors—lawyers, scholars, and judges who had direct contact with legal and judicial litigation in the empire—usually start off their works by justifying the necessity of the *Mecelle* project and explaining its functions and the key jurisprudential canons incorporated within its articles. It appears that these *Mecelle* commentaries garnered their legitimacy as well as the license to be published after their approval by the Ottoman legal establishment. Moreover, these commentators unanimously affirm that the *Mecelle* was based on authoritative late Hanafi legal commentaries. They refer the reader to late Hanafi works that make the connection between the *Mecelle* articles and late Hanafi jurisprudence, such as *al-Durr al-Mukhtār* and its commentaries, *al-Bahr al-Rā'iq*, *al-Nahr al-Fā'iq*, *Majma' al-Anhur*, and Abū Saʿīd al-Khādimī's *Majāmiʿ al-Haqā'iq*.

Here, I limit myself to one of the authoritative commentaries in the field, namely: *Durar al-Hukkām Sharh Majallat al-Ahkām*. I explore how this commentary discussed the project of the *Mecelle*, and how the commentator viewed the relationship between *Mecelle* and the late Hanafi legal tradition. Also, I discuss how this commentary understood the role of legal maxims in the process of legal reasoning.

In his *Durar al-Hukkām Sharh Majallat al-Ahkām*, Alī Haydar (d. 1935), a prominent Ottoman judge and lawyer, reiterates that legal scholars agree that the science of *fiqh* is a "sea without a shore," and that the extraction of the key principle is contingent upon a "sublime skill and established knowledge."[65] Haydar follows the *Mecelle* by asserting that the authoritative Hanafi commentaries have plenty of differences. In his opinion, summarizing the preponderant opinions with the supporting evidence and collecting them in a significant work, such as the *Mecelle* is one of the most difficult matters in need of careful research and investigation. Haydar explains that due to his career in the Ottoman judicial system, he was able to record some key and subtle cases by collecting them in a commentary on the *Mecelle*. Haydar emphasizes that the *Mecelle* was extracted from *fiqh*; thus, a commentary on it should explicate its articles based on *fiqh* manuals. Also, he affirms that it should be in agreement with the opinions that were chosen by the *Mecelle* drafters. Haydar points out that the scholars and jurists in the High Fatwā Council reviewed this work. His commentary was approved because it "agrees with *al-sharʿ al-sharīf*,"[66] meaning that it was consistent with the current norms of jurisprudence.

We observe that Ottoman Hanafi jurists, and especially their *fatāwā* works, significantly influenced later Hanafi legal articulations as reflected in the *Mecelle*.

---

65. Ali Haydar, *Durar al-Hukkām Sharh Majallat al-Ahkām*, trans. Fahmī al-Husaynī (Beirut: Dar ʿĀlam al-Kutub, 2003), 7.
66. Ibid.

Ottoman Hanafi jurists were immensely ingrained in the Hanafi legal tradition, and they were able to employ the techniques of the tradition to revisit, suspend, or introduce legal rulings. The ideational framework for the *Mecelle* is important for evaluating the Hanafi texts consulted and whether or not the *Mecelle* is faithful to the Hanafi tradition.

The Process of Legal Continuity and Change in the Mecelle

The following three case studies pinpoint the process by which the *Mecelle* drafters embraced and preserved Hanafi norms and categories, and transformed key doctrines to produce standardized judicial rules to guide litigation. The transformations that were introduced in the *Mecelle* were justified from within the Hanafi legal tradition and in the name of its authorities. Many of these doctrines in the *Mecelle*—which clearly rescind early Hanafi doctrines—were incorporated in the late Hanafi tradition as part of its organic doctrinal development.

Ahkām al-ghasb (Rules of Usurpation)[67]

Although the introduction of the *Mecelle* alludes to a few cases of legal change within the Hanafi school, I located many other subtle transformations within the *Mecelle* articles. One of the central aspects of the *Mecelle* is that it confirms a process of legal continuity and change by which Hanafi doctrines were shifted or altered. This early modern process relies upon techniques similar to those in late Hanafi legal literature in order to address a new social reality.

In the introduction to the chapter on wrongful appropriation (*ghasb*), the definition of *ghasb* in the *Mecelle* does not reflect its classical authoritative provisions stated by Abū Hanīfa and Abū Yūsuf. Instead, the stated definition in the *Mecelle* endorses the opinion of Muhammad b. al-Hasan al-Shaybanī over the professed opinion of the school.[68] The *Mecelle*, unlike the classical definition, defines *ghasb* in Article 881 as the act of taking and seizing someone's *mal* without the owner's permission.[69] It explicates that the one who wrongfully takes another's property is called usurper (*ghāsib*), the seized *mal* is called usurped (*maghsūb*), and the valid owner of the usurped property is the one whose property is usurped (*maghsūb minhu*).[70] Clearly, the *Mecelle* turns away from the

---

67. This is a legal term that refers to the unlawful assumption of the use of property which belongs to another, an interruption, or disturbing a man in his right and possession. It also refers to the act of wrongful appropriation.

68. *Mecelle*, 147.

69. The *Mecelle* defines *mal*, in Article 126, as to what a person naturally is inclined and which can be saved/stored until the time of need, whether it was movable or immovable. In Article 127, the *Mecelle* offers two definitions for *al-māl al-mutaqawim*; first, it denotes what is permissible to be utilized; the second, it refers to the acquired secured property, thus, the fish in the water is not a *mutaqawim māl*, yet once it is acquired it becomes *mutaqawim* by securing its possession.

70. *Mecelle*, 129.

definition of *ghasb* coined by Abū Ḥanīfa and Abū Yūsuf, who conditioned the ability of the usurper to affect legal actions (selling, buying, etc.) into the usurped objects in order to be considered a *ghasb*.⁷¹ By contrast, Muhammad b. al-Hasan al-Shaybānī only stipulated the act of seizing *mal* without the owner's permission. This change of the concept of *ghasb* as a legal concept does not only express the internal development of the school, but also addresses the new social realities and commercial activities within the empire.

At the same time, the *Mecelle* adheres faithfully to key late Hanafi doctrines and norms. For instance, Article 887 of the *Mecelle* reinstates the premodern Hanafi doctrine in the cases of duress, wrongful appropriation, and spoilage. Article 887 states, "causing damage by direct causality (*mubāsharatan*) is to cause direct damage to the object itself. The one who causes this damage is called *mubāshir*." ⁷² This doctrine is further explained in Article 888 in which the *Mecelle* defines secondary causality (*tasabbuban*) as the inflicting of damage on another with [full knowledge of how such an action would cause damage]. The one who commits this act is called *mutasabbib*. An example of this is a person who cuts the rope of a hanging lamp: this person would be the cause for its fall to the ground, as well as the secondary cause of any damage to it. The cutting of the rope is by direct execution (*mubāshara*), while the damage to the lamp is by secondary causation (*tasabbub*).⁷³

By the same token, the *Mecelle* follows the late Hanafi formulations in Article 890. It demands the return of the usurped *mal* to its rightful owner at the location of wrongful appropriation. Yet, if the *mal*'s valid owner and the usurper met by a sheer accident in a different place (country) and the seized *mal* is with the usurper, the owner would have the option either to recuperate his *mal* at this location or request to reacquire his *mal* in the location of the wrongful appropriation. In this case, the usurper will shoulder the financial cost of transporting the usurped object.⁷⁴ Additionally, the *Mecelle* establishes the central doctrine of transgression (*al-taʿdī*), which is the sole criterion that triggers financial liability in the late Hanafi legal reasoning. According to Article 898, if the usurper changed some of the intrinsic features of the usurped material by spending some of his money on it, the valid owner would have the choice: (1) to give the money for the extra value and recuperate his exact usurped thing; (2) to hold the usurper financially liable for the whole value of the object.⁷⁵ For example, if the usurped substance is a garment and the usurper dyed it, the valid owner would have the

---

71. Ibn ʿĀbidīn, *Radd al-Muhtār*, 9:260; al-Baghdādī, *Majmaʿ al-Damānāt* (Cairo: Dār al-Kitāb al-Islāmī, n.d) 1:287.
72. Khadimī, *Manāfiʿ al-Daqāʾiq* (Istanbul: Dār al-Ṭibāʿa al-ʿĀmira, 1980), 308.
73. *Mecelle*, 129, 130.
74. Ibid.
75. Muhammad b. Sulayman al-Kalibulī, *Majmaʿ al-Anhur fi Sharh Multqā al-Abhur* (Beirut: Dar Ihyaʾ al-Turath al-ʿArabi, n.d.), 4:96.

choice either to ask for financial compensation for the garment or he may give the usurper the value of dying and be returned his garment.[76]

The *Mecelle* adopted late Hanafi revisions of persistent early Hanafi doctrines on the rejection of imposing any liability for the *manāfiʿ* (profitable utility). It also incorporates late Hanafi opinion on the issue of *zawāʾid* (natural outgrowth) of the usurped objects. For instance, Article 903 affirms that the *zawāʾid* of the usurped substances belongs to its valid owner.[77] If the usurper consumed them, he will be held financially liable for them. Thus, if the *ghāsib* consumed the baby of a usurped animal that was born during his possession of the animal, he will be liable for it. The same applies to the case of the fruits of a usurped garden. The *Mecelle* gives a third example of a usurped apiary, the valid owner would also reclaim the value of what was produced while the apiary was in the possession of the usurper. In short, the *Mecelle* sets out a revised doctrinal attitude of affirming financial liability for both the *manāfiʿ* and *zawāʾid* of the usurped objects.

Moreover, these remedial rules of wrongful appropriation of property are addressed in Article 905 in the *Mecelle*. It states that the usurper must return the usurped property to its owner without changing it or decreasing its value. Yet, if the value of the property decreased due to an action by the usurper, he would be financially liable for its value. Also, if someone destroyed the location of the usurped house or it was damaged because of his residence, which resulted in the decrease of its value, the usurper would be liable for the decreased value. Also, if a house were burned down by fire that was lit by the usurper, he would be financially liable for its value.[78]

The most important shift, in my view, was transforming the definition of *ghasb* in the legal literature of the *Mecelle* to reflect the transformation of the *madhhab* opinions, not breaking with its fundamental norms by shifting from the authoritative opinions of Abū Ḥanīfa and Abū Yūsuf to the opinions of Muhammad al-Shaybānī. Thus, even this change was induced within the internal plurality of the school opinions from within its hierarchical positions.

Written Proofs: Admitted Without Reservations

The *Mecelle* settles completely the issue of accepting written proofs as sufficient legal evidence in courts. Late Hanafis specifically address this issue in their legal commentaries. For instance, Ibn ʿĀbidīn shows the gradual acceptance of some types of written proofs such as imperial edicts, sultanic decrees, endowment registers and court records. He explains that ʿAlāʾ al-Dīn al-Ḥaskafī accepts these types of written documents as legal proofs once they are cleared of

---

76. *Mecelle*, 131.
77. Ibn ʿĀbidīn, *Radd al-Muḥtār*, 9:286; *al-Fatāwā al-Hindiyya*, 6 vols. (Cairo: Dār al-Fikr, 1991), 5:150–151.
78. *Mecelle*, 151.

fraud or forgery.⁷⁹ This is also the same position of most of the Ottoman Hanafi jurists.⁸⁰ However, Ibn 'Ābidīn points out that Khayr al-Dīn al-Ramlī (d. 1671) showed resistance to accepting written documents as sufficient proofs to endowment claims.⁸¹ Most importantly, the process by which Ibn 'Ābidīn is able to accept some of these written documents as legal proofs is by introducing exceptions to the rule.⁸²

By contrast, the *Mecelle* discusses this issue under the title, "Written Proofs," in which it stipulates the acceptance of all authenticated written proofs in four Articles. First, in Article 1736, the *Mecelle* states that a sultanic decree or a seal—on its own—has no legal validity, but if they are established to be free from forgery and imitation, they have full demonstrative proof in court. Second, in Article 1737, the *Mecelle* stresses that imperial assignments/certificates (*berats*) and the books of the management of the Land Registry Office have full demonstrative force because they are secure against every kind of fraud. Third, in Article 1738, the *Mecelle* accepts court registers and grants them full demonstrative force as valid legal proofs, if they are exact and clear of any forgery. Fourth, in Article 1739, the *Mecelle* declares that endowment certificates are valid as legal proofs as long as they are registered in authentic court records.

The Prerequisites for Valid Testimony (shurūt al-shahāda) Revisited

In the discussion of the required qualification of the witness, the *Mecelle* requires all traditional qualifications of a witness, but not the quality of being a Muslim.⁸³ In a complete departure from Hanafi legal thought,⁸⁴ the section on testimony and evidence in the *Mecelle* does not address the religion of the witnesses. The focus is primarily on the exactitude and justice of the witness as well as his/her reputation in Article 1705. The just person is defined in the same article as the one whose good deeds are dominant over his/her bad deeds.⁸⁵ This is the first time in Islamic jurisprudence that the religious identity of the witness is not considered as an issue affecting the validity of a testimony. Although Islamic jurisprudence acknowledges the testimony of non-Muslims in courts, it consistently resisted the testimony of non-Muslims against Muslims.⁸⁶ The *Mecelle* shifted these norms and introduced more egalitarian conditions for valid testimony in front of a judge. It also reflects the frequent complaints of the European powers

79. Ibn 'Ābidīn, *Radd al-Muhtār*, 4:413.
80. Ibid., 4:414.
81. Ibid.
82. Ibid., 4:413. Ibn 'Ābidīn discusses these issues under the title: "A written document is not relied upon except in specific issues."
83. *Mecelle*, 344. See also the footnote in Schacht, *An Introduction to Islamic Law*, 93.
84. Ibn 'Ābidīn, *Radd al-Muhtār*, 5:472.
85. *Mecelle*, 344.
86. Ibn 'Ābidīn, *Radd al-Muhtār*, 5:472–73.

that their citizens could not litigate in front of the Sharia courts because their testimony was not accepted against Muslims in cases of litigation.

Conclusion

The drafters of the *Mecelle* maintained that it was inspired by the already existing genre of legal maxims (*al-qawāʿid al-fiqhiyya*) within the Hanafi school. The emergence of the *Mecelle* should be understood, not in terms of an epistemic break from the Islamic legal reasoning, but in terms of a continuation and transformation within the structure of a legal tradition. The *Mecelle* necessarily emerged out of an existing genre of *qawāʿid* in a manner that made it an authentic representation of the legal tradition for experts of the profession. Moreover, the *Mecelle* itself was circulated among legal authorities and the Ottoman religious establishment to approve it and endorse its formation, as an indispensable process of legitimacy. The articles of the *Mecelle* are not randomly selected norms or doctrines from the Hanafi legal tradition as has been claimed by some scholars. The central doctrines codified in the *Mecelle* as well as its predominant articles are faithful to late Hanafi opinions. Still, some legal doctrines of premodern Hanafi jurisprudence were transformed in the *Mecelle* through the internal mechanisms and rationalization of the *madhhab*, such as customs, change of time, and necessity. These shifts should be understood within the Hanafi doctrinal development, because they are justified in the name of the *madhhab* and its authorities.

The *Mecelle* represents a shift in the function of the law in the late nineteenth-century Ottoman Empire. This function changed to reflect new emergent state institutions. In this context, Hanafi jurisprudence was called to address this transformation and fulfill this role. While I acknowledge that continuity and change are key features of the premodern Islamic jurisprudence, the scale of transformation reflected in the *Mecelle* and its new function denote that it was formulated to address specific circumstances. The *Mecelle* as a systematic codification of a legal tradition successfully incorporated and introduced new "modern" concepts and premises, such as the systemic distinction between public and private property, the restriction of absolute authorities (*wilāyat*), revisiting key remedial rules and legal liabilities (*damānāt*), and the introduction of new types of contractual agreements (*ʿuqūd*). The *Mecelle* introduced these changes by rooting them into the legal tradition itself, reflecting a new legal order.

Additionally, one of the purposes of the *Mecelle* was the standardization of legal and judicial reasoning. The *Mecelle* was the first step in the process of developing a written law that was designed to assist judges to render similar legal judgments on similar issues. While I affirm that the context that shaped the discussions around the *Mecelle* is intertwined with the questions of Western hegemony, the key issue in the minds of the drafters of the *Mecelle* was how to formulate an

Islamically informed response to Western hegemony.[87] The *Mecelle* is not only a manifestation of such debates and a response to these questions, but also a successful strategy to meet the demands of the Ottoman bureaucracy.

The *Mecelle* is particularly faithful to the late Hanafi doctrines and norms. The drafters of the *Mecelle* imagined themselves within the *madhhab*, as active participants and contributors to it. For instance, the *Mecelle* adopts Ibn Shubruma's opinions, leaving behind Abū Ḥanīfa's opinion, on stipulating conditions for the sale of contracts on the basis of customary practice among craftsmen. Some late Hanafis invoke Ibn Abī Laylā's and Ibn Shubruma's opinions to depart from Abū Ḥanīfa's opinions.[88] As I have shown, the *Mecelle* embodies the daunting and complex process in which the legal and doctrinal change targeted a nucleus of legal concepts and values to be replaced with "new" norms and doctrines for which the Hanafi tradition was the point of departure. These changes and transformations are not achieved in opposition to the legal tradition. Rather, this tradition, in its various articulations, is invoked to address the foreign legal hegemonies by asserting, revising, and rescinding its own norms and doctrinal boundaries.

The problem with attributing any legal or doctrinal change in the Hanafi school during the late nineteenth century to the influence of European codes is that it overlooks the process by which legal transformation was entrenched in legal tradition itself. Also, what is "modern" about the transformation of Hanafi legal doctrines in the *Mecelle* is not that it imitates European codes, but the underlying premises that the *Mecelle* is trying to articulate from within an Islamic legal tradition. Most importantly, the point of departure for Muslim lawyers has always been Islamic legal tradition. In short, the *Mecelle*, at its core, is a Muslim response to modernity and its legal order argued and justified from within the tradition.

SAMY AYOUB is a lecturer in Islamic Studies at the University of Texas, Austin.

---

87. Şenturk, "Intellectual Dependency," 294.
88. Ibn 'Ābidīn, *Radd al-Muhtār*, 5:602; Ibn al-Humām, *Fath al-Qadīr*, 10 vols. (Beirut: Dār al-Fikr, n.d) 6:441.

Appendix A

Thematic tables of the *Mecelle* Articles:
I. Deposit for Safe-Keeping (*al-Wadīʿa*)

The Mecelle Articles	Hanafi Works
كتاب الوديعة	كتاب الوديعة
المادة ٧٦٣ الوديعة هي المال الذي يوضع عند شخص لأجل الحفظ	مجمع الأنهر في شرح ملتقى الأبحر الوديعة ما يترك عند الامين للحفظ مالا كان أو غيره
المادة ٧٧٥ يشترط كون الوديعة قابلة لوضع اليد عليها و صالحة للقبض فلا يصح إيداع الطير في الهواء	درر الحكام شرح غرر الأحكام شرطها كون المال قابلا لاثبات اليد عليه لأن الايداع عقد استحفاظ و حفظ الشيئ بدون إثبات اليد عليه محال، فإيداع الطير في الهواء و المال الساقط في البحر غير صحيح
المادة ٧٧٤ لكل من المودع و المستودع فسخ عقد الإيداع متى شاء	البحر الرائق شرح كنز الدقائق حكم الوديعة كون المال أمانة عند المستودع مع وجوب الحفظ و الأداء عند الطلب
المادة ٧٧٧ الوديعة أمانة في يد الوديع بناء عليه إذا هلكت بلا تعد في المستودع و بدون صنعه و تقصيره في الحفظ لا يلزم الضمان إلا إذا كان الإيداع بأجرة علي حفظ الوديعة فهلكت أو ضاعت بسبب يمكن التحرز منه لزم المستودع ضمانها. مثلا لو وقعت الساعة المودعة في يد الوديع بلا صنعة فانكسرت لا يلزم الضمان ، أما لو وطئت الساعة بالرجل أو وقع من اليد عليها شيئ فانكسرت لزم الضمان كذلك إذا أودع رجل ماله عند اخر واعطاه أجرة علي حفظه فضاع المال بسبب يمكن التحرز منه كالسرقة يلزم المستودع الضمان	مجمع الأنهر شرح ملتقى الأبحر الوديعة أمانه فلا يضمن المودع الوديعة بغير تعد بالهلاك سواء أمكن التحرز عنه أو لا الفتاوي الانقروية الوديعة أمانة لا تضمن إلا بالتعدي البحر الرائق شرح كنز الدقائق أمانة فلا تضمن بالهلاك سواء أمكن التحرز عنه أو لا هلك معها للمودع شيء أو لا تغييرا

The Mecelle Articles	Hanafi Works
	المحيط البرهاني إذا هلكت الوديعة في يد المودع ، يستوي فيه الهلاك بأمر يمكن الاحتراز عنه أو لا يمكن التحرز، لأن الهلاك مما يمكن التحرز عنه يعني العيب في الحفظ وصفة السلامة عن العيب إنما يصير مستحقا في المعاوضات دون التبرع ، و المودع متبرع
المادة ٧٧٩ فعل ما لا يرضي به المودع في حق الوديعة تعد في الفاعل	الفتاوي الانقروية المتعدي هو الذي يفعل بالوديعة ما لا يرضي به المودع
المادة ٧٩٨ منافع الوديعة لصاحبها. مثلا نتاج حيوان الوديعة أي فلوه و لبنة و شعرة لصاحب الحيوان	رد المحتار على الدر المختار منافع الوديعة لصاحبها
المادة ٨٠٣ الوديعة إذا لزم ضمانها فإن كانت من المثليات تضمن بمثلها وإن كانت من القيميات تضمن بقيمتها يوم لزوم الضمان	تنقيح الفتاوي الحامدية وإن مات وصارت دينا فإن كانت من ذوات الأمثال وجب مثلها وإلا فقيمتها

II. Trusts and Trusteeship (al-'Āriya)

The Mecelle Articles	Hanafi Works
كتاب العارية	كتاب العارية
المادة ٧٦٥ العارية هي المال الذي تملك منفعته لآخر مجانا أي بلا بدل و يسمى معارا و مستعارا	مجمع الانهر في شرح ملتقى الأبحر العارية هي تمليك منفعة بلا بدل رد المحتار على الدر المختار تمليك المنافع مجانا

	المادة ٨٠٤
رد المحتار على الدر المختار	الإعارة تنعقد بالإيجاب و القبول وبالتعاطي
أفاد بالتمليك لزوم الإيجاب والقبول ولو فعلا أي كالتعاطي في القهستاني	
حاشية الطحطاوي على الدر المختار	
عقد التبرع إنما يتوقف علي الايجاب و القبول ، و القبول ليس بشرط عند أصحابنا استحسانا ، ولو فعلا كالتعاطي كما في القهستاني	

	المادة ٨٠٥
رد المحتار على الدر المختار	سكوت المعير لا يعد قبولا، فلو طلب شخص من اخر إعارة شئ فسكت صاحب ذلك الشئ ثم أخذه المستعير كان غاصبا
ولهذا قال القبول صريحا غير شرط بخلاف الإيجاب في	
التتارخانية : إن الإعارة لا تثبت بالسكوت	

	المادة ٨٠٦
مجمع الأنهر في شرح ملتقى الأبحر	للمعير أن يرجع عن الإعارة متى شاء
للمعير أن يرجع عن الإعارة متى شاء	
رد المحتار على الدر المختار	
وله أن يرجع متى شاء لما تقرر أنها غير لازمة	
المحيط البرهاني	
وللمعير أن يرجع فيها متى شاء	

	المادة ٨٠٧
المحيط البرهاني	تنفسخ الإعارة بموت المعير و المستعير
و تبطل بموت أحدهما أيهما مات	

	المادة ٨١٣
تنوير الأبصار	المستعير يملك منفعة العارية بدون بدل فليس للمعير أن يطلب من المستعير أجرة بعد الإستعمال
العارية تمليك المنافع مجانا	
الفتاوي الهندية	
تمليك المنافع للمستعير بغير العوض و ما هو معلق بالمنفعة عرفا و عادة	

المادة ٨١٤	فتاوي الأنقروي
إذا حصل من المستعير تعد أو تقصير بحق العارية ثم هلكت أو نقصت قيمتها فبأي سبب كان الهلاك أو النقص يلزم المستعير الضمان. مثلا إذا ذهب المستعير بالدابة المعارة إلي محل مسافته يومان في يوم واحد فتلفت تلك الدابة أو هزلت و نقصت قيمتها لزم الضمان و كذا لو استعار دابة ليذهب بها إلي محل معين فتجاوز بها ذلك المحل ثم هلكت الدابة حتف أنفها لزم الضمان و كذلك إذا استعار إنسان حليا فوضعه علي صبي و تركه بدون أن يكون عند الصبي من يحفظه فسرق الحلي، فإذا كان الصبي قادر علي حفظ الأشياء التي عليه لا يلزم الضمان، و إن لم يكن قادرا لزم المستعير الضمان	العارية أمانة في يده إذا هلكت من غير تعد لا يضمن، لو ضرب المستعير الدابة أو كبحها أو ركض ضمن عنده خلافا لهما، ولو استعار دابة إلي موضع فسلك لها طريقا ليس بالجادة ضمن رد المحتار علي الدر المختار ولا تضمن بالهلاك من غير تعد ولو استعار ذهبا فقلده صبيا فسرق الذهب من الصبي فإن كان الصبي يضبط حفظ ما عليه من اللباس لم يضمن وإلا ضمن لأنه إعارة والمستعير يملكها ص ٦٨٤

III. Gift Giving (*al-Hiba*)

The Mecelle Articles	Hanafi Works
كتاب الهبة	كتاب الهبة
المادة ٨٣٣ الهبة هي تمليك مال لاخر بلا عوض، و يقال لفاعله واهب ولذلك المال الموهوب و لمن يقبله موهوب له، والايهاب قبول الهبة	مجمع الانهر في شرح ملتقي الابحر: هي تمليك عين بلا عوض رد المحتار علي الدر المختار هي تمليك العين مجانا أي بلا عوض
المادة ٨٣٧ تنعقد الهبة بالايجاب و تتم بالقبض	مجمع الانهر في شرح ملتقي الأبحر وتصح بإيجاب و قبول و تتم بالقبض الكامل رد المحتار علي الدر المختار و شرطها في الموهوب أن يكون مقبوضا و ركنها الايجاب والقبول لايشترط

رد المحتار على الدر المختار و تتم الهبة بالقبض الكامل	
درر الحكام في شرح غرر الاحكام و تصح بإيجاب كوهبت فإنه صريح فيها و نحلت أيضا كذلك يقال نحلة كذا أي أعطاه إياه بطيب نفسه بلا عوض و كذا اعطيتك وبعض ألفاظ في معني التمليك مثل واعمرتك رد المحتار على الدر المختار و تصح بإيجاب كوهبت و نحلت و أطعمتك هذا الطعام، وحاصلة : أن اللفظ إن أنبأ عن تملك الرقبة فهبة	المادة ٨٣٨ الايجاب في الهبة هو الألفاظ المستعملة في معني تمليك المال مجانا كأكرمت ووهبت و أهديت و التعبيرات التي تدل علي التمليك مجانا ايجاب للهبة أيضا كإعطاء الزوج زوجته قرطا و حليا و قوله لها خذي هذا وعلقيه
فتاوي قاضيخان إذا قال رجل لصاحب الثوب أعطينه فقال اعطيتك، عن محمد أنها تكون هبة البحر الرائق شرح كنز الدقائق لأن جوازه باعتبار الرضا ، ويلزم البيع بالتعاطي وقد وجد ، وقد بناه في الهداية على أن المعتبر في هذه العقود هو المعنى والإشارة إلى العقود التمليكية مثل الهبة	المادة ٨٣٩ تنعقد الهبة بالتعاطي أيضا
رد المحتار على الدر المختار في كالنكاح والخلع والهبة والرهن ونحوها ، فإن الوكيل فيها كالرسول	المادة ٨٤٠ الإرسال و القبض في الهبة و الصدقة يقوم مقام الإيجاب و القبول لفظا
فتاوي قاضيخان أذا أكرهت علي الهبة فوهبت لا تصح و يسمع دعواها بدائع الصنائع في ترتيب الشرائع الإكراه على الهبة يوجب فسادها كالإكراه على البيع	المادة ٨٦٠ يلزم في الهبة رضاء الواهب فلا تصح الهبة التي وقعت بالجبر و الإكراه

		المبسوط
		الإكراه على الهبة إكراها على التسليم ، ثم بسبب الإكراه تفسد الهبة
المادة ٨٦٤		رد المحتار على الدر المختار
للواهب أن يرجع من الهبة و الهدية بعد القبض برضا الموهوب له و ان لم يرض الموهوب له راجع الواهب الحاكم و للحاكم فسخ الهبة و ان لم يكن ثمت مانع من موانع الرجوع		يصح الرجوع في الهبة بعد القبض مع انتفاء مانعه

مجمع الأنهر في شرح ملتقى الأبحر

يصح الرجوع في الهبة بعد القبض كلا أو بعضا
رد المحتار على الدر المختار

وإذا رجع أحدهما بقضاء أو رضا كان فسخا لعقد الهبة من الأصل وإعادة لملكة القديم لاهبة الواهب |
| المادة ٨٦٥ | | رد المحتار على الدر المختار |
| لو استرد الواهب الموهوب بعد القبض بدون حكم الحاكم و قضائه و بدون رضي الموهوب له يكون غاصبا و بهذه الصورة لو تلف أو ضاع في يده يكون ضامنا | | ولا يصح الرجوع إلا بتراضيهما أو بحكم الحاكم

فتاوي قاضيخان

رجل وهب لرجل ثوبا فسلمه إليه ثم اختلسه منه فاستهلكه ضمن الواهب قيمة الثوب للموهوب له لأن الرجوع في الهبة لايكون إلا بقضاء أو رضا

حاشية الطحطاوي على الدر المختار

ولا يصح الرجوع إلا بتراضيهما او بحكم الحاكم فلو استردها بغير قضاء ولا رضي كان غاصبا حتى لو هلكت في يده يضمن قيمتها للموهوب له |
| المادة ٨٦٧ | | مجمع الأنهر في شرح ملتقى الأبحر |
| لو وهب كل من الزوج و الزوجة صاحبه شيئا حال كون الزوجية قائمة بينهما فبعد التسليم ليس له الرجوع | | الزوجية مانعة من الرجوع لأن المقصود فيها الصلة

رد المحتار على الدر المختار

الزوجية تمنع من الرجوع في الهبة

فتاوي قاضيخان

إذا وهب أحد الزوجين لصاحبه لا يرجع في الهبة و إن انقطع النكاح بينهما |

8 Criminal Codes, Crime, and the Transformation of Punishment in the Late Ottoman Empire

Kent F. Schull

By the end of World War I, the Ottoman Empire had significantly transformed its criminal justice system to include modern centralized penal codes, policing organizations, criminal courts, modern law schools, and a centralized prison system wherein the vast majority of convicted criminals received incarceration as punishment. These transformations did not happen overnight, but often came about in fits and starts as imperial and local officials attempted to deal with the challenges and crises experienced during this period. This "modern" criminal justice system was not borrowed wholesale from Western Europe. Instead, it possessed deep roots and antecedents in Ottoman "classical" criminal justice practices and Islamic law. Themes such as prisoner rehabilitation, prison labor, the Circle of Justice, and legitimizing imperial practice through Islamic law still functioned and took precedence in the late Ottoman legal system.[1] The assumptions and world view associated with Ottoman modernity governed this transformation. Ottoman officials implemented these reforms in order to centralize power over criminal justice through the rationalization and standardization of legal procedure, criminal codes, court practices and jurisdictions, policing, and criminal punishment.[2] These transformations, however, should not be viewed as simple impositions of state authority detached from societal norms

---

1. The Circle of Justice possesses deep roots in the Middle East dating back to ancient Mesopotamia and appropriated by Islamic polities including the Ottomans. This self-referential ruling strategy linked sovereignty and prosperity to the maintenance of justice and protection of the population from administrative exploitation, "There can be no government without men; No men without money; No money without prosperity; And no prosperity without justice and good administration." See Linda Darling, *A History of Social Justice and Political Power in the Middle East: The Circle of Justice from Mesopotamia to Globalization* (New York: Routledge, 2013), 2–12.

2. For an overview of this transition from the "classical" Ottoman criminal justice system to the "modern", see Kent F. Schull, *Prisons in the Late Ottoman Empire: Microcosms of Modernity* (Edinburgh: Edinburgh University Press, 2014), 19–25.

or mores.³ Instead, they should be seen as an imperfect outcome of negotiated, collaborative, and contentious exchanges between and among central and local state actors and societal forces, with the central state holding a distinct power advantage.

This article investigates the transformation of criminal law, practice, and punishment within the nineteenth and twentieth-century Ottoman Empire utilizing a socio-legal approach. It focuses closely on five intertwined aspects of this "modern" criminal justice system, namely the concrete links between newly codified penal codes, the extensive delineation of crimes, the adoption of incarceration as the primary form of criminal punishment, incarceration rates for particular crimes, and the deployment of Islamic legal norms and mores to legitimize these reforms. Through the promulgation and then expansion of these new penal codes together with other aspects of its overhauled criminal justice system, the Ottoman administration gradually gained a monopoly over the adjudication of criminal matters. This effectively circumscribed the autonomy of local magistrates and Islamic court judges in adjudicating criminal cases and meting out punishments, thus making the prison the primary site of criminal punishment within the empire. This transformation constitutes a dynamic process of adoption and adaptation, continuity and change, and innovation that thoroughly undermines the worn-out narrative of rupture, Westernization, secularization, and cosmetic reform often utilized to characterize such attempts at reinvigorating the empire. In fact, this process of transformation and amalgamation of new methods of governance with its already existing institutions and practices represents a distinct Ottoman modernity.⁴ Throughout the entire process of criminal justice transformation, Ottoman officials continued to legitimate their reforms with Islamic legal norms, practices, statutes, and mores augmented to meet the constraints of the modern world.

This article first provides a short overview of penal code codification in the Ottoman Empire with a central focus on the creation and expansion of the 1858

---

3. Ruth Miller problematically argues that the codification of criminal law in the nineteenth and twentieth-century Ottoman Empire and Turkey created "an abstract system . . . divorced from its social relevance . . . in which purity of function or purity of idea is more important than utility of function or utility of idea . . . it is a system in which crime is purely discursive." In other words, Ottoman and Turkish criminal law was devoid of its social context and represented a complete imposition of central authority on society absolutely free of any societal norms or influence, thus disregarding the critical contribution of socio-legal studies to Ottoman history. Ruth A. Miller, *Legislating Authority: Sin and Crime in the Ottoman Empire and Turkey* (London: Routledge Press, 2005), 1–2.

4. For a detailed discussion of Ottoman modernity as it relates to criminal justice, see Schull, *Prisons in the Late Ottoman Empire*, 5–6; idem, "Comparative Criminal Justice in the Era of Modernity: A Template for Inquiry and the Ottoman Empire as Case Study," *Turkish Studies* 15 (2014): 621–37.

Imperial Ottoman Penal Code (IOPC) during the last century of the empire's existence, with a particular emphasis on the 1911 reforms to the IOPC. It then discusses general connections between the IOPC and prison statistics to see how this penal code reflected views on criminality and actual incarceration. Finally, it looks more closely at the relationship between these penal codes, criminality, and incarceration through a detailed analysis of four major areas of criminal codification and prison statistics specifically related to crimes against state officials, honor, theft, and violent crime.

Penal Codes and the Delineation of Crime: Transforming Punishment and Circumscribing Autonomy

Ottoman bureaucrats created the empire's first codified penal code in 1840 (*Ceza Kanunnamesi*) shortly after the declaration of *Gülhane Hatt-ı Hümayun* in 1839.[5] This code contained thirteen articles in forty-two sections and an epilogue, and dealt with crimes related to treason, incitement to rebellion, embezzlement of state funds, tax evasion, and resistance to authority. The code was not comprehensive regarding the many crimes and punishments stipulated by Sharia law (*hadd, qisas, diyet*, and *ta'zir*), nor those crimes and punishments enforced by state executive authority (*siyaset*).[6] It did stipulate that the punishment for ho-

---

5. The 1839 *Gülhane Hatt-ı Hümayun* called for, "guarantees to all Ottoman subjects of perfect security for life, honor, and property; a regular system of assessing taxation; and an equally regular system for the conscription of requisite troops and the duration of their service." See J.C. Hurewitz, *The Middle East and North Africa in World Politics: A Documentary Record*, vol. 1: *European Expansion, 1535–1914* (New Haven: Yale University Press, 1975), 268–70. This decree combined with the *Islahat Fermanı* (discussed below) were the backbone of Ottoman reform programs during the *Tanzimat* (restructuring and reform). These decrees declared that all Ottoman subjects, regardless of religious affiliation, ethnicity, or socio-economic status, were equal before the law.

6. Peters defines *hadd* crimes as "offenses with fixed, mandatory punishments based upon the Koran or the Sunna . . . that include theft, banditry, unlawful sexual intercourse, an unfounded accusation of unlawful sexual intercourse, the drinking of alcohol, and apostasy" (Rudolph Peters, *Crime and Punishment in Islamic Law: Theory and Practice from the Sixteenth to the Twenty-First Century* (Cambridge: Cambridge University Press, 2006), 53). *Qisas* and *diyet* are closely related punishments sanctioned by Islamic law that constitute "retaliatory death or mutilation" and "monetary compensation for death and bodily harm in lieu of *qisas*" respectively (Ibid., 49–53). *Siyaset* crimes deal with issues of social order and state preservation and their punishments are defined as "discretionary justice exercised by the head of state and executive officials, not restricted by the rules of the Shari'a." They are, however, sanctioned and legitimated by Islamic law, which gives authority to a ruler to preserve social order and enforce justice all closely linked with the Circle of Justice ruling philosophy. *Ta'zir* are "discretionary punishments" meted out by the Islamic court judge and authorized by Islamic law in cases where the accused could not be convicted according to the stipulations of Islamic law, but who were obviously guilty. *Ta'zir* punishments, therefore, could not exceed Sharia punishments. Both *siyaset* and *ta'zir* consisted of corporal punishments, such as flogging, amputation, fines, incarceration, and in the case of *siyaset*, exile and the death penalty (Ibid., 196 and 127–33).

micide would now include incarceration with hard labor in addition to the traditional penalty of blood-money (*diyet*). Generally speaking, though, this code did not change traditional forms of punishment. It still allowed discretionary corporal punishments and fines (*ta'zir* and *siyaset*), meted out respectively by *kadıs* and local magistrates. In other words, local Islamic court judges and magistrates continued to possess great autonomy in identifying, trying, and punishing criminals according to their discretionary powers; all of which were sanctioned under official Ottoman-Islamic legal authority.

Other items covered in the 1840 code included changes in legal procedure and clearly stipulated punishments for select criminal offenses. Although some of these ascribed punishments included incarceration, a range of "traditional" punishments continued to be employed. For the first time in the Ottoman Empire, this code stipulated specific punishments for offenses such as reprimands, corporeal punishments, incarceration, banishment, and hard labor, thus removing some of the discretionary authority held by judges and magistrates. The 1840 Penal Code did not, however, place the adjudication of all these offenses under the authority of one court, be it Islamic or divan council. Some offences continued to be adjudicated by separate authorities with others being handled jointly. Islamic legal procedures, however, still applied to all criminal proceedings.[7] Reformers intended this code to serve as a bulwark against administrative corruption and abuse of power, thus maintaining the Circle of Justice.[8] The majority of its articles dealt with such issues and was intended to centralize power by expanding the notion and practice of rule of law in government administration.[9] The 1840 Penal Code constituted an important combination of executive and religious law not previously found in an Islamic society wherein *hadd, qisas, diyet, ta'zir*, and *siyaset* crimes *and* punishments were completely intertwined and indistinguishable from each other in a common codified code legitimated by Islamic legal principles, practices, and mores. This code set the precedent for all subsequent penal codes promulgated within the empire until its demise.

Ottoman legal reformers addressed some of the inadequacies of the 1840 Penal Code by promulgating the 1851 New Penal Code (*Kanun-i Cedid*). This new code better fulfilled the demands of the 1839 *Gülhane* Decree by expanding criminality to offences involving crimes against life, honor, and property, such as forgery, abduction of girls, and the making of indecent sexual advances to minors. Additionally, it better clarified procedures adjudicating homicide; addressed some of the needs of sick and indigent prisoners; and regulated the

---

7. See John A. Strachey Bucknill and Haig Apisoghom Utidjian, *The Imperial Ottoman Penal Code: A Translation from the Turkish Text* (London: Oxford University Press, 1913), xii–xiii; Peters, *Crime and Punishment in Islamic Law*, 127–33.

8. Peters, *Crime and Punishment in Islamic Law*, 71–75; Darling, *A History of Social Justice*, 2–12.

9. Miller, *Legislating Authority*, 26–31.

punishment of slaves. The general purpose of the 1851 Penal Code was to assist in the maintenance of public order, prevent tyranny and corruption by government officials, and protect individual rights.[10] In essence, the code expanded its predecessor without any major changes to criminal legal procedure or practice.

In 1858 Sultan Abdülmecid and Reşid Pasha replaced the 1851 Penal Code with the Imperial Ottoman Penal Code (*Ceza Kanunname-i Hümayunu*). Over the final sixty years of the empire's existence, law makers regularly expanded and augmented the IOPC.[11] It, therefore, became the foundation for criminal justice transformation, including the transition from corporeal punishment to fines and incarceration as the primary forms of criminal punishment. In addition to the penal codes of 1840 and 1851, the origins of the IOPC are also closely linked to broader imperial reforms, specifically the 1856 *Islahat Fermanı*.

Reşid Pasha penned the *Islahat Fermanı* with assistance and pressure from the British ambassador to the Ottoman Empire, Sir Stratford Canning. Sultan Abdülmecid issued this declaration for multiple reasons, two of which were to rejuvenate the Tanzimat reforms and fulfill a host of European Powers' designs on the empire. The decree included a crucial passage related to criminal justice that specifically discussed the need to transform the empire's penal codes, criminal courts, punishment (including discontinuance of torture), and prisons.

> Penal, correctional, and commercial laws ... shall be drawn up as soon as possible and formed into a code ...
>
> Proceedings shall be taken, with as little delay as possible, for the reform of the penitentiary system as applied to houses of detention, punishment, or correction, and other establishments of like nature, so as to reconcile the rights of humanity with those of justice. Corporal punishment shall not be administered, even in the prisons, except in conformity with the disciplinary regulations established by my Sublime Porte, and everything that resembles torture shall be entirely abolished.[12]

The *Islahat Fermanı*, therefore, constitutes the impetus for creating a "modern" criminal justice system in the empire by calling for comprehensive criminal codes and reforming punishment.

In accordance with the *Islahat Fermanı*, the empire promulgated the Imperial Ottoman Penal Code on 9 August 1858.[13] Portions of the new code included

---

10. Peters, *Crime and Punishment*, 127–33; Gabriel Baer, "The Transition from Traditional to Western Criminal Law in Turkey and Egypt," *Studia Islamica* 45 (1977): 143–44.

11. Peters, *Crime and Punishment*, 127–33; Bucknill and Utidjian, *The Ottoman Imperial Criminal Code*.

12. Hurewitz, *The Middle East and North Africa*, 315–18.

13. For a brief, but useful discussion of the source and significance of the initial 1858 Imperial Ottoman Criminal Code, see Baer, "The Transition from Traditional to Western Criminal Law," 139–58; Buckhill and Utidjian, *The Imperial Ottoman Penal Code*, ix–xvi.

adaptations of the 1810 French Criminal Code. The most striking difference between this new penal code and its predecessors was that it possessed an entire section devoted to the protection of individual rights. Crimes against individuals were divided into three distinct categories of crime: crimes against life and personal protection, honor and dignity, and personal property.[14]

The adoption of the IOPC represents a fundamental shift in Ottoman and Islamic criminal law and practice. For the first time in Ottoman history the preservation of personal rights was codified and rationalized within an Islamic legal framework with the state acting as guarantor. Contrary to contemporary scholarship, this does not represent the Westernization of Ottoman criminal law. While it was the bureaucratic Ottoman state that codified these laws, Islamic court judges (*kadıs*) still rendered judgments and presided over all criminal proceedings. Ottoman administrators legitimated the IOPC by claiming that it was in harmony with Islamic legal principles and practices.

> Article 1: Whereas the punishment of offences taking place directly against the Government lies with the State, and the consideration that offences taking place against a person disturb the public tranquility likewise concerns the State, this Code also guarantees and secures the determination of the degrees of the punishment the fixing and execution of which lie with the order of the Supreme Authority according to the Sher'; without prejudice, however, in any case to the personal rights prescribed by the Sher'.[15]

The IOPC also continued to combine both state and Islamic criminal law within the same code as established in the 1840 Penal Code, but did so much more extensively.

The rationalization and codification of these rights, however, greatly circumscribed the autonomy of Islamic court judges and local magistrates by standardizing punishments for criminal behavior.[16] Instead of characterizing these reforms as secularization, they should be viewed as the continuation of the standardization and rationalization of executive and Islamic criminal law and practice begun with the 1840 and 1851 penal codes that brought all forms of criminal punishment sanctioned by Islamic law (*hadd*, *qisas*, *diyet*, *ta'zir*, and *siyaset*) under a uniform penal code and regulated adjudication. For example, Articles 168–172 of the IOPC continued to make provisions for *qisas* and *diyet* punishments in cases of premeditated murder in addition to incarceration with hard labor, thus demonstrating the preservation and balancing of administrative and Islamic legal needs and stipulations.[17]

---

14. Günihal Bozkurt, "The Reception of Western European Law in Turkey (From the Tanzimat to the Turkish Republic, 1839–1939)," *Der Islam* 75 (1998): 283–95.
15. Buckhill and Utidjian, *The Imperial Ottoman Penal Code*, 1.
16. Baer, "The Transition from Traditional to Western Criminal Law," 144–45.
17. Buckhill and Utidjian, *The Imperial Ottoman Penal Code*, 124–27.

The IOPC was the forerunner to larger reform efforts intended to overhaul the entire Ottoman justice system. This restructuring eventually included the drafting of the first codification of Islamic civil law known as the *Mecelle*.[18] As mentioned above, it also laid the ground work for the circumscription of *kadı* interpretive autonomy, because judicial reforms, the standardization of procedure, practice and punishment, and codified legal codes all limit a judge's right to legal interpretation. The IOPC also facilitated the creation of *Nizamiye mahkemeleri* or civil/criminal courts. While the *Nizamiye* and Sharia courts worked in very close cooperation for the first couple of decades, the *Nizamiye* courts eventually superseded Sharia courts in all civil and criminal matters except for inheritance and family law.[19] Avi Rubin convincingly demonstrates, though, that these *Nizamiye* courts should not be considered "secular" in contra-distinction to the "religious" Sharia courts, because the *kadı* presided over the adjudication of law in both courts. Ottoman administrators maintained the same Islamic legitimating structures for these new courts as they had for centuries, thus demonstrating continuity with long-held legal practices, but transforming them to meet the strictures of the modern world.[20] This is Ottoman modernity at its clearest: Ottoman rulers and law makers simultaneously built off the empire's own traditions by adopting and adapting modern instrumentalities of governance to the empire's specific context.

An analysis of the transformation of the IOPC from 1858 to 1911 clearly demonstrates the shift in the conceptualization of crime and punishment in the Ottoman Empire over the long nineteenth century. Lawmakers greatly expanded the code through the expansive delineation of new crimes with fixed punishments. With the exception of execution for very serious offenses, such as premeditated homicide, banditry, rebellion, and treason, lawmakers eventually discontinued all forms of corporal punishment and the use of torture, thus completely circumscribing the ability of local magistrates and judges to utilize discretionary punishments (*ta'zir* and *siyaset*). Administrators replaced these punishments with clearly delineated fines and prison sentences according to the crime committed. Occasionally, exile was still employed as a possible criminal punishment. Some prison sentences also continued to include hard labor (*kürek*), especially for serious crimes (*cinayet*).

---

18. Adopted as the empire's civil code in 1877, the *Mecelle* represented the first systematic attempt to codify and modernize Islamic law (Sharia). It was prepared and written from 1869–76 by a commission under the direction of Ahmet Cevdet Pasha and consists of sixteen volumes containing 1,851 articles. See C.R. Tyser, D.G. Demetriades, and Ismail Haqqi Efendi, *The Mejelle: Being an English Translation of Majallah El-Ahkam-i-Adliya and a Complete Code on Islamic Civil Law* (Kuala Lumpur: The Other Press, 2001).

19. Avi Rubin, *Ottoman Nizamiye Courts: Law and Modernity* (New York: Palgrave Macmillan, 2011), 1–54; Peters, *Crime and Punishment*, 131.

20. Rubin, *Ottoman Nizamiye Courts*, 1–54.

By 1911 the IOPC consisted of 264 articles dealing with criminal legal procedures, crimes, liabilities, and punishments. Lawmakers divided the code into four main sections: a "Preliminary" and three chapters. The "Preliminary" consisted of forty-seven articles broken into four parts that stipulated the general grades and degrees of offenses and punishments with specific attention to delineating the punishments for serious (*cinayet*) and lesser crimes (*cünha* and *kabahat*). The "Preliminary" also specified the guidelines for determining criminal liability and culpability.[21]

The second section of the IOPC delineated crimes carried out against the Ottoman state and the general well-being of its populace and their associated punishments. This section included 121 articles divided into sixteen subsections. The sixteen subsections deal with crimes that disturb the external and internal security of the empire, such as espionage, incitement to riot and civil war, brigandage, banditry, abrogation of the constitution, and so forth. Other subsections enumerate the crimes of bribery, theft of state property, abuse of office, power, and negligence of duties, disobedience or opposition to government officials, aiding and abetting criminals, impersonating Ottoman officials, interfering with religious privileges, disrupting imperial telecommunications, censorship and printing, counterfeiting, forgery, and arson.[22]

The third section of the IOPC is divided into twelve subsections containing eighty-six articles detailing crimes and punishments against individuals. The enumerated crimes against persons include homicide in its various forms, bodily injuries, threats, abortion, selling adulterated beverages and medicines, violations of honor (rape, molestation, and kidnapping), improper arrest and incarceration, perjury, slander, vituperation, theft, bankruptcy, embezzlement, breach of contract, fraud, and the destruction of private property.[23] The fourth and final section of the IOPC consists of twelve articles associated with minor crimes (*kabahat*) and punishments and includes matters pertaining to sanitation, cleanliness, and the police, such as improper maintenance of chimneys and furnaces, disturbing the peace with loud noise or raucous behavior, public drunkenness, and the improper burial of corpses.[24]

The reforms of the 1858 IOPC during the Second Constitutional Period culminated a continuous process of revision begun with the code's initial promulgation. However, since its adoption, the IOPC had never been more comprehensively augmented than during the Second Constitutional Period. On 4 June 1911, the Ottoman Parliament reissued the 1858 IOPC in its most modified and

21. Bucknill and Utidjian, *The Imperial Ottoman Penal Code*, 1–36.
22. Ibid., 37–123.
23. Ibid., 124–98.
24. Ibid., 199–208.

expanded form.²⁵ Most CUP penal code reforms focused on four separate, but related areas: rationalizing punishments and criminal proceedings; expanding and centralizing governmental power to determine and adjudicate criminal activity; gaining a greater monopoly over the use of force by assuming sole authority in exacting, determining, and imposing punishments; and eliminating intermediaries between state centralized power and criminals. These changes in turn enabled the CUP and the Ottoman administration to gain greater access to the populace and assume more responsibility for its welfare through the protection of individual rights and private property. These changes range widely over various issues important to the empire and its peoples and deal with private property, personal rights, prevention of government oppression and corruption, protection of honor, protection of state officials, and so forth. Every section of the code was revised, expanded, and updated. In fact, out of the 265 articles contained in the IOPC, a total of fifty-six articles were rescinded, revised, and/or expanded.²⁶

As the CUP revised the IOPC, it also implemented the first of its extensive prison reforms in late 1911 and early 1912 including the creation of the first centralized prison administration, a comprehensive prison survey, a wide-ranging program to completely refurbish and modernize the empire's prisons and jails, and efforts to professionalize the prison cadre and rehabilitate prisoners. Prison reform had been an ongoing process within the empire since the 1850s. As criminal punishment transitioned from being multifaceted to primarily incarceration and fines, there was an increasing need for additional prison space, especially since the empire's prisons suffered from massive overcrowding.²⁷ The need for more prison space reached its greatest point during the Second Constitutional Period with the CUP's agenda of totalizing criminal justice reform. It is, therefore, no accident that the CUP enacted judicial, criminal, and penal reforms together in 1911–12, especially since the Ministry of the Interior overhauled its entire administration as well.

Penal Code Revisions, Crime Statistics, and Ottoman Sensibilities to Criminality

There are, of course, deep connections between the 1911 revisions to the IOPC, the 1912 Ottoman prison survey, the resulting crime statistics, and CUP and Ottoman sensibilities to criminality, crime, and punishment. The majority of crimes listed on the prison survey closely coincide with those most heavily augmented by the sweeping changes to the 1911 penal code. An analysis of the intersection between these penal code reforms and the prison survey also offers intriguing

---

25. Ibid., xiv.
26. Ibid., xiv. For a comprehensive list of all the changes made to the IOPC by the CUP, see Schull, *Prisons in the Late Ottoman Empire*, 29–30.
27. For a comprehensive discussion of Ottoman prison reform in the nineteenth and twentieth centuries, see Schull, *Prisons in the Late Ottoman Empire*.

insights into Ottoman predilections concerning modern state formation, particularly regarding the consolidation of authority in the hands of the state in criminal matters, threats to power and the state, and issues dealing with social order and control.

This section is divided into five subsections. The first deals with the crimes listed on the 1912 Ottoman prison survey. The other five subsections discuss major crimes listed on the prison survey, how they relate to the revisions made in the IOPC, and the number of prisoners incarcerated for these crimes. This discussion provides critical insights into late Ottoman sensibilities towards crime, criminal justice, and punishment. These four subsections are "Crimes against State Officials," "Crimes against Honor," "Theft," and "Violent Crimes."

Crime and the Ottoman Prison Survey[28]

The Ottoman Prison Administration divided the category for crimes, entitled "Types of Crimes" (*Nev'i-i Ceraim*) into two sections: "*Cünha ve Kabahat Kısmı*" ("Section for Lesser Crimes") and "*Cinayet Kısmı*" ("Section for Serious Crimes").[29] The first section contained twenty separate lesser offences:

1. Disrespecting civil servants, gendarme, and soldiers
2. Aiding and abetting the escape of a convict and concealing habitual perpetrators of serious crimes
3. Being without good character, i.e., a vagrant without skills or profession
4. Forgery of travel permits and passports
5. Assault and battery
6. Offering abortions and harmful medications
7. The seduction and dishonoring of a virgin
8. Indecent sexual behavior
9. The verbal and physical molestation of youth

---

28. For a detailed discussion of the 1912 Ottoman prison survey, see Ibid., Chapter 3; "Conceptualizing Difference during the Second Constitutional Period: New Sources, Old Challenges" in *Religion, Ethnicity and Contested Nationhood in the Former Ottoman Space*, ed. Jorgen Nielson (Leiden: Brill, 2012), 63–87; idem, "Identity in the Ottoman Prison Surveys of 1912 and 1914," *International Journal of Middle East Studies* 41:3 (2009): 365–67.

29. There is no clear English translation for the Turkish words *cünha, kabahat ve cinayet*. *Cünha* and *kabahat* are less serious crimes in comparison with *cinayet*. *Cünha* crimes carry a variety of punishments including incarceration from one week to three years, fines, dismissal from office and discontinuance of salary, and even temporary banishment from three months to three years. A combination of these punishments may also be imposed as punishment for *cünha* crimes. *Kabahat* crimes are the least severe and carry a punishment of incarceration lasting between twenty-four hours to one week or a fine not exceeding one Turkish lira. Examples of *kabahat* crimes include violations of civil and state codes on sanitation. *Cinayet* crimes are roughly equivalent to felonies. Punishment consists of incarceration from three years to life imprisonment with hard labor, banishment, incarceration in a citadel, or execution. Bucknill and Utidjian, *The Imperial Ottoman Penal Code*, 5–7.

10. Unlawful arrest and incarceration
11. Switching, concealing, and stealing a child and kidnapping a girl
12. Providing false witness, oath, or evidence during a judicial proceeding
13. Vituperation, insulting, and slandering
14. Fraud
15. Theft
16. Breach of confidence/embezzlement
17. Wasting or destroying a person's goods, property, and documents/papers
18. Opposition to regulations, announcements, and the warnings of a police officer
19. Miscellaneous lesser crimes and misdemeanors
20. Debtors[30]

These lesser crimes carried a much lighter sentence than those of the second section (*cinayet*) and constituted just over a third of the Ottoman Empire's 1911–12 prison population.[31] The second section (*Cinayet Kısmı*) contained fifteen categories of serious crimes:

21. The harboring of highway robbers/bandits and embezzling state goods
22. Premeditated homicide/first degree murder
23. Homicide without premeditation
24. Willful homicide without premeditation
25. Severe assault and battery and cutting off of a body member/limb/organ
26. The intentional or forced aborting of a fetus
27. Forced violent indecent sexual behavior/rape or sodomy
28. Forcibly abducting a female who has reached puberty
29. The forgery of seals and official items
30. Arson
31. Theft with severe conduct and injury
32. Theft via breaking and entering by breaking the door or breaching the wall
33. Theft carried out with severe conduct but without injury
34. Possession of weapons forbidden by the Ministry of War
35. Prisoners awaiting trial from martial law courts[32]

Those convicted of or awaiting trial for serious offenses made up almost two-thirds of the Ottoman Prison population of 1911–12.[33]

The vast majority of the crimes listed on the prison survey questionnaire correspond to crimes against property, life, honor, and social order. Eighteen of

---

30. BOA, DHMBHPSM 8/3 doc. 13.
31. BOA, DHMBHPS 145/31.
32. BOA, DHMBHPSM 8/3 doc. 13.
33. BOA, DHMBHPS 145/31.

the above crimes deal in some way with violent behavior against an individual. Fourteen crimes deal with theft or fraud. Nine relate to honor in terms of character and sexual purity. Nine are associated with function, authority, and the power of the state. Finally, all of the offenses, in one way or another, deal with crimes against social order, discipline, and control. None of these crimes, however, are associated with espionage, bribery, the selling of government secrets, dereliction of duty, or corruption. The CUP was interested in collecting information on very specific types of crimes and the number of those who perpetrated them. The crimes collected by the Ottoman prison survey were the ones most substantially altered or created by the 1911 penal code reforms.

According to the IOPC, there were hundreds of *cinayet, cünha,* and *kabahat* crimes punishable by incarceration. The Ottoman Prison Administration, however, only requested data for a small portion of those crimes. The survey listed some crimes as a general category, such as theft, but most crimes listed on the survey were quite specific. A close analysis of these crimes, their relation to the 1911 revisions of the IOPC, and the number of criminals convicted of each of these crimes offers revealing insights into Ottoman society and CUP ideology regarding what criminal behavior represented threats to public order and safety.

Crimes against State Officials

Throughout the history of empires and other polities, governments have placed a high priority on protecting officers while performing official duties, such as tax collection, law enforcement, maintenance of the regime, and protecting public order. Ottoman interest in these issues is, therefore, not surprising. The amount of attention paid to these issues, however, reveals their importance to the CUP-led government, even though Ottoman courts prosecuted very few individuals for these crimes.

The prison administration listed two crimes on the Ottoman prison survey dealing with offenses against state officials. The survey labeled those crimes as "Disrespecting civil servants, gendarme, and soldiers" and "Opposing regulations, announcements, and warnings of the gendarme/police." Regulations and punishments associated with these crimes are contained in Articles 112–116 of the IOPC. The Ottoman Parliament in 1911 significantly augmented these articles by more clearly delineating these offences and their penalties. The only article not repealed and substituted with a new version was Article 112. Article 112 deals with the crime and punishment for disrespecting or maligning civil servants. Article 113 concerns the crime and punishment for disrespectful, disruptive, or abusive behavior and intimidation against soldiers and police and their associated punishments. The Ottoman Parliament repealed and replaced this article with a similarly worded one. The punishment, however, was doubled to fifteen days–six months incarceration.

Lawmakers expanded Article 114 to include low ranking gendarme together with police and soldiers. In its earlier version, this article only related to the beating of one of these officials. As a result of the 1911 revisions, however, it now included offenses related to any kind of compulsive treatment, threats, or violence against these government officials. The punishment for such an offense, however, was reduced from six months-two years to six months-one year incarceration. The Ottoman Parliament also made revisions to Article 115 (wounding any government official charged with carrying out his duty) in order to define this crime's punishment more clearly as double that of normal assault, i.e., "imprisonment for six months to three years."[34]

Article 116 was the most significantly revised. The 1858 version of Article 116 dealt only with the crime of failure to appear in court when officially summoned. This crime carried a small fine determined by circumstances, such as seriousness and if the accused was a repeat offender.[35] In contrast, the 1911 version of Article 116 was significantly expanded. Ironically, the new version completely elides the crime of failure to appear in court. It does, however, clearly stipulate crimes associated with organized protests against state officials, especially police, military personnel, and tax collectors. Punishments for such an offense range from twenty-four hours to two years of incarceration depending on the size, actions, and whether or not the protesters were armed.[36]

It is ironic, but not surprising, that such an article would be written and passed during the Second Constitutional Period. In fact, the CUP armed, organized, instigated, and directed a series of violent protests and uprisings against government officials attempting to collect two very unpopular taxes prior to the Revolution of 1908. These 1905–07 tax riots occurred in various places around the empire, including Erzurum, Trabzon, Kastamonu, Mosul, and Sivas.[37] With the passage of this newly revised article, the CUP and Ottoman Parliament further strengthened the 1909 laws banning strikes and public protests. It appears that the masses had served their purpose in assisting the 1908 Constitutional Revolution and reversing the 1909 counter coup, but now had to be controlled in order to maintain social order and to protect the power of the new regime.

According to the prison surveys, the number of prisoners arrested, convicted, and incarcerated for "Crimes against State Officials" was very low. In the provinces (*vilayet*) of Istanbul, Beirut, Baghdad, and the Hijaz, and in the admin-

---

34. Bucknill and Utidjian, *The Imperial Ottoman Penal Code*, 86–92.
35. Ibid., 91.
36. Ibid., 91–92.
37. For a detailed discussion regarding tax revolts organized by the CUP from 1905–1907, see Aykut Kansu, *The Revolution of 1908 in Turkey* (Leiden: Brill, 1997), 29–72. For a detailed discussion of the laws passed by the CUP prohibiting public protest and strikes, see idem, *Politics in Post-Revolutionary Turkey, 1908–1913* (Leiden: Brill, 2000).

istrative district (*sanjak*) of Canik, there was a total prison population in 1911–12 of 15,091. This represented over half of the total prison population of 27,700.[38] Out of these 15,091 prisoners only 300 were incarcerated for "Crimes against State Officials" and most of them served very short prison terms. Two hundred and sixty out of the 300 prisoners were either pardoned or received punishments of one day-one month's incarceration. The other forty prisoners received varying sentences ranging from one month-one year, with just a hand full of prisoners being incarcerated for the maximum sentence of two years.[39] In other words, most offenses were not serious. Unfortunately, without the documents from the actual court cases it is impossible to know the exact nature of these prisoners' crimes. Notwithstanding the low numbers of prisoners convicted of this crime, it was still important to the CUP to track the numbers of prisoners arrested, convicted, and serving time for disturbing the peace and attempting to abrogate state authority.

Crimes against Honor

The Ottoman Parliament in 1911 also significantly altered the IOPC section dealing with crimes against an individual's honor, including sexual offenses, perjury, calumny, and vituperation and proceeded to collect prison statistics associated with these crimes. IOPC Articles 197–215 delineate the abovementioned crimes against honor.[40] Although these crimes also do not represent a significant number of incarcerations, they do constitute a significant portion of the crimes for which prison statistics were collected. Out of the thirty-five crimes listed on the Ottoman Prison Survey, ten crimes were related to this offence.

The most significant modifications relating to "Crimes against Honor" are Articles 197, 201, 206, 213, and most extensively, Article 214. Article 197 concerns the commission of the "abominable act", i.e., "unlawful unnatural or natural intercourse, with a minor."[41] In the original 1858 version of the article, a child over the age of eleven was held accountable for the action and was subject to punishment. This standard for adulthood and criminal culpability is based on Islamic law according to when a child manifests having attained puberty. The age of discernment or accountability was raised to fifteen years old in 1911. The significance of this change in regards to changing notions of childhood constitutes a clear

---

38. For the total number of prisoners in the Ottoman Empire for 1911–12 organized according to severity of crime and those awaiting trial, see BOA, DHMBHPS 145/31.

39. For the complete 1911–12 prison statistics for Istanbul, Beirut, Baghdad, the Hicaz, and Canik, see BOA, DHMBHPSM 4/4, DHMBHPSM 5/9, DHMBHPSM 4/21, DHMBHPSM 3/36, and DHMBHPSM 5/1 respectively. The breakdown of the prison population in 1911–1912 for the provinces of Istanbul, Beirut, Baghdad, the Hicaz, and for the administrative district of Canik are as follows: Istanbul: 5,738, Beirut: 4,586, Baghdad: 2,528, The Hicaz: 460, Canik: 1,779.

40. Bucknill and Utidjian, *The Imperial Ottoman Penal Code*, 149–70.

41. Ibid., 149–50.

example of CUP attempts to standardize and rationalize legal codes and punishment, particularly related to criminal culpability since, according to Islamic law, puberty begins at different times for each individual depending on the sex of the child. The Ottoman administration rationalized this to a specific age that was regarded in Islam as the latest age of accountability, even if puberty had not yet manifested itself. This is an excellent example of Ottoman administrators attempting to rationalize and standardize legal practice through the legitimization of and adherence to Islamic law and practice.[42]

The revisions and addenda adjoined to Article 201 are surprisingly progressive for anywhere in the world in the early twentieth century. Originally Article 201 only dealt with the "corruption of youth," for which the 1912 prison survey specifically collected statistics, however, in 1860 this article was expanded to include adultery and its related punishments. The punishments called for in the 1860 version were very one-sided and harsher on a wife who committed adultery than a husband. This revision mirrored exactly the 1810 French Penal Code. In 1911, however, the punishments of incarceration were made almost exactly equal for both the wife and husband, but unlike the wife taken in adultery, the husband also had to pay a fine in addition to incarceration.[43]

Statistics for "Indecent Sexual Behavior" were also very low, but still found on the Ottoman prison survey. According to the survey, the vast majority, over ninety-five percent of all prisoners arrested, convicted, and incarcerated for "Indecent Sexual Behavior" were males. The ratio of males to females convicted for this crime was 325 males to thirty-one females.[44] This statistic has several possible meanings. One, men were arrested, convicted, and punished for committing unlawful sexual behavior, such as fornication, prostitution, adultery, or same-sex sexual acts, more than women. Two, the crime of "Indecent Sexual Behavior" was not vigorously prosecuted. Three, males typically dealt with wives or female rela-

---

42. Regarding Islamic law and determining the age of accountability in the nineteenth and early twentieth-century Ottoman Empire, see Tyser, et. al., *The Mejelle*, Articles 985–987; Bucknill and Utidjian, *The Imperial Ottoman Penal Code*, 26–30; Peters, *Crime and Punishment*, 20–1. For a detailed discussion of the transformation of definitions of juvenile criminal culpability, delinquency, incarceration, and rehabilitation, see Schull, *Prisons in the Late Ottoman Empire*, Chapter 6.

43. Perhaps this was the case because women tended to have very little money of their own, particularly if they were married and not part of the labor force. Bucknill and Utidjian, *The Imperial Ottoman Penal Code*, 152–56.

44. The references for 1912 Ottoman Prison Survey statistics are Istanbul: BOA, DHMBHPSM 4/4; Baghdad: BOA, DHMBHPSM 4/21; Bitlis: BOA, DHMBHPS 145/8 and 145/78, Mosul: BOA, DHMBHPS 145/2, 146/69, and 146/70; Canik: BOA, DHMBHPSM 5/1; Kastamonu: BOA, DHMBHPSM 145/56 and 53/34; the Hicaz: BOA, DHMBHPSM 3/36, Beirut: BOA, DHMBHPSM 5/9; Mamüretülaziz: BOA, DHMBHPSM 12/70, 14/65, and DHMBHPS 145/26; Edirne: BOA, DHMBHPSM 4/1; Yanya: BOA, DHMBHPSM 4/20; and Manastır: BOA, DHMBHPSM 6/27.

tives who committed sexual crimes extra-judicially, through so-called "honor killings." Finally, perhaps sodomy was more commonly prosecuted than other sex crimes, thus targeting males more readily in the empire's patriarchal society, wherein men dominated the public sphere.

Article 206 represents another example of the CUP in 1911 completely rescinding the previous versions of the article and replacing it with a highly modified and more comprehensive version of the 1858 article. All versions of the article deal with the crimes of kidnapping children and girls at the age when puberty was supposed to begin (nine years old for females and eleven years old for males). The most significant changes carried out in 1911 consisted of first, expanding the victims of kidnapping to include adults as well as children. Second, the victims of the crime included both males and females, whereas the original version only stipulated females. Third, even though victims now included both sexes, female victims were still the primary focus of the article and the associated punishments. Fourth, the ages of childhood and accountability were also changed from being determined by strict adherence to Islamic legal norms to being set at the maximum age of accountability (fifteen years old) in reference to Islamic legal stipulations concerning the latest date of accountability for all individuals, even if puberty had not manifested itself. Finally, unlike the 1858 version of Article 206, the 1911 version removed all jurisdiction regarding "Crimes of Honor" from Sharia court procedural directives. Only the *Nizamiye* courts could adjudicate these types of crimes.[45]

Statistics for these crimes were collected by the 1912 prison survey did not include kidnapped adults, but rather focused on the kidnapping of children of both sexes and the kidnapping of females near the age of puberty, but not yet considered an adult (*mashriqa*). The first crime dealing with the kidnapping of children was considered a lesser crime (*cünha*) and the second was considered a serious offense (*cinayet*).[46] This was a crime for which very few were incarcerated during the Second Constitutional Period, but notwithstanding its rarity, the collection of statistics for this offense demonstrates the administration's clear interest in protecting the welfare of the empire's children and expanding state-patriarchy.[47]

Article 213 of the IOPC dealt with crimes against an individual's honor related to slander. In the original version of the article, distinctions were made between slandering a normal civilian and a government official with the punishment for slander against a government official carrying a much heavier punish-

---

45. Bucknill and Utidjian, *The Imperial Ottoman Penal Code*, 159–62. However, as Avi Rubin has clearly demonstrated, criminal and Islamic courts were often presided over by an Islamic court judge (*kadı*), thus preserving the legitimizing link of Islamic law to state reforms and administration. See Rubin, *Ottoman Nizamiye Courts*.

46. BOA, DHMBHPSM 8/3 doc. 13.

47. See Schull, *Prisons in the late Ottoman Empire*, 176–79.

ment. The 1911 version made no distinction between slandering a civilian and a government official in terms of gravity or punishment. In fact, government officials were not even mentioned in the 1911 article, since this crime was dealt with in Articles 112 and 113 discussed above.[48]

The crime of vituperation and its associated punishments was the subject of IOPC Article 214. The original 1858 version was very short and outlined only the basics of the crime, i.e., "[falsely] ascribing some vice or otherwise" to another person, and stipulated a punishment of brief incarceration or fine for the offense.[49] In 1911, however, parliament rescinded the 1858 version and replaced it with a substantially larger article, stipulating in minute detail the definition of vituperation, how it must be committed, i.e., in a public setting with witnesses, etc., the rights of the accused, and the requisite punishments (from twenty-four hours to six months incarceration and/or a fine of between five and fifteen liras). In fact, the original article is only fifty-six words long, but the 1911 version is almost one thousand words in length.[50] It should be clearly evident that from the sheer length and detail of the 1911 version of Article 214 that vituperation was a key concern for the Ottoman Parliament and the CUP.

The CUP was not above using strong arm tactics to pressure, intimidate, and even assassinate its detractors and rivals. The 1912 general election which occurred less than a year after these extensive revisions to the IOPC and three months after the completion of the Ottoman prison survey is a clear example of the CUP's strong arm electioneering tactics.[51] Regardless of the reasons for such a detailed and extensive reformation of Article 214 on vituperation, Article 214 was the most revised of all IOPC articles in 1911. This article and its revisions demonstrate yet again CUP desires to control criticism and protect its power.

In the 1912 prison survey the crimes of slander and vituperation were listed under the same heading and their statistics combined. It is, therefore, impossible to distinguish between these two closely associated offences as tabulated by the prison questionnaires.[52] The crimes of slander and vituperation had a moderate rate of incarceration during the Second Constitutional Period. In each of the provinces and administrative districts previously mentioned (Baghdad, Hijaz, Istanbul, Beirut, and Canik) there were only 423 out of 15,091 total prisoners convicted of slander and vituperation in 1911–12. Over ninety percent of these prisoners received and served prison sentences of twenty-four hours to one month.[53]

48. Bucknill and Utidjian, *The Imperial Ottoman Penal Code*, 164–66.
49. Ibid., 166.
50. Ibid., 167–70.
51. Feroz Ahmad, *The Young Turks: The Committee of Union and Progress in Turkish Politics, 1908–1914* (Oxford: The Clarendon Press, 1969), 92–120; Erik J. Zürcher, *Turkey: a Modern History* (London: I.B. Tauris, 2001), 112–14.
52. BOA, DHMBHPSM 8/3 doc. 13.
53. BOA, DHMBHPSM 5/1, 4/4, 5/9, 4/21, and 3/36.

Their crimes could not have been too serious, especially since the maximum penalty for felony (*cinayet*) slander was ten years hard labor. If a particular slander or vituperation constituted a less serious offense (*cünha*) the maximum penalty was between one and three years of incarceration.[54] The prison survey results, therefore, indicate the prevalence of short prison sentences.

Theft

The second most prevalent crime committed in the Ottoman Empire was theft (*sirkat*) in all of its related forms, including petty theft, violent theft, breaking and entering, fraud, embezzlement, and robbery. Theft-related crimes constituted seven of the thirty-five crimes listed on the prison survey questionnaire. More prisoners were incarcerated for crimes associated with theft than any other crime except assault and battery (*derb ve cerhi*). Not surprising, it was also a key area of revision in the IOPC by the Ottoman Parliament in 1911. In fact, several of the IOPC's articles relating to theft were among the most heavily revised. For example, out of the twenty-six theft related articles, six were revised in 1911 (Articles 220, 222, 224, 225, 226, and 230). Articles 216–241 of the IOPC stipulate the various offenses and punishments associated with theft related crimes.[55]

The specific types of revisions made in 1911 to theft related articles include strengthening the punishments and expanding the criteria for breaking and entering. In the 1858 version of Article 220, breaking and entering only referred to drilling through, digging under, or climbing a wall or breaking down a door or window of a building of any sort. In 1911 this type of crime was expanded to include the breaking and entering into any type of closed structure, be it a building, safe, cupboard, or the like.[56] This inclusion greatly expanded the definition of this type of theft and was designed to protect private property more thoroughly. It also expanded the Islamic definition of breaking and entering, upon which the 1858 definition was based. Islamic criminal law was still the basis of the definition for this crime, however. Ottoman authorities did not abrogate Islamic law here, but simply expanded it to fit the interests of a modern capitalist state fully integrated into the world economy.

Revisions to Article 222 in 1911 simply increased the punishment according to the circumstances under which people perpetrated theft, such as whether the theft occurred at night or day, whether the thief was armed or not, and whether the crime was committed by a servant or apprentice against her/his master. The punishment was increased from six months-three years to one-three years of in-

---

54. Bucknill and Utidjian, *The Imperial Ottoman Penal Code*, 165–69.
55. Ibid., 171–90.
56. Ibid., 174.

carceration.⁵⁷ Punishing servants and apprentices more harshly for theft represents the continuation of Islamic norms and mores in the IOPC.

Other revisions enacted in 1911 dealt mainly with imposing harsher penalties for theft-related crimes. In many cases officials doubled the stiffest penalties of incarceration. This was certainly the case for Articles 224–226. An additional revision to Article 224 expanded the list of items for which a certain punishment could be imposed for theft. These items were mainly related to agriculture, such as horses, other draft animals, and tools.⁵⁸

The most extensively revised theft-related article was Article 230. The original version dealt only with petty theft and pick pocketing. The Ottoman administration, however, greatly expanded and revised this article several times over the course of the second half of the nineteenth and early twentieth centuries. The most significant changes dealt with expanding liability for these crimes to those who purchase, receive, and/or sell stolen goods. Revisions also included the mitigation and reduction of punishments for those who voluntarily came forward regarding their crimes, confessed them, and made restitution prior to court proceedings or arrest.⁵⁹

The prison survey questionnaire of 1912 included nine crimes, associated in one form or another with theft. These consisted of fraud, embezzlement, breaking and entering, violent robbery, and others. The prison population of 1911–12 in the administrative regions of Istanbul, Bagdad, Beirut, the Hijaz, and Canik incarcerated for misdemeanor theft consisted of 2,596 out of a total population of 15,091.⁶⁰

The protection of private property was a key facet of CUP penal reform as reflected by the amount of revisions made to the IOPC regarding theft and the number of prisoners arrested, convicted, and sentenced for theft related crimes. Protecting private property was important to Ottoman officials and society dating back at least as far as the sixteenth century, when Sultan Süleyman issued his famous *kanunname*s and brought Islamic and bureaucratic laws and punishments into harmony with each other. Over the course of the nineteenth century these regulations and laws were even more closely synchronized. Many scholars characterize these rationalizing legal reforms as the Westernization and secularization of Ottoman legal norms eventually resulting in the abrogation of Islamic law.⁶¹ This is incorrect. Many of these crimes had been punished over the

---

57. Ibid., 175–76.
58. Ibid., 177–79.
59. Ibid., 180–83.
60. BOA, DHMBHPSM 3/36, 4/4, 4/21, 5/1, and 5/9.
61. Niyazi Berkes, *The Development of Secularism in Turkey* (New York: Routledge, 1998), 161–72, 417, 467–73; Kemal Karpat, *The Politicization of Islam* (New York: Oxford University Press, 2001), 421–22; Peters, *Crime and Punishment*, 127–33.

empire's existence through a combination of *hadd, qisas, diyet, ta'zir,* and *siyaset* punishments. Ottoman bureaucrats during the nineteenth century were not abrogating Islamic criminal or civil law, but were codifying, standardizing, and rationalizing these crimes and punishments. Islamic law was central to the IOPC and its legitimacy, but now transformed to fit the needs of a modern imperial state. No Ottoman administration did this more than the CUP during the Second Constitutional Period. The protection of private property was particularly important to the CUP, because of its attempts to build a Muslim middle class, increase private enterprise, foster industrialization, and promote the economic development and independence of the empire.[62]

Violent Crimes

Violent crime represents the most prevalent crimes in the Ottoman Empire, according to the 1912 prison survey. In fact, the survey collected statistics on fourteen different violent crimes. The articles related to violent crimes found in the IOPC, such as threats, physical assaults, and homicide, were also amongst those most substantially altered by the Ottoman Parliament in 1911. The IOPC contains twenty-four articles related to violent crimes (Articles 168–191).[63]

Concerning homicide, lawmakers significantly changed Article 174. The original Article 174 read as follows:

> If a person has killed an individual without premeditation he is placed in kyurek [*kürek*] for a period of fifteen years; but if this matter of destruction of life has taken place while committing another Jinayet [*cinayet*] either before the commission or after the commission, or for the sake of committing a Junha [*cünha*], the person destroying life is punished with the punishment of death according to law.[64]

The 1911 article expanded the 1858 version by providing greater protection for government officials while performing their duties and made significant clarifications regarding punishments associated with accidental homicides.[65] In preservation of Islamic law, the IOPC still preserved the right of victims' relatives to *qisas* and *diyet* punishments stipulated in Articles 171 and 172.[66]

---

62. Regarding CUP economic policies during the Second Constitutional Period see Zafer Toprak, *"Milli İktisat" 1908–1918* (Ankara: Yurt Yayınları, 1982); idem, *İttihad-Terraki ve Cihan Harbi: Savaş Ekonomisi ve Türkiye'de Devletçilik, 1914–1918* (Istanbul: Homer Kitabevi, 2003); idem, *Milli İktisat, Milli Burjuvazi* (Istanbul: Tarih Vakfı Yurt Yayınları, 1995).
63. Bucknill and Utidjian, *The Imperial Ottoman Penal Code*, 124–45.
64. Ibid., 127–28.
65. Ibid., 128–29.
66. Ibid., 126–27.

Other articles changed in 1911 associated with homicide include more severe punishments for accomplices.[67] Articles 177, which dealt with assaults that result in the loss of use of a bodily member, was further strengthened and clarified in 1911. Punishment now included the payment of medical expenses and incarceration of not less than six years hard labor.[68] Other articles associated with assault and homicide that were augmented in one way or another by the CUP in 1911 include Articles 180, 188, 189, 190, and 191, but most changes dealt with the crimes' associated punishments.[69]

The actual number of prisoners convicted of violent crimes, particularly assault and homicide constitute almost half of all those incarcerated in Ottoman prisons in 1911–12. For example, 2,926 out of the 5,738 individuals incarcerated in Istanbul prisons in 1911–12 were convicted and sentenced for violent crime. In Beirut, out of the 4,591 incarcerated persons 2,121 were serving time for either assault or homicide in 1911–12. In Baghdad the number of violent crimes was less than half of the prison population in 1911–12, but still constituted the majority of any type of crime committed. Out of a prison population of 2,528, there were 799 prisoners convicted of violent crimes. In the Hijaz, the percentage of those incarcerated for violent crimes was also not as high as other places, but it still accounted for more than any other class of crime. Eighty-four individuals were serving time for violent crimes out of a population of 460. In Canik, 631 were convicted of assault or homicide out of 1,779 total prisoners.[70]

The most prevalently convicted and incarcerated offense during the Second Constitutional Period was misdemeanor (*cünha*) "Assault and Battery" (*darb ve cerh*). More than any other crime, this constituted the largest percentage of convictions and incarcerations. Most punishments related to this crime, however, indicated that the types of assaults were relatively minor, such as fisticuffs. The vast majority of prisoners incarcerated for misdemeanor assault served less than one month's incarceration in the administrative regions of Istanbul, Beirut, Baghdad, the Hijaz, and Canik. The overwhelming majority of females incarcerated in Ottoman prisons (which was a miniscule percentage compared to males) were guilty of misdemeanor assault and battery. Female punishments were also primarily twenty-four hours to one month's incarceration.

The prosecution and prevention of violent crimes, such as assault, rape, and homicide comprised a major portion of Ottoman penal reforms. Central to Ottoman administrative goals was the need to maintain public order and discipline. As the state relied less and less on intermediaries and increasingly centralized its

---

67. Ibid., 129.
68. Ibid., 131.
69. Ibid., 136–37 and 141–45.
70. BOA, DHMBHPSM 5/1, 4/4, 5/9, 4/21, and 3/36.

authority over the use of force, maintaining public order, and meting out punishment, there was an increased confluence of what has been characterized as "secular" and "religious" law and legal practice. Islam was not being abrogated, but increasingly standardized to fit the demands of a rapidly changing world. This confluence of the need for social order and discipline and the state having greater access to and control over the lives of individuals is clearly reflected in both the 1911 alterations to the IOPC, in terms of violent crime against individuals, theft, the prevalence of these crimes, and in the results of the 1912 prison survey. Even the crimes where few individuals were actually incarcerated, but still monitored by the prison surveys, add additional insight into Ottoman administrative goals regarding its desire to consolidate power within its hands and protect government officials in their duties. Both of these goals are essential for creating and running a strong, central, and efficient government that possesses a monopoly on the use of force and can project and enforce its policies and laws over the empire's population.

Conclusion

The codification of Ottoman-Islamic criminal law and practice over the course of the second-half of the nineteenth and early twentieth centuries resulted in several key transformations concerning conceptions of criminality, punishment, and the modernization of Islamic criminal law and practice to meet the rigors of modern statecraft and societal changes. Codification comprehensively rationalized and standardized crime and punishment for the first time in the empire by combining crimes and punishments from Islamic law with executive/state crimes and punishments (*hadd*, *qisas*, *diyet*, *ta'zir*, and *siyaset*) within the same code. This effectively circumscribed the autonomy of Islamic court judges and state magistrates to mete out discretionary punishments (*ta'zir* and *siyaset* respectively) through the extensive delineation of crimes and ascribed punishments, along with the adoption of new criminal case procedural laws. Besides execution for capital offenses, corporeal punishments including torture were discontinued and banned respectively, thus making incarceration and fines the primary punishment for criminal offenses.

These were not simply cosmetic changes to satisfy Western demands for reform and secularization. They reflect the development of a unique Ottoman modernity that blended the practices and institutions of "classical" Ottoman criminal justice with new methods of governance and practices to create a thoroughly modern criminal justice system still predicated and legitimized by Islamic legal practices, principles, and standards now updated to meet the strictures of the "modern" world. The IOPC was updated, modified, and enforced until the end of the empire as demonstrated by prison statistics draw from the 1912 Ottoman prison survey. These changes and transformations were not devoid of their cultural, political, or societal basis, but wholly rooted in traditional practices, norms, and mores that reflected generally held sensibilities towards crime and punishment in terms of Islamic law, the Circle of Justice ruling philosophy, the protection of individual rights, preserving state power, and maintaining social order.

KENT F. SCHULL is an Associate Professor in the Department of History at Binghamton University and is the editor of *The Journal of the Ottoman and Turkish Studies Association*.

9 Refugees, Locals and "The" State

Property Compensation in the Province of Izmir Following the Greco-Turkish Population Exchange of 1923[1]

Ellinor Morack

THE MUTUAL AND compulsory population exchange between Greece and Turkey marks a crucial event in the demographic, economic and social history of both countries. Signed on 30 January 1923, the agreement between both governments sealed the fate of about 800,000 Greek-Orthodox citizens of the Ottoman state (known as *Rum*) who had involuntarily left Anatolia and Thrace between 1912 and 1922, banning them from ever returning to their homeland again. Those who were still in place were also forced to emigrate to Greece. The same rules were applied to the Muslim population of Greece (including those who had already left during the Balkan Wars), which was to emigrate to Turkey. Exceptions were made for the Greeks living in Istanbul (including Greek citizens who were known as *Yunan* in Ottoman Turkish), the Muslims of Western Thrace, and the *Rum* island populations of Imros and Tenedos at the mouth of the Dardanelles.[2]

As an internationally sanctioned forced migration, the exchange helped to legalize and make permanent the ethnic cleansing of the Ottoman Greeks that had taken place during the Balkan Wars, World War I, and the Turkish War of Independence.[3] By providing Turkey with about 400,000 Muslim immigrants,

---

1. I would like to thank all the participants of the graduate student workshop on "Turks in Conflict" at Columbia University who provided feedback on an early draft of this article. Special thanks go to the two anonymous *JOTSA* reviewers for their very helpful criticism and suggestions.

2. Onur Yıldırım, *Diplomacy and Displacement: Reconsidering the Turco-Greek Exchange of Populations, 1922–1934* (London: Routledge, 2006); Renée Hirschon, ed., *Crossing the Aegean: An Appraisal of the 1923 Compulsory Population Exchange between Greece and Turkey* (New York: Berghahn, 2003).

3. As in all previous forced migrations on the Balkans, many refugees had actually hoped to return. See Ayhan Aktar, "Türk-Yunan Nüfus Mübadelesi'nin İlk Yılı: Eylül 1922– Eylül 1923," in *Yeniden Kurulan Yaşamlar. 1923 Türk-Yunan Zorunlu Nüfus Mübadelesi*, ed. Müfide Pekin (Istanbul: Bilgi Üniversitesi Yayınları, 2005), 41–84.

it helped to replace at least some of the lost non-Muslim populations, but the exchange involved not only people. A crucial part of the agreement dealt with the appraisal and indemnification of all the property, whether rural or urban, movable or immovable, owned by the "exchangeable" populations. It was this part of the exchange that turned out to be most problematic.[4] According to the exchange agreement, a Mixed Commission comprised of Greek, Turkish, and neutral members was supposed to deal with the gigantic task of registering and appraising all property of the exchanged, and provide them with documents stating its value. The receiving state would then indemnify them with property of equal value. At the end of the process, the values on both sides should have been balanced with the difference being paid in gold currency. This plan, however, was never implemented. The Greek and Turkish delegations at the Mixed Commission spent years discussing possible appraisal schemes only to eventually drop the idea altogether in the Ankara agreement of 1930, which formally ended the exchange.[5] Rather than the Mixed Commission, it was national legislation and its implementation by local administrations that shaped compensation policies. While Greece depended heavily on international aid and the League of Nations, Turkey managed the task alone.

Studies of the population exchange in Turkey have generally focused on settlement of people, paying very little attention to the accompanying policies of property distribution and indemnification for "exchangees" (*mübadil* in Ottoman Turkish). Yet, it is this aspect of the exchange that connects "exchangees" to a much broader issue in early Republican history, namely, the project of economic "Turkification" (the forced transfer of economic resources from non-Muslim to Muslim hands).[6] This endeavor clearly mattered not only for those chosen few who made fortunes by taking over Armenian- and Greek-owned companies and landed estates.[7] It also involved countless humble people who took part in the boycott movement that started to target first mainland Greeks and later *Rum*

---

4. Dimitri Pentzopoulos, *The Balkan Exchange of Minorities and Its Impact upon Greece* (Paris: Moutonon, 1962).

5. Stephan Ladas, *The Exchange of Minorities: Bulgaria, Greece and Turkey* (New York: MacMillan, 1932); Yıldırım, *Diplomacy*.

6. Çağlar Keyder, "The Consequences of the Exchange of Populations for Turkey," in *Crossing the Aegean*, 39–52; Ayhan Aktar, "Homogenising the Nation, Turkifying the Economy: The Turkish Experience of Population Exchange Reconsidered," in Ibid., 79–95. Both Keyder and Aktar link the exchange to the project of "Turkification." However, their conceptual work has so far not been taken up in source-based studies of the exchange in Turkey.

7. For a discussion of popular (and especially female) participation in the plundering of Armenian possessions, see Mehmet Polatel and Uğur Ü. Üngör, *Confiscation and Destruction: The Young Turk Seizure of Armenian Property* (London: Continuum International, 2011), 88f.

from 1909 onwards.[8] Moreover, many Muslim refugees and homeless people were settled in houses of both *Rums* and Armenians between 1912 and 1922.[9] Their desire to keep this stolen wealth possibly was an important reason for widespread Muslim support for the Turkish War of Independence (of which the Greco-Turkish War forms a part).[10] Legal or illegal occupation of such property became the subject of a lively debate after 1922, especially in Izmir (where the great fire of September 1922 destroyed most of the inner city) and the surrounding towns, some of which had also burned down.[11] At first, the debate mainly targeted the Ministry of Finance and its local branches, which evicted people from *Rum* and Armenian houses in order to auction them off.[12] However, in many cases an eviction was impossible because the occupants themselves were soldiers, policemen, or other state officials.[13] Illegal occupation of houses and agricultural land (often by state employees, such as policemen and officers) continued to be a major headache for authorities trying to settle exchangees from 1923 onwards.[14] There is, however, no detailed, source-based study dealing with this problem that takes into account both exchangees and locals. This article provides a first step into this direction, thus making an important contribution to a better understanding of local politics and state-society relations in early Republican Turkey.

Those few scholars dealing with the details of property distribution to exchangees have used records (*tahsis defterleri*) that were drawn up by local settlement authorities at the very beginning of the settlement process.[15] Organized in tabular form, these registers convey the impression of accuracy and order. However, recent research has shown that an internal investigation in the province of Manisa, which was performed in 1927, actually found the registers to be largely fictitious.[16] On a general level, we already know that property compensation re-

---

8. Y. D. Çetinkaya, *The Young Turks and the Boycott Movement: Nationalism, Protest and the Working Classes in the Formation of Modern Turkey* (London: I.B. Tauris, 2014), 41.

9. Polatel and Üngör, *Confiscation*; Ryan Gingeras, *Sorrowful Shores: Violence, Ethnicity, and the End of the Ottoman Empire, 1912–1923* (New York: Oxford University Press, 2009).

10. Fuat Dündar, *Modern Türkiyenin Şifresi. İttihat ve Terakkinin Etnisite Mühendisliği (1913–1918)* (Istanbul: İletişim, 2008), 245.

11. Kemal Arı, "Yunan işgalinden sonra İzmir'de 'Emval-i Metruke' ve 'Fuzuli İşgal' Sorunu," *Atatürk Araştırma Merkezi Dergisi* 15:5 (1989), http://www.atam.gov.tr/index.php?Page=DergiIcerik&IcerikNo=891 (accessed 3 June 2010).

12. Ibid.

13. Yıldırım, *Diplomacy*, 148.

14. Ibid.; Kemal Arı, *Büyük Mübadele: Türkiye'ye Zorunlu Göç (1923–1925)* (Istanbul: Tarih Vakfı Yurt Yayınları, 1995),117–19.

15. These are Nedim İpek, *Mübadele ve Samsun* (Ankara: Türk Tarih Kurumu, 2001); Tülay A. Baran, "İzmir'de Çiftçi Mübadiller," *Kebikeç* 4 (1996).

16. Mehmet Öz and Ferhat Berber, "Mübadele Sürecinde Yaşanan Sorunlar ve Merkezden Müdahaleye Bir Örnek: 1927 Manisa Teftişi," *Atatürk Araştırma Merkezi Dergisi* 78 (2010).

mained highly contested, creating large amounts of red tape and keeping local courts busy well into the 1930s.[17]

The historiography of the population exchange in Turkey continues to be plagued by a certain state-centeredness.[18] While scholars are interested in the immigrants' experience, they have found very few sources produced by non-state actors, such as exchangees themselves.[19] Oral history projects only started in the late 1990s, too late to record the memories of people who had immigrated as adults.[20] On a conceptual level, there is an ongoing tendency to focus on the central state's agenda and to assume that the state was the most important (if not only) force driving social change—in this case, the settlement and compensation policies for exchangees.[21] Very much like contemporary critics of the settlement process in Turkey, historians of the exchange usually explain the gap between laws and their application, with corruption, incompetence, or lack of funds, in short: a lack of state power.[22] In this view, the state remains a monolithic abstraction whose practices perpetually fall short of fulfilling its own promise of perfect, rational administration.

This article takes a different approach to the "failures" of settlement and compensation schemes. Taking up Joel Migdal's state-in-society model, it argues

---

17. Tülay A. Baran, *Bir Kentin Yeniden Yapılanması (İzmir 1923–1938)* (Istanbul: Arma Yayınları, 2003).

18. This can no longer be said of Republican history in general. Recent contributions to the field include Hale Yılmaz, *Becoming Turkish: Nationalist Reforms and Cultural Negotiations in Early Republican Turkey, 1923–1945* (Syracuse: Syracuse University Press, 2013); Gavin D. Brockett, ed., *Towards a Social History of Modern Turkey* (Istanbul: Libra, 2011); Metin Metinsoy, "Fragile Hegemony, Flexible Authoritarianism, and Governing from Below: Politicians' Reports in Early Republican Turkey," *International Journal of Middle East Studies* 43:4 (2011); Yiğit Akın, "Reconsidering State, Party and Society in Early Republican Turkey: Politics of Petitioning," *International Journal of Middle East Studies* 39:3 (2007).

19. Neither Kemal Arı nor Onur Yıldırım had access to the exchangee petitions that are now available in the Republican Archive in Ankara. Arı works with an interesting collection of private letters, while Yıldırım uses the few available autobiographies.

20. For instance, see Bruce Clark, *Twice a Stranger: The Mass Expulsions that Forged Modern Greece and Turkey* (Cambridge: Harvard University Press, 2009); İskender Özsoy, *İki Vatan Yorgunları Mübadele Acısını Yaşayanlar Anlatıyor* (Istanbul: Bağlam, 2003); Tolga Köker, "Lessons in Refugeehood: The Experience of Forced Migrants in Turkey," in *Crossing the Aegean*, 193–208.

21. This state-centeredness can be traced back to political theory in Ottoman times and the mind-set of early Republican bureaucratic and military elites: Şerif Mardin, "Projects as Methodology: Some Thoughts on Modern Turkish Social Science," in *Rethinking Modernity and National Identity in Turkey*, ed. Sibel Bozdoğan and Reşat Kasaba (Seattle: University of Washington Press, 1997), 64–80; Erik J. Zürcher, "The Ottoman Legacy of the Turkish Republic: An Attempt at a New Periodization," *Die Welt des Islams* 32 (1992).

22. For instance, see Arı, *Büyük* and to a lesser extent, Yıldırım, *Diplomacy*. A more recent example is Öz and Berber, "Mübadele."

that the early Turkish Republic, like any other modern state, was characterized both by "the image of a coherent controlling organization in a territory" and through the "actual practices of its multiple parts."[23] Seen from this angle, various practices in the application of law do not necessarily appear as corruption or other forms of "weakness" on the part of state agencies.[24] Rather, they can be understood as results of multiple, and at times contradictory, objectives of various institutions and people, both within the state apparatus and in the surrounding society. In fact, it may at times be difficult to distinguish between "state" and "society," as their boundaries, especially on a local level, tend to blur.

Very much like the "state," law can hardly be conceptualized as a single, rational body of rules which, once written, are simply implemented. Societies have an impact on legislation which may start to make itself felt even before specific laws are written. The Ottoman Land Code of 1858 is a case in point: Far from being simply a reaction to Great Power demands, it includes many provisions that can be read as reactions to the needs and practices of Ottoman society: Legal practice in the Ottoman Empire had already started to regard land as a commodity, and the new law merely codified this idea.[25] On the other hand, its writers were careful to accommodate older, collective forms of land-use.[26]

Modern times have seen a proliferation of laws that normalize behavior rather than punish it. These types of law (for instance those regulating welfare policies) encourage certain types of behavior and discourage others, often penetrating the most mundane realms of everyday life—they are tools of governance.[27] As such, they must remain flexible and adjustable to popular demands or to the necessities arising in administration.[28] This type of law is accompanied by a flexible notion of legality, which does not emphasize the application of universal principles, but rather tends to find temporary solutions for particular problems, especially in matters concerning resource allocation.[29]

---

23. Joel S. Migdal, *State in Society: Studying How States and Societies Transform and Constitute One Another* (Cambridge: Cambridge University Press, 2001), 16.

24. Ibid., 12.

25. See Richard S. Smith's discussion of this tendency in Martha Mundy and Richard S. Smith, *Governing Property, Making the Modern State: Law, Administration and Production in Ottoman Syria* (London: I.B. Tauris, 2007). Also, see Attila E. Aytekin, "Agrarian Relations, Property and Law: An Analysis of the Land Code of 1858 in the Ottoman Empire," *Middle Eastern Studies* 45:6 (2009).

26. Huri İslamoğlu, "Politics of Administering Property: Law and Statistics in the Nineteenth-Century Ottoman Empire," in *Constituting Modernity: Private Property in the East and West*, ed. Huri İslamoğlu (New York: I.B. Tauris, 2004), 276–319.

27. Alan Hunt and Gary Wickham, eds., *Foucault and Law: Towards a Sociology of Law as Governance* (London: Pluto Press, 1994).

28. Ben Golder and Peter Fitzpatrick, *Foucault's Law* (London: Routledge, 2009), 54.

29. Ibid., 38.

This article analyzes the implementation of property compensation laws for exchangees as a case study for this type of legality, which arguably had repercussions for central state legislation. The relevant laws were often changed and re-written, a fact which in itself suggests a certain degree of responsiveness and flexibility towards popular discontent. Based on a conceptualization of the "state" as multifaceted and of law as responsive to popular demands, this article studies how laws for exchangee compensation were implemented in several small towns and villages in the environs of Izmir. In order to do so, it makes use of administrative correspondence produced by two central state agencies (namely, the Ministry of Internal Affairs and the Ministry of Finance) and the provincial administration (*valilik*) of Izmir. These letters also provide some insights into the activities of village and regional councils, and crucially, into the demands made by local people. The perspective of the exchangees is studied through petitions that were sent to the settlement office (which was a part of the Ministry of Internal Affairs) at Ankara. Given low rates of literacy, these texts were often written by or with the help of petition-writers. While not representing the voices of the petitioners themselves, they can certainly provide us with an idea of what petition writers knew about the legal categories and rules in place, and how they—probably together with their clients—interpreted them.[30]

Taken together, laws, bureaucratic correspondence, and petitions allow us to discover the complicated relationship between legality and legitimacy: They make it possible to study how administrations actually applied settlement and compensation laws. Most importantly, they offer clues as to objectives that were not formulated in positive law, but nevertheless were regarded as legitimate. Petitions, on the other hand, help us to understand how people made sense of law and administrative practice. These questions are discussed first with regard to the supposedly privileged status of exchangees (as opposed to other groups) and then to the administrative procedure of property allocation to them. Laws pertaining to compensation schemes and settlement policies were drawn up very hastily during the first months of the population exchange and later underwent frequent changes. Many of these changes can be read as reactions to popular protests, suggestions, and claims which did not only surface in newspapers and the parliament, but also in individual petitions that have been preserved in the Republican Archive in Ankara.[31] Taken together, petitions, administrative texts,

---

30. For the problems and limitations on the use of petitions as sources for social history, see Andreas Würgler, "Voices from among the 'Silent Masses': Humble Petitions and Social Conflicts in Early Modern Central Europe," *International Review of Social History* 46, Supplement 9 (2001). For a methodologically sophisticated study of petitions from 1930s Turkey, see Akın, "Reconsidering State, Party and Society in Early Republican Turkey."

31. In September 2009 the petitions cited here were part of the Toprak İskân Genel Müdürlüğü Kataloğu (Muhacirin Fonu, no. 272.1) of the Republican Archive in Ankara. The

and laws allow us to study the complex relationship between administrative practice, popular notions of justice, and the law, each of which arguably had an impact on the others.

Exchangee Settlement and Property Compensation: A Priority over the Needs of Other Groups?

The task of settling incoming refugees in Turkey was at first assigned to a special Ministry for the Population Exchange, Repairs and Settlement Affairs (*mübâdele, imâr ve iskân vekâleti*), which was established in November 1923. When the relevant bill was discussed in the National Assembly, the newly appointed minister Mustafa Necati Bey, made the following statement: "I will settle refugees wherever I can. This is the right of the people who are subject to the population exchange."[32]

At a first glance, the minister's statement seems to imply that the settlement of exchangees had priority over the housing needs of other groups. The freshly established ministry was indeed empowered to evict people who were currently living in abandoned property houses (including those paying rent for them) in order to settle refugees. These refugees, however, also included various groups other than exchangees, such as people who had fled from countries other than Greece and those who had left their houses due to wartime destruction.[33] The minister's statement propagated a privileged status for exchangees that was not (yet) part of positive law. It is, however, important to note that he spoke both of "people who are subject to the population exchange" and of "refugees" in general. His statement may well have been directed not so much against the interests of other refugees but against a rivaling institution, the Ministry of Finance, which had been collecting rents from refugees who had been settled in "abandoned" property of *Rum*s, *Yunan*s, and Armenians since about 1913. The possible eviction of these people, and their replacement with new refugees, therefore, threatened this source of revenue. (The law which spelled out the competences of the ministry of the exchange actually went on to discuss with how the loss of these rents would be dealt).

---

catalog has in the meantime been reorganized and no longer includes files related to the population exchange. The file numbers cited here may, therefore, be outdated.

32. "Mübadeleye tabi olan halkın hakkı olarak, bulduğum mahallere muhacir koyarım... Her nerede muhacirin hakkı olan hane mevcut ise, [görevim] oraya muhacir koymaktan ibarettir." Cited by Kemal Arı, *Büyük*, 116.

33. "Mübadele ve imar ve iskân vekâleti bilûmum gayrimenkul emvali metrukenin muhacirin ile düşman tarafından meskenleri tahrip ve ihrak edilen muhtaciıne tahsis ve tevziine ve bu emvalden elyevm isticar ve suveri saire ile eşhası salise tarafından meşgul olanlarını idareten tahliyeye salâhiyettardır." Mübadele, İmar ve İskan Kanunu, No. 368, Article 8, http://www.tbmm.gov.tr/tutanaklar/KANUNLAR_KARARLAR/kanuntbmmc002/kanuntbmmc002/kanuntbmmc00200368.pdf (last accessed on 12 March 2015).

A distinction between exchangees and other people in need only became part of positive law in the Spring of 1924. Issued on 13 March 1924, Law No. 441 regulated the distribution of "real estate (*emlâk*) that is abandoned and therefore currently under control of the government."[34] Here, it was explicitly stated that only property "owned by people not subject to the exchange" (*mübadeleye gayri tabi eşhasa ait olup*)[35]—i.e., Armenians, and Greeks who were not Ottoman citizens—would be distributed among people who had lost their homes during the war, according to their losses (*hedmü tahrip veya harp dolayısıyle ihrak edilmiş olan emlâk sahiplerine, muhtaç olanlar tercih edilmek şartile, zayiatlarının derecesi nisbetinde tevzi ve temlik olunur*). About a month later, on 16 April 1924, a law (no. 488) regulating the terms and administrative procedure for the distribution of property to *mübadil* followed.[36] It stated that exchangees would be given property whose value would not exceed twenty percent of the sums inscribed in the documents they had brought with them from Greece. Pending the completion of the population exchange, they would only receive temporary and revocable property rights and would not be allowed to make any but petty alterations to it. Neither were they allowed to mortgage land or houses received in the course of this preliminary procedure (§7). The law did not assign a particular kind of abandoned property to them.

The first-mentioned law (no. 441) for locals foresaw that full, private property rights (*mülk*) would be granted through the procedure of *temlik*. The procedure for exchangees was different: They were only given preliminary, revocable usage rights which did not allow them to alter the property or mortgage it. The administrative procedure through which these limited rights were granted was called *tefviz*. This terminology points back to pre-modern Ottoman land law, which conceptualized almost all agricultural land as state-owned (*miri*), merely allowing for the transfer of usage rights—this transfer was called *tefviz*.[37]

Both laws taken together suggest that locals, at least by Spring 1924, were better off than exchangees. Not only was "their" law issued first, but they were eligible for full property rights—if only for Armenian abandoned property, which was relatively scarce in Western Anatolia. (The reverse was true for Eastern Anatolia). Exchangees, though only receiving revocable rights, had reason to expect

---

34. *Hükumet yedinde sahipsiz olarak mevcut bulunan emlâkin; emval ve emlâki düşman, usat ve hasbellüzum Hükumet tarafından tahrip edilmiş olanlara nisbet dahilinde tevzii hakkında kanun*, 13 Mart 1340, No. 441, *Düstur*, 3. Tertip, vol. 5, 1231-35, §11, 690.

35. Unless otherwise indicated, I cite laws and regulations from transliterated, published texts without altering the transliteration.

36. *Mübadeleye tabi ahaliye verilecek emvali gayri menkule hakkında kanun* No. 488, 16 Nisan 1340, Ibid., 844-46.

37. On the pre-modern meaning of *tefviz*, see İpek, *Mübadele*, 135; Anton Minkov, "Ottoman Tapu Title Deeds in the Eighteenth and Nineteenth Centuries: Origins, Typology and Diplomatics," *Islamic Law and Society* 7:1 (2000): 259. İpek also discusses its meaning in Republican times.

that they would eventually be given more than just twenty percent of their rightful claims.

The first legal text that explicitly reserved a certain class of abandoned property for exchangees was issued in October 1924. This regulation (*talimatname*), stipulated numerous exceptions to the rules issued in April.[38] According to §11, people who were not *mübadil*, but nevertheless held [abandoned] property, would be allowed to rent it on condition that they were actually controlling it (*fiilhal vaziyet olmak*) and if the property was either owned by Armenians or not needed for *mübadil* (*mephus emval Ermeni emvali metrukesinden bulunmak veyahut mübadil ahalinin ihtiyacından fazla olduğu tahakkuk eylemek*). The condition of *de facto* control over a piece of property makes it very clear that this regulation was aimed at legalizing the widespread illegal occupation of abandoned property. In March 1926, this rule was changed from rent to purchase by mortgage, with a law clearly stating that it only applied to property "abandoned by people not subject to the population exchange," i.e., Armenians and Greek citizens. These houses and fields would not be claimed back by the state from people "apart from those subject to the exchange, who have a legal right to settlement and have already been settled."[39] Non-exchangees would be allowed to purchase real estate according to the rules of the law of obligations (*borçlanma kanunu*) issued in January 1926. The property's 1915 value would be transferred to the custodian accounts of the former owners, the rest of the money being distributed to the respective administrative units (*idarei hususiyelere ita olunur*).[40]

The Application, Case One: Exchangees Against Locals in Urla, 1927

On 17 January 1927, three refugees sent a telegram from the town of Urla, forty km south of Izmir, to the Minister of Internal Affairs in Ankara, Cemil Bey:

> In contradiction to procedure, fire-victims (*harikzedegân*) from the village of Kuşçular are still living in the abandoned property houses in Urla. Your state order for their removal to their village has not been put into effect, making it impossible for exchangees to be settled and bringing them into a most terrible condition. It has been decided to let the fire-victims stay until March. Due to

---

38. *Bazı muhacirine tasfiyei katiyeye değin icar mukabilinde ita ve bedeli icarının tecili hakkında talimatname*, 8 Teşrinievvel 1340 (Oct. 1924), *Düstur*, 3. Tertip, vol. 5, 1231–35.

39. *Mübadeleye gayri tabi eşhastan metruk olup hakkı iskânı haiz olanlara verilmiş ve verilecek emvali gayri menkule hakkında kanun*, No. 781, 13 Mart 1926, *Düstur*, 3. Tertip, vol. 7, 655.

40. These custodian accounts must have been the ones that had been established in the course of the Armenian Genocide in 1915/16. Their contents were never paid to the actual owners (or their heirs), but transferred to the treasury with a law issued in 1928, see Polatel and Üngör, *Confiscation*, 56; Nevzat Onaran, *Emvâl-i Metrûke Olayı: Osmanlı'da ve Cumhuriyette Ermeni ve Rum Mallarının Türkleştirilmesi* (Istanbul: Belge, 2010), 209. The text of the law can be found in Salâhaddin Kardeş, "Tehcir ve emval-i metruke mevzuatı," (2008): 111ff. http://eskiportal.sgb.gov.tr/Publications/Tehcir%20ve%20Emvali%20Metruke%20Mevzuat%C4%B1.pdf

this, the exchangees, who, according to the law, have a legal right to be settled, will face the danger of dying in the streets. We, therefore, ask for [your] mercy in this matter. Urla: Mustafaoğlu Musa, Ismailoğlu Hüseyin and Şerif Hüseyin of the Mübadil from Kavala, in Urla.[41]

The text mentions all the actors usually involved in such disputes: the exchangees (*mübadil*) and local people whose houses had been burned down towards the end of the Turkish-Greek War (*harīkzede*). (Today, there is a village called Kuşçular only three kilometers distance from Urla. If this was the village mentioned in the petition, the locals would really not have been strangers at all). Both groups' common objects of desire were "abandoned property houses" (*emvāl-ı metrūke hāneleri*), houses, as this petition makes clear, to which the *mübadil* considered themselves to have a legal right, but found occupied by the *harīkzede*. The petition points to the law and its violation on three different levels: It states that the *harikzedes*' dwelling in the houses is "against procedure" (*hilāf-i usūl*), that the minister's order for their eviction was not implemented (*emr-ü devletleriniz icrā edilmediğinden*), and, finally, argues that the exchangees had a legal right to the houses in question. Their claim is further supported by an argument of need: the danger of dying in the streets.

In this case, the state agencies involved were Izmir's provincial administration and the settlement directorate (*iskân müdürlüğü*) in Ankara, which was part of the Ministry of Internal Affairs. (The Exchangee Ministry had been dissolved in 1924). The other telegrams included in the file tell us more about the background of this story: In a telegram dated 15 December 1926, the governor (*vali*) of Izmir, Kazim Pasha, appealed to the settlement directorate concerning this matter. According to his letter, an imperial decree (*emirnāme-yi hümāyūn*)[42] issued in 11 September 1926 ordered that the *harīkzede* be allowed to stay. Local agencies, therefore, tried to accommodate as many people as possible, often by squeezing several families into one house. This practice, however, still left fifty *mübadil* families "out in the open." One hundred and fourteen houses continued to be occupied by *harīkzede*, including employees of the state (*memūr*) and army

---

41. "*Urla'da hilâf-i usūl emvāl-i metrūke hānelerinde ikāmet eden Kuşçular karyesi harikzedegānınıñ hemān köylerine naklı ve hānelerinde henüz iskān edilemeyen mübādillere i'tāsı hakkındaki emr-ü devletleriñiz icrā edilmediğinden iskān görmeyen mübādiller fecī bir vaż'iyet içindedir harikzedegānıñ Mārta kadar hānelerinde kalmaları için tesīsāt-ı icrā kılındığı işcār kılındı. harikzedegānıñ hānelerinde temdīn-i ikāmetine me'zūniyet verildiği takdīrde kānūnen iskāna tābi' olan mübādiller açıklarda ölmek tehlīkesine ma'rūż kalacaktır. Emr-ü devletleriñiziñ hemān tatbīki hakkında (. . .) iş'âr-i keyfiyet buyurulması merhâmet.*" Cumhuriyet Arşivi (CA) 272 . . . 12.51.114.06, p. 3.

42. Words, phrases, and titles like this one appear quite often in early Republican documents. It would be worthy of a close investigation concerning how long and in which contexts Ottoman imperial language like this continued into the Republican era, and how their meanings might have changed.

officers (*zābıtān*). The *vali* pointed out that it was absolutely necessary to return as many *harīkzede* as possible to their villages in order to make room for the *mübadil*. He asked the central settlement agency to give orders to that effect to "the local" (*mahallına*)—possibly the local settlement office.

The Ankara settlement directorate answered in December 1926, stating that it was "necessary to remove the *harīkzede* from the houses in Urla, bring them to surrounding villages and place the exchangees in the emptied houses."[43] Apparently, this order was communicated to the local authorities, but met with resistance by the *harīkzede*. As the governor reported in another telegram to Ankara, they had successfully turned to a local court, arguing that there was in fact a decree favoring them, and, moreover, that the exchangees were actually not homeless at all. Both the district governor (*kaymakam*) and the municipality (*belediye*) had supported the *harīkzede*, again leaving the provincial governor unable to enforce their eviction. The last letter in this file was written on 1 February 1927. In it, the general director of settlement affairs (in Ankara) declared that the *harīkzede* must be evicted by 15 March 1927, and requested information regarding the number of people who would have to be resettled.

In their petition, the three refugees from Kavala argued that they had a legal right to be settled in abandoned property houses. How did they come to such a conclusion? Apparently, the Ministry of Internal Affairs had previously decided in favor of the local *harīkzede*, notwithstanding the existing legislation clearly allocating former *Rum* property to *mübadil*. For reasons unknown to me (but possibly as a result of the exchangees' petition) this decision was later revoked. According to the governor's report, the fire-victims' claims were accepted by both the local court and the municipality. This information suggests that "the state" was represented by a variety of different actors (the central settlement office, the provincial governor, the local governor, the local court and municipality), who had quite conflicting objectives. It seems that in order to force through its decisions, the settlement office in Ankara needed the cooperation of local administrations, which, as this document shows, sometimes decided to openly support local populations rather than incoming refugees. Whether or not the local government finally complied with orders from Ankara remains unclear.

The Çiftlik Mahmudlar in the District of Tire

For this case, I only have a report written by the governor of Izmir dated 14 July 1925.[44] In it, the governor explained that the people of the village Mahmudlar, which was adjacent to an agricultural estate (*çiftlik*) of the same name, had sent a petition—it is not made explicit to whom, probably to himself. The petition asked that their eviction from that estate to be revoked. The eviction is called *tahliye-i*

---

43. CA 272 . . . 12.51.114.06, p. 9.
44. CA 272 . . . 12.45.75.14.

mukteza, an eviction required by law. The village dwellers were apparently working the land of the *çiftlik*, which was now about to be allocated to exchangees. In their petition, they argued that the loss of that land would "forever sentence them to be captives of poverty" (*illelebed mahkūm-u sefālet olacakları*). An investigation had established that the amount of land that the villagers owned as private property (*mülk*) was indeed very limited: 195 people in fifty-four households had only 238 *dönüm*s of land at their disposal, while the estate covered about 15,000 *dönüm*s.[45] So far, the villagers had been able to make a living as workers and sharecroppers of the landowning family.[46] The report's actual subject was not the petition but its results. The district council had decided to sell the land to the villagers, and the Ministry of Finance had given permission for such a sale.[47] This was to be done in accordance with a clause of the 1925 "law of public equilibrium" (*muvāzene-yi umūmiye kānūnu*), i.e., the official budget law. The governor now asked for permission from the Ministry of Internal Affairs for the transaction to be completed.

The budget law of 1925 indeed contains a passage regulating the sale of "national land" (*mevcūd olan arāzi-i millīye*), repayable within ten years, to people in need, on the condition that no household would be given more than 200 *dönüm*s.[48] The law had only been issued three months earlier, possibly against the backdrop of many similar requests of landless or nearly landless people. This is suggested by a cabinet decision of October 1924, which explicitly regulated the sale of *çiftlik* estates to those people who were working on the land as sharecroppers or day-laborers.[49]

The governor's report carefully avoided discussing whether the owners in question were "subject to the population exchange" (*mübādeleye tabi'i*). Instead, it referred to them as "disappeared people" (*eşhās-ı mütegayyibe*), indicating that they had fled the country during or towards the end of the War of Independence. Only the names of the owners, which are cited in great detail, make it clear that they were ethnic Greeks. The very fact that the governor was asking the Ministry

---

45. One *dönüm* corresponded to 919.3 square meters (slightly less than 0.1 hectares) in pre-1928 Turkey.

46. "Şimdiye kadar mezkūr el-esāmi mutasarrıfları hesābına ve ortaklık suretiyle zırāat ederek tesis-i ma'işet edebildikleri anlaşılmış ve bu hālde temaādisi mebden fi'āl ve hakiki rençber olan mezkūr karye ahālisinin mağdūriyeti mūcib olacağı bedihi bulunmuş olmakla (:..).'' Ibid.

47. "Mezkūr karye-yi muhtāciye zırā'ata tefvīziye hazīne-yi celilece ruhsat itāsı każā-yı mezkūr meclis idāresinde vārid olan mażbatada bildirilmiştir." Ibid.

48. 1341 *senesi muvazenei umumiye kanunu*, No. 627, 18 Nisan 1341, Düstur 3. Tertip, vol. 6, 335–552, §23338–39.

49. "Emlāk-ı milliye derhāl tatbīki ve emlākı metrukeden olan çiftliklerde hiç arāziye sāhib olmayan ve bu çiftliklerde yarıcı ve gündelikçi olarak çalışan çiftçileri (. . .) uzun vādeli taksītlerle arāzi sāhibi etmek esāsı itibāriyle kabul edilmiş." CA 30.18.01.01.11.48.3, 8 Oct. 1924.

of Internal Affairs for permission to sell the land suggests that the Mahmudlar estate was owned by *Rums,* and therefore subject to the population exchange. Therefore, not only the Ministry of Finance, but also Internal Affairs (which was in charge of exchangee settlement) had to approve of the planned sale, and thus decide which rules would be applied.

Rich Exchangees Against Poor Locals? Selçuk/Çirkince, 1926

The reference to the budget law, though appearing to be a sound argument at first glance, might not have convinced the settlement officials. This is suggested by a similar case in Selçuk in which the Ministry of Internal Affairs insisted on distribution among exchangees (in December 1926). In this case, the local chairman of the People's Party in Kuşadası and his wife petitioned the Ministry of Finance in Ankara on behalf of certain villagers in Selçuk and Çirkince (present day Şirince). The file archived at the settlement office does not contain the original petition, which was sent back to the Ministry of Finance, but a copy of an inspector's report from the provincial financial administration (*defterdarlık*) in Izmir has survived. The inspector reported that he had been approached by the local municipal council (*belediye hey'eti*) and local people, who had complained that certain orchards, which they had been renting for a long time (*ötedenberi bilisticār irāde ettikleri*), had been taken away from them and given to "rich exchangees" (*zengin birkaç mübādile tahsīsi*). As a result, many locals had become "idle and jobless" (*bu kasaba halkından pek çoklarıñ da işsiz ve idāresiz kalarak*). They now wished to buy the land from the Treasury. The inspector approved of this idea, stating that auctioning the orchards would benefit the locals, help to rebuild the wealth of the region, and that the property claims of the exchangees were of low value.[50] The settlement office in Ankara was not convinced by these arguments. It pointed out that the compensation claims of the exchangees were not small and that a sale of exchangeable land to other people could not be approved. Somewhat annoyed, the official added that this was exactly similar to "earlier requests along the same lines which were also turned down."[51] While the Ministry of Finance was keen to auction the land, that of Internal Affairs prioritized the satisfaction of exchangee claims.

While these cases suggest that the settlement office usually upheld the principle that locals would not receive exchangeable land and houses, there is some

---

50. "Esāsen bu bahçeleriñ kıymet-ı mukayyedesi dūn olmakla berāber mübādilleriñ ibrāz ettikleri evrākıñ māhiyeti dahī (. . .) hem bir kasaba halkınıñ terfīhi hem de bu servet-i mahalliyesinde devām-ı imārisi için bilmüzāyede ahāli-yi mahalliye satılması pek muvāffık ve müsāittir (. . .)" CA 272 . . . 12.50.110.7 p. 2.

51. "Selçuk ve Çirkince mevkiilerindeki bahçelerin mübādillerden gayrisine itā ve tahsīsine görülememiş olduğu ve mukaddiman vekāleti celīleye vukuʿ bulan aynı mürācaʿat üzerine 'alākadarlara evvel sūretle cevāb verilmesi olduğu." Ibid., p. 3.

evidence that the matter was treated quite differently when the other people in question were also refugees (though not *mübadil*). A circular published in 1924 stated that refugees who had arrived after 1912 from countries other than Greece and who had already been settled since would be allowed to stay.[52]

Legality and the Revocability of Tefviz

In June 1927, a certain Hasanoğlu Ahmed sent a petition from the town of Söke to the Ministry of Internal Affairs in Ankara. Identifying himself as "[one] of the exchangees from Salonica resident in Söke," he explained that a settlement inspector had come to town and "witnessed the unlawful and corrupt decision of the local settlement administration for my eviction."[53] Ahmed complained that after the inspector's departure, the local district governor (*kaymakam*) was again, contrary to the inspector's orders, and despite all necessary documents being in place, "insisting on the same treatment in order to destroy my home and family." Ahmed asked "for immediate action in the name of law and justice" for the matter to be corrected.[54]

The said inspector's report dated 6 June 1926 narrates the affair quite differently. According to him, forty-eight houses in Söke had been allotted to exchangees in August 1924. On his visit, he had walked through the town with a list showing the previously allotted houses, only to find out that the list had almost nothing to do with reality. As for the *mübadil* Ahmed, he was indeed part of the list, but there was a [more recent] decision in place to give the house to another exchangee. Many houses, especially income-generating property such as hotels, depots, shops, and so forth had been given to several people at once. It was "this point which has caused conflict and complaints."[55] The inspector concluded his report by saying that it would be necessary to reclaim the distributed houses and start the whole allotment process anew.

In his reply to the provincial administration in Izmir, the Minister of Internal Affairs cited a report written by the *kaymakam*, which admitted that a lot of property had indeed been "given both to exchangees and to people who pretend to have rightful claims" (*müteda'i*). The minister argued that it was "legally im-

---

52. "*Yunanistan'ın mübadeleye tabi olmayan yerlerile 328 [1912] senesinden sonra Yugoslavyadan, Romanyadan, Bulgaristandan ve sair memaliki ecnebiyeden gelmiş muhacirlerden usulen iskan muamelesi görmüş olanlar bulundukları yerlerde ipka edileceklerdir.*" Tamim no. 5870/56, §7. T.C. Sıhhat ve İctimai Muavenet Vekaleti, İskan Umum Müdürlüğü, *İskan Mevzuatı* (Ankara, 1936), 189–90 cited in Öz and Berber, "Mübadele."
53. "*İskân müfettişi Nâmık Bey Söke'ye geldi . . . iskân idâresinden hakkımda tatbîkına kalkıştığı kānunsuz ve yolsuz tahliye kararına şāhiddir.*" CA 272 . . . 12.49.97.12, p. 3:
54. "*Müfettiş bey gidince ka'imakām bey meskenimi ve yuvamı bozmak için yine eski icrāda ısrār ediyor. Hukūk-u 'adālet nāmına hukūk ve hayāt . . . ? miz için serî' ve müdāhaleñiz . . . suz şeyle(re) istirhām ederim.*" Ibid.
55. "*İztırāb ve şikâyet bu noktadan doğmuştur.*" Ibid, 2.

possible to distribute this kind of property," and that it would, therefore, "have to be claimed back." The only possible exception would be made for people whose documents matched the value of the property in question. Additionally, they were to be asked to pay rent for the time they had been using it illegally.

Again, similar to the Urla case, we do not know how the story ended. The documents do, however, offer a number of clues as to the bureaucratic view on property distribution on the ground. The minister made a distinction between exchangees and "people who pretend to have rightful claims," implicitly arguing that only exchangees were rightful claimants. Both official documents make it perfectly clear that people such as the petitioner had become illegal occupiers due to a change in policy. The inspector even mentioned that this was the initial starting point of the whole affair.

This last statement of the minister is rather interesting, because it seems to conflate all categories and procedures mentioned in the laws. His suggestion that exchangees and other people with a right to settlement would be legalized, but asked to pay rent for the time of their illegal occupation seems to be an adaptation of the 1926 law which had legalized illegal occupation by other groups by asking them to pay rent. The minister thus applied a principle laid down in non-exchangee legislation to exchangees, trying to resolve a situation that had admittedly been created by the government's own contradictory policies. The minister's letter suggests that early allotment procedures had given houses to people who could not show proof of having owned sufficiently valuable property in Greece. The local settlement agency might later have started to take the category of matching value more seriously, revoking a decision that had already been taken. Both the petition of Hasanoğlu Ahmed and the inspector's report make clear that this policy was considered unfair and unjust, and led to considerable problems on the ground. In terms of legality, however, it may well have been closer to the letter of the law than the inital distribution in 1924.

The inspector's report on the situation in Söke was not the only one to find that distribution policies carried out in the beginning of the exchange had almost nothing to do with the legal rules they were supposed to follow. A similar report on the whole province of Manisa (written in 1927) found the situation to be so chaotic as to require the whole allocation process to be repeated.[56] While it seems highly unlikely that the settlement authorities would have really reconsidered all decisions for property allocations in a given province, there is plenty of evidence for cases in which property that had initially been given to exchangees was later repossessed. This was legally possible as long as the procedure of *tefviz* (which granted only preliminary rights) had not been followed by *temlik* (which was only performed from 1928 onwards). Many petitions sent from Izmir in 1926 and

---

56. See Öz and Berber, "Mübadele."

1927 show that people did not care for the subtleties of the law. Keenly pointing out that they had received official documentation for it, they considered a house or piece of land they had received from the state as their private property. Most of these petitions were sent by people who were eligible for actual compensation in accordance with their losses, and whose houses were taken back from them once the value of these claims were found to be insufficient.

The following petition was sent from Bornova (a suburb-village near Izmir) by a certain Hacı Hüseyinoğlu Ramazan, an exchangee from Kavala, on 22 June 1926. He claimed to have been given a house in accordance with the number of household members in the course of a procedure known as default settlement (*iskān-ı 'ādi*).[57] Default settlement was supposed to provide poor exchangees with the bare minimum of land and housing necessary for a family. The petitioner explained:

> The garden and field that were given to me in the course of default settlement in order to support my family of nine, and that are necessary for our subsistence, [are taken away from me], and they are giving them to another exchangee as *tefviz*. [This is happening] despite state orders that property distributed in the course of default settlement would not be taken back. Although my family and I work the land ceaselessly, trusting in [illegible] and despite my being in possession of definitive documents of possession (*tasarruf senedinde*) [illegible] issued by the settlement office in Izmir, the aforementioned garden is taken away from me, and all our work is counted for nothing.[58]

The petition made a point about the difference between *tefviz* vs. *iskān-ı 'ādi*. The distinction made here, however, was probably incorrect. *Tefviz* signified the character of the rights granted, not whether they were granted in the course of compensation or merely to provide the basic means for subsistence. While I have not come across any order stating that default settlement decisions were irrevocable (as the petition claims), pointing to such an order, if it existed, must have constituted a powerful argument in favor of the petitioner. Even if no such order existed, the petitioner might have thought so, simply because he knew that the procedure was supposed to provide for his bare subsistence. How could the state possibly take that minimum away from him?

---

57. A booklet published in 1932 contains a detailed list of these minimum standards. See *İskân Tarihçesi* (Istanbul: Hamit, 1932).

58. "Muhācirine iskān-i 'ādi sūretiyle verilmiş emvālı kimseden istirdād edilmemesi ve şahsi? emr?-i tefvîz edilmemiş hakkındaki evāmir-i devletlerine rağmen dokuz nüfūsundan 'ibāret olan efrād-ı 'ā'ilemiñ ittifāk ve i'āşesi için 'uhdemize iskān-i 'ādi sūretiyle verilmiş (....) taşlı tarla merhametinde 12 dönüm bāğ ve dört dönüm tarladan 'ibāret olan mālımızı şimdi başka bir mübādiline tefvîzen veriyorlar. Çoluk çocukla gece gündüz dinmeyerek mezkūr bāğ ve tarla (....) çalıştığım hālde ve elimde Izmir iskān müdüriyetinden verilmiş bir kat'i tasarruf senedinde (...) hālde 'arż ettiğım mebāliğ ile mezkūr bāğıma efrād-i 'ā'ilemizden geçen bütün emeklerimiziñ dahil edilmeyerek elimizden almak mukarrer (...)." CA 272.12...53.129.06.

The petition refers to the documents that the petitioner had received as "*tasarruf senedi*," a term that had in earlier times referred to a document for usage rights, but by the 1920s was regularly used to signify documents of full property ownership. As full property rights were only granted from 1928 onwards, it seems unlikely that Hacı Ramazan had really received these documents. He had probably been given proof of the *tefviz* procedure, which, in his case, was performed in accordance with his needs, not his property in Greece. His use of the term *tasarruf senedi* indicates that he had not grasped (or rejected) the difference between *tefviz* and *temlik*. Indeed, the concept of revocable property rights must have been difficult to understand even for those who could read the documents they received. Moreover, as the petition made clear by repeatedly mentioning the number of household members, and the work that they all invested in the garden and field, the decision to give the property to another exchangee was threatening their basic means of living, and thus contradicted the very purpose of default settlement. The reaction of the settlement office in Ankara unfortunately does not offer any clues as to the impression Ramazan's arguments made upon central government officials. As in most of these cases, the bureaucrat in charge simply sent the petition back to Izmir, asking the provincial settlement office to look into the matter.

Full rights to property distributed in the course of *tefviz* were only granted by Law No. 1331, which was issued on 30 May 1928.[59] Its application, as well as that of a follow-up law issued in 1931, proceeded painfully slowly and was fiercely criticized in Izmir's local press.[60] Many decisions for allocation and property compensation ended up in local courts whose records are unfortunately not available to researchers. There were, however, some cases in which decisions of lower courts ended up at the Council of State (*şūrā-yi devlet*), which functioned as an appeal court and also dealt with inter-ministerial conflicts. Some of its decisions were sent to the Prime Minister's Office and archived there.

One decision taken in May 1932 concerns a conflict between the Ministry of Internal Affairs and the Ministry of Finance. In order to recover the debts of former owners, the Treasury had sold immovable property that had already been distributed by *tefviz*. Upon protests of the Ministry of Internal Affairs, the Treasury declared that it was ready to leave the property in question with the exchangees—provided they pay the debts of previous owners at once and in cash. The matter was referred to the Council of State, which decided that the Treasury ought to have recovered such debts by liquidating the property *before* it was as-

---

59. *Mübadil, gayri mübadil, muhacir vesaireye kanunlarına tevfikan tefviz veya adiyen tahsis olunan gayri menkul emvalin tapuya raptına dair kanun*, May 30, 1928, in: Kardeş, "Tehcir," 107ff.

60. Baran, *Bir Kentin Yeniden Yapılanması*.

signed to exchangees. The court ruled unanimously that debts of former owners could not be recovered from new ones.[61]

In another case, a certain Fatma Zehra Hanım from Salonica who had received both *tefviz* and *temlik* property was later found not eligible for exchangee status. Following the Ministry of Internal Affairs' decision to revoke her *mübadil* status, the local *tefviz* commission (the document does not mention the location) revoked its decision to grant her property by *tefviz*. On grounds of this revocation, the Ministry of Finance then initiated a case against her in a court of first instance (*asliye*) in order to have her full property title (*tapu*, which had been granted by *temlik*) cancelled. Fatma Zehra appealed to the State Council against the *tefviz* commissions' decision and won the case. As a result, the commission reinstated her *tefviz* rights. Later, the *asliye* court rejected the Ministry of Finance's court case against her, arguing that the decision to revoke *tefviz*, which had been the legal basis of the demand for *tapu* cancellation, had in the meanwhile been reversed. The Ministry of Finance informed the Prime Minister's office in 1940 that it would not pursue the case any further.[62]

This last case is important for showing that exchangees could turn to the courts, successfully challenge the decisions of local *tefviz* commissions and have them overturned. This case also illustrates the importance of the difference between *tefviz* and *temlik*: the first could be revoked by a simple, local commissions' decision, while the second could only be reversed in court.

Conclusion

This article has utilized some petitions and administrative documents to clarify the legal, administrative, and social context in which property compensation for "exchangee" immigrants was performed. It sheds light on the question of if and how early Republican settlement agencies actually applied laws regulating settlement and property compensation for "exchangees." Rather than simply explain their shortcomings in fulfilling compensation laws as failure or corruption, I have shown that settlement policies had to be negotiated against a background of local resistance and competing objectives of other institutions of the Turkish state, namely that of the Ministry of Finance to create income for the Treasury. How can these practices be understood in terms of legality on the one hand and legitimacy on the other? Which patterns of interaction between the two can be observed?

The first three cases discussed here concerned people who were already occupying houses (Urla) and land (Mahmudlar, Selçuk/Çirkince), and who tried to receive or keep property for themselves despite this property being earmarked for exchangee immigrants. In all three cases, these claims were supported by local

---

61. Şurayi Devlet, 28 March 1932, CA 30.10...140.2.11.
62. Maliye Vekaleti Müşavirliği to Başvekalet, 22 July 1940, CA 30.0.11.001.000.140.25.1.

institutions (the respective district councils, a municipality, and a local court). The Ministry of Internal Affairs initially issued an order to let the fire-victims in Urla stay. This order was later used to justify their case in a local court, even after the ministry had changed its stance on the matter. Local institutions apparently interpreted this order as equivalent to a law, thus creating more leeway for their particular notion of legality.

In the Mahmudlar case, it was not only local institutions, but also the Ministry of Finance that approved the selling of land to villagers who had already worked the land as sharecroppers of the *Rum* landowning family. It is unclear which institution first pointed to the budget law of 1925 as a legal basis for this decision. The law indeed stipulated that landed estates could be sold among former sharecroppers or agricultural workers, and thus, upon first glance, may be taken to have contradicted or challenged compensation laws for exchangees. It could, however, only be interpreted in this way if the terminological distinction between "exchangeable" and "non-exchangeable" people and property was ignored. (The governor's report did exactly that). The relevant laws that were issued from 1924 onwards earmarked *Rum* "exchangeable" property for exchangees and all other, "non-exchangeable" land for other people. In reality, however, these categories were challenged, negotiated, and blurred, not least because both the Ministry of Finance *and* that of Internal Affairs were in charge of the relevant property. The cases at hand suggest that the Ministry of Internal Affairs had the final say in matters concerning "exchangeable" property. However, the very fact that the Ministry of Finance repeatedly asked for permission to sell land of this category suggests a certain degree of ambiguity regarding the division of competences between both agencies. The case of Selçuk/Çirkince shows that the settlement office usually rejected such requests, and that the officials there prioritized the needs of exchangees over those of local populations, even if this hurt the local population by leaving them without land or jobs. The court case that was finally decided in 1932 indicates that the conflict between both ministries intensified in later years, with the Ministry of Finance no longer asking for permission, but simply selling houses even after they had been allocated to exchangees. Again, this was only possible because the immigrants had not yet received full property rights.

Taken together, all the cases discussed here show that the state, far from being monolithic, was actually comprised of several institutions whose objectives often contradicted each other, and who had different notions of legality. The divide between local, provincial, and central authorities is most pronounced in the Urla case, where the settlement office in Ankara (and the provincial governor) were utterly unable to enforce the eviction of locals from formerly *Rum* homes. Those locals who would have enforced such an eviction (gendarmes and army officers) were themselves among the squatters. The central government, too, was divided between the Ministry of Finance and that of Internal Affairs, who more often than not worked against each other. As far as the Ministry of Finance was concerned, it was legally possible (and desirable) to sell the land in Mahmudlar and Selçuk to local people. Selling land to locals potentially served the double purpose to help the landless and to create revenue. The competing Ministry of Internal Affairs, however, objected and prioritized the legal claims of exchangees over revenue creation and local needs.

With regard to legality, both ministries followed a rather strict approach. Their competing policies were not driven by disparate interpretations of the same law, but by recourse to different sets of legislation. Though there are traces of flexible solutions for which there (probably) was no legal basis (such as the initial order to let the fire-victims in Urla stay), to-the-letter implementation of laws was clearly considered important by administrators, who sought to *present* their decisions as legal. The governor's report about the Mahmudlar case is especially interesting for proposing a creative solution to a settlement problem by basing it on a different set of legislation (budget rather than compensation law). The report did so by ignoring the basic terminological distinction between exchangeable and non-exchangeable land.

Among ordinary people, there clearly was a notion of extra-legal legitimacy. The populations of Mahmudlar and Selçuk/Çirkince petitioned against administrative decisions that clearly had a legal basis, namely, compensation laws for exchangees. Rather than turn to the exchangee ministry and ask for an exception to those rules, the locals petitioned the Ministry of Finance which was more likely to support their claims: the fiscal interest to create revenue coincided with theirs to buy the land in question. Though the locals' petitions have not survived in their original form, it is clear from the official reports citing them that they mainly operated with a logic of need: the Mahmudlar people were in danger of staying "captives of poverty," those in Selçuk had become "idle and jobless," while those in Urla argued that their adversaries were "not homeless at all."

Exchangee petitions are more mixed in their approach towards law and legality. The Urla case actually stressed three different levels of law: the violation of proper procedure, the exchangees' own rights to compensation, and the non-implementation of a ministerial order. Additionally, the petitioners argued that they were in danger of dying in the streets. The man in Söke complained about unlawful treatment and accussed the local official of trying to destroy his family. The exchangee in Bornova employed a legal argument that was probably based on a popular misconception of *tefviz*, which he (incorrectly) presented as a procedure different from that through which he had received "his" garden. He, too, additionally made a point of his (and his large family's) dire need for the property in question.

The question most difficult to assess is that of bottom-up influences on central state legislation. Such a mechanism was probably at work in the case of the miniature land reform which allowed landless peasants to purchase abandoned property. The Mahmudlar petition, though submitted somewhat later, was certainly not the only one addressing the plight of sharecroppers and agricultural workers on "abandoned" estates. The law of 1926 which turned squatters of abandoned property into tenants was clearly inspired by strong popular resistance against evictions.[63] At least from 1926 onwards, locals had to pay for the property they received, while exchangees got certain amounts "for free," i.e., in accordance with the values recorded in their documents from Greece. Other groups seem to have been able to first rent and later buy property through mortgage (this point, however, would also need to be checked for its actual application). While *tefviz* "for free," i.e., in accordance with rightful compensation claims, may at first look like privileged treatment, the cases discussed here suggest that the procedure had the rather serious down-side of providing only revocable property rights. In cases such as Söke, where houses were distributed at least twice, the lack of permanent, enforceable property rights must have made it hard for people to counter the arbitrary conduct of local officials.

Courts must have been an important instrument for people in their quest for justice, and the one case discussed here shows that there were at least some people who succeeded. The case of Fatma Zehra Hanım is especially interesting as she was admittedly not eligible for exchangee treatment, and her receiving property through *tefviz*, therefore, had been illegal in the first place. However, the Council of State seems to have ruled that a decision once taken (possibly years before) could not be so easily revoked, apparently even an illegal decision was a decision. The case in which the Ministry of Finance sold houses that had already been distributed via *tefviz* once again points to the importance of inter-ministerial competition. In this case, it was the intervention of one ministry that protected exchangees from the policies of another.

ELLINOR MORACK is a Postdoctoral Research Fellow of the Martin Buber Society of Fellows in the Humanities, The Hebrew University of Jerusalem, Israel.

---

63. As early as 1923, there was a governmental order which stated that illegal squattings would be legalized if the occupants paid rent. See Yıldırım, *Diplomacy*, 242.

Index

abandoned property, 185, 186, 187, 188, 189, 198, 199
Abd al-Rahman ibn Nasr Shayzari (Abu'l-Nacib al-Shayzari), 75
Abduh, Muhammad, Grand Mufti of Egypt (1899–1905), 95, 106
Abdülmecid I, Sultan, 160
accused, 158n6, 168, 172
administrative council, 6, 65, 66, 110, 111, 115, 116, 116n36, 117, 118, 118n46, 121, 124, 125, 126, 126n72, 127
Agmon, Iris, 2, 3, 22n47, 87, 94, 109
agricultural land, 110, 112, 114, 115, 120, 122, 181, 186
agricultural workers, 197, 199
Ahkām al-ghasb (Rules of Usurpation), 144
Ahmed III, 57, 61
Ahmed Cevdet Pasha, 77
Aleppo, 5, 11, 19n38, 20, 23, 23n52, 23n53, 23n55, 24, 72n30
al-Mahdi, Muhammad al-Abbasi, Grand Mufti of Egypt (1847–97), 95
al-Marghinani, 98
al-Ramli, Khayr al-Din, 98, 102, 147
Anatolia, 54, 58, 61, 73, 97, 104, 130, 179, 186
application of laws, 3, 8, 183
Arabic language, 23
archive, 5, 13, 18, 21, 21n42, 23, 124, 182n19, 184, 184n31
Armenian property, 180, 181, 185, 186
asesbaşı, 36, 37, 38
askeri, 27, 28, 32, 33

Baldwin, James, 98
blood money (*diyet*), 39, 40, 159
bridal tax, 20
British, 89
British ambassador 160
Bucakbağı (Bucakbahçe), 6, 26, 27, 31, 31n24, 32, 33, 35
bureaucracy, 4, 12, 29, 72, 72n30, 81, 111, 111n11, 112n20, 119, 120, 127, 130, 135, 139, 149
bureaucratic expansion, 7, 111, 127, 128

cadastral survey, 10, 12, 53, 55
Cairo, 12, 13, 14, 17, 19, 22n51, 25, 95, 97, 98
Canning, Stratford, 160
centralization, 5, 41, 133
children, 19, 102, 103, 104, 106, 171
Çirkince/Şirince, 191, 196, 197, 198
civilization (civilizational), 75, 139, 140
classical patriarchy, 30
codification, 4, 5, 7, 20, 88, 91, 93, 94, 106, 129, 132, 133, 135, 138, 139, 148, 157, 157n3, 158, 161, 162, 177
commanding right and forbidding wrong, 68, 69
compensation, 8, 146, 158n6, 180, 181, 182, 184, 191, 194, 195, 196, 197, 198, 199
concubine, 98
Constitutional Revolution (1908), 168
convicted, 156, 158n6, 166, 167, 168, 169, 170, 172, 174, 176
corruption (misconduct), 73, 79, 80, 159, 160, 164, 167, 170, 182, 183, 196
Council of State (şura-yı devlet), 195, 199
court, 3, 5, 6, 7, 19, 21, 22, 22n47, 23, 26, 27, 29, 30, 31, 32, 33, 34, 35, 36, 37, 38, 40, 41, 42, 46, 54, 56, 60, 62, 63, 64, 85, 92, 94, 95, 97, 100, 101, 102, 103, 104, 105, 108, 111, 114, 115, 117, 117n42, 118, 120, 123, 124, 127, 135, 136, 139, 140n52, 146, 147, 156, 159, 160, 162, 166, 167, 168, 169, 174, 195, 196, 197, 199
    court of first instance, 115, 117, 118, 120, 123, 127, 196
    court procedures, 6, 94, 139
    court records, 3, 7, 40, 40n59, 46, 56, 100, 101, 108, 115, 118, 119, 127, 146, 147
    court registers, 30, 105, 117, 121n56, 147
    Islamic court, 8, 157, 158n6, 159, 161, 171n45, 177
    law court, 5, 19, 22n47, 166
    law court records, 10, 15, 20, 23, 24
    local court, 46, 61, 182, 189, 195, 197
    Nizamiye court (criminal court), 3, 85, 108, 109, 110, 115, 118, 120, 122, 123, 124, 127, 134, 138, 162, 171
    Ottoman state court, 136

201

court (*continued*)
  shar'i court, 85n99
  Sharia court, 3, 5, 6, 7, 92, 93, 94, 95, 96, 97, 100, 102, 103, 104, 104n38, 105, 106, 108, 109, 110, 115, 116, 117, 117n42, 118, 119, 120, 121, 121n56, 121n57, 121n58, 122, 123, 124, 126, 127, 134, 138, 140, 148, 162, 171
courthouse, 13, 21, 29
crime, 5, 8, 27, 37, 53, 80, 86, 90, 157, 157n3, 158, 158n6, 159, 161, 162, 163, 164, 165, 165n29, 166, 167, 168, 169, 170, 171, 172, 173, 174, 175, 176, 177, 178
  adultery, 170
  assault, 168, 175, 176
  assault and battery, 165, 166, 173, 176
  banditry, 85, 158n6, 162, 163
  cinayet (*jinayet*) (serious offense), 162, 163, 165, 165n29, 166, 167, 171, 173, 175
  cünha (lesser offense), 163, 165, 165n29, 167, 171, 173, 175, 176
  embezzlement, 158, 163, 166, 173, 174
  fraud, 147, 163, 166, 167, 173, 174
  hadd, 158, 158n6, 159, 161, 175, 177
  homicide, 26, 36, 37, 38, 39, 39n55, 39n56, 41, 85, 159, 162, 163, 166, 175, 176
  honor, 105, 158, 158n5, 159, 161, 163, 164, 165, 166, 167, 169, 171
  indecent sexual behavior (deviant), 165, 166, 170
  kabahat (misdemeanor), 163, 165, 165n29, 167
  kidnapping, 163, 166, 171
  murder, 37, 38, 39, 41, 161, 166
  rape, 163, 166, 176
  sexual crimes, 158n6, 159, 165, 166, 167, 169, 170, 171
  slander and vituperation, 172
  theft, 82, 83, 158, 158n6, 163, 165, 166, 167, 173, 174, 177
  violent crimes, 158, 165, 166, 167, 173, 174, 175, 176, 177
criminal, 8, 23, 36, 37, 37n50, 41, 42, 53, 80, 81, 86n104, 92, 110, 115, 136, 156, 157, 158, 159, 160, 161, 162, 163, 164, 165, 167, 169, 170, 170n42, 177
  criminal code, 156, 160
  criminal punishments ('*uqūbāt*), 136, 140
  criminal justice, 156, 157, 160, 164, 165, 177
  criminal justice system, 8, 36, 39, 156, 157, 160, 163, 177
criminality, 158, 159, 164, 177
cultivators, 43, 44, 56, 89n117, 112, 114n26, 118, 119, 124, 125, 128

Damascus, 23n51, 47, 48, 54, 55, 56, 73, 112, 113, 121n56, 121n57, 121n58, 125
debt, 7, 23, 85, 97, 98, 99, 101, 110, 114, 119, 122, 123, 124, 166, 195, 196
direct causality (*mubāsharatan*), 145
district (*kaza*), 7, 56, 57, 58, 59, 60, 81, 84, 85n98, 97, 108, 110, 111, 111n12, 112, 112n16, 113, 114, 115, 116, 117, 118, 118n46, 119, 119n52, 120, 121, 122n60, 124, 125, 126, 126n72, 127, 169, 169n39, 172, 189, 190, 192,
divorce (judicial or annulment), 93, 94, 95, 96, 98, 99, 101, 103, 104, 106, 106n44
dizdar, 6, 27, 29, 33n38, 34
documents, 7, 8, 10, 12, 13, 15, 16, 17, 19, 19n38, 20, 21, 22, 23, 23n52, 41, 46, 47, 48, 50, 54, 55, 56, 64, 69n12, 86, 93, 94, 96, 100, 101, 103, 104, 132n13, 146, 147, 166, 169, 180, 186, 188n42, 192, 193, 194, 195, 196, 199
Düstur, 67, 67n2

endowments, 6, 23n55, 31, 33, 47, 48, 52, 55, 57, 58, 63, 64, 135
  endowment deed (*waqfiyya*), 15, 23n53, 32, 47
Erzurum, 47, 48, 49, 50, 57, 58, 59, 60, 61, 63, 82n86, 168
eviction, 181, 185, 188, 189, 190, 192, 197, 199
extra-judicial actors, 6, 27, 29, 30, 36, 41
executive officers (*ehl-i örf*), 28, 29, 36, 37, 37n47, 37n50, 38

fatāwā, 131n10, 132n13, 138, 139, 143
fatwas, 95, 98, 99, 100, 101, 102, 103, 104
Feyzullah Efendi, 6, 47, 48, 48n17, 50, 52, 53, 57, 58, 59, 60, 61, 63, 64
fiqh (jurisprudence), 5, 28, 65, 68n12, 70, 78, 87n106, 88, 121n58, 130n4, 132n18, 136, 139, 140, 140n52, 143
forgery, 147, 159, 163, 165, 166
forum shopping, 7, 16, 95, 96, 98, 105, 107, 109, 110, 111, 120, 127, 128
Foucault, Michel, 78, 80, 83n89, 91n123
four humors (or four pillars) of society, 72
four virtues, 73

gender, 5, 27, 40, 42
Gönelü salt works, 47, 49, 50, 57, 59, 61, 63
governance, governing, government, 10, 15, 20, 21, 23, 38, 43, 46, 50, 51, 56, 58, 61, 64, 66, 67n2, 70, 72, 73, 75, 76, 76n55, 78, 79, 80, 81, 83, 83n89, 84, 85, 86, 87, 88, 89, 90, 91, 91n123, 94, 96, 104, 105, 108, 109, 110, 112, 113, 114, 115,

117, 118, 119, 120, 124, 126, 127, 157, 159, 160, 161, 162, 163, 164, 167, 168, 171, 172, 175, 177, 179, 183, 186, 189, 193, 195, 197
   Ottoman government/governance/governing, 6, 7, 16, 20, 21, 22n47, 57, 58, 64, 65, 66, 67, 82, 88, 91, 108, 111, 112, 113, 117, 119, 120, 126, 127
   provincial government/governance, 83, 112, 121, 125, 126
grand vizier, 6, 26, 27, 29, 35, 36, 41, 42, 49, 54, 61, 135
Greco-Turkish War, 181
Greece, 8, 179, 180, 185, 186, 192, 193, 195, 199
Greek property, 180, 186, 187

Hamidian, 111, 112, 122, 127
Hanafi School of law, 78
Hanbali, 70, 78, 95, 98, 99, 101, 102,
harikzede (internal migrants), 188, 189
hisba, 69, 70
historiography, 11, 27, 40, 72, 94, 182
homicide, 26, 36, 37, 38, 39, 39n55, 39n56, 41, 85, 159, 162, 163, 166, 175, 176
Hududname (demarcation document), 6, 46, 47, 48, 49, 54, 55, 56, 59, 61, 63, 64
husband, 32, 93, 94, 95, 97, 98, 101, 102, 103, 104, 105, 106, 106n44, 170
   absent or missing husband, 7, 94, 96, 97, 98, 99, 101, 102, 104, 105, 106
   husband and marital authority, 98, 102

Ibn ʿĀbidīn, 131, 135, 136, 137n40, 139n50, 147, 147n82
Ibn Khaldun, 17, 74, 75, 76, 77, 79, 90
Ibn Nujaym, 7, 130, 132n18, 138
Ibn Tawq, 18, 18n34
Ibn Taymiyah, 68n10, 71, 74, 77, 78
immorality, 106
imperial assignments/certificates (*berats*), 59, 147
interpreter, 21, 24, 24n58, 77
Iraq, 97
Islahat Fermanı (1856 Imperial Decree of Reform), 158n5, 160
Islam/Islamic, 7, 8, 9, 10, 13, 15, 18, 28, 38, 41, 50, 53, 54, 58, 66, 68, 69, 70, 70n22, 71n25, 73, 77, 78, 95, 96, 106n44, 129, 130, 131, 132, 133, 135, 136, 139, 139n51, 147, 148, 149, 156n1, 157, 159, 161, 162, 170, 171, 173, 174, 177
Islamic taxes (*tekalıf-i şeriyye*), 53
Izmir, 181, 184, 187, 188, 189, 191, 192, 193, 194, 195

jail (*tevkifhane*), 164,
judge (*kadı, hakim, naib*), 7, 16, 17, 19, 20, 21, 22, 22n47, 24, 25n61, 26, 28, 29, 34, 36, 46, 52, 54, 55, 56, 59, 60, 61, 63, 64, 67n7, 73, 85, 87, 93, 94, 95, 96, 97, 98, 99, 100, 101, 102, 103, 105, 106, 110, 115, 116, 117, 118, 121, 121n58, 122, 123, 131n8, 138, 139, 139n50, 143, 147, 148, 159, 161, 162
   Hanafi judge, 19, 20, 99, 104
   Islamic court judge (*qadi*), 8, 157, 158n6, 159, 161, 171n45, 177
judicial
   Egyptian judicial system, 92, 96
   judicial discretion, 27, 42
   judicial practice (*amal*), 104
   judicial reform, 162
   judicial system, 93, 105, 127, 143
   Ottoman judicial system, 143
jurisprudence, 95, 96, 97, 99, 100, 101, 104, 107, 134, 136, 138, 143
juristic preference (*istiḥsān*), 142
justice, 2, 10, 16, 19, 66, 71, 73, 74, 75, 78, 88, 89, 90, 140, 147, 160, 185, 192, 199
   Circle of Justice, 74, 79, 156, 156n1, 158n6, 159, 178
   justice and legitimacy, 71
   justice as equilibrium or balance, 66, 71, 73, 74, 75
   justice as virtue, 73, 74, 75
just (or fair) price, 68n10, 68n12, 77

kadı, 27, 28, 29, 30, 36, 37, 37n47, 37n50, 38, 40, 41, 42, 54, 67n7, 69, 71, 159, 161, 162, 171n45
kadıasker, 6, 26, 27, 35, 41
keşif, 26
Khayr al-Dīn al-Ramlī, 98, 147
kin, 36, 38
Kınalızade Ali Efendi, 73
Kömör village and salt works, 59, 61, 159, 162, 163, 166, 175, 176
Kuşadası, 191

land code, of 1858, 111, 113, 114, 116, 122, 127, 183
landless, 190, 198
land registration, 116, 119
late Hanafis (*almutaʾakhkhirīn*), 129, 129n1, 139n50, 146, 149
law, 1, 2, 3, 4, 5, 6, 7, 8, 10, 11, 12, 13, 15n22, 16, 17, 18, 20, 21, 24, 25, 27, 29, 30, 34, 35, 36, 40n59, 43, 47, 49, 53n39, 54, 56, 63, 67n2, 68, 70, 73n41, 74, 78n70, 79, 88, 92, 93, 94, 95, 96, 100, 101, 102, 103, 104n38, 106, 109, 115n29, 117,

204 | Index

law (*continued*)
   124, 129, 131, 131n8, 132, 134, 135, 136, 137n40, 139, 140, 141, 148, 157, 157n3, 158n5, 159, 160, 161, 162, 168, 168n37, 174, 175, 177, 182, 183, 184, 185, 186, 186n35, 187, 187n40, 188, 190, 191, 192, 193, 194, 195, 196, 197, 198, 199
     budget law, 190, 191, 197
     civil law, 92, 93, 110, 129, 132, 136, 162, 175
     codification of law, 4, 5, 7, 20, 88, 93, 94, 106, 129, 132, 133, 135, 138, 139, 148, 157, 157n3, 158, 162, 177
     customary law, 21, 42
     Egyptian law, 7, 93, 94, 95, 96, 97, 106, 107
     family law, 7, 93, 94, 95, 96, 106, 107, 162
     French law, 92, 131, 134, 161, 170
     Hanafi law, 7, 102
     Islamic criminal law, 161, 173, 177
     Islamic law (*shari'a* and *şeriat*), 3, 5, 6, 7, 28, 39n56, 43, 47, 49, 56, 68, 129, 130n4, 132, 133, 134, 135, 136, 139, 156, 156n6, 161, 162n18, 169, 170, 171n45, 173, 174, 175, 177, 178
     law and legality, 198
     law code, 7, 20, 92, 94, 107, 129
     Muslim law (sharia), 4, 29, 30, 30n18, 36, 43, 54, 63, 71, 74, 94, 109, 110, 121n58, 122, 129, 134, 136, 140, 158, 158n6, 162n18
     Ottoman law, 9, 12, 14, 19, 20, 23, 24, 29, 77, 80, 108
     property law, 7, 92, 108, 110, 127
     statutory law (*nizam*), 136
     sultanic law (*Kanun*), 4, 14n18, 20, 21, 27, 28, 43, 47, 53, 63, 136, 158, 159, 160, 174, 187, 190
legal agent, 102
legal code, 1, 129, 162, 170
legality, 1, 2, 3, 5, 8, 10, 35, 79, 90n122, 183, 184, 193, 196, 197, 198
legal maxims (*al-qawā'id al-fiqhiyya*), 8, 130, 138, 139, 143, 148
legal pluralism, 7, 9, 19, 96, 97, 108, 109, 110, 124, 127, 130n4
legitimacy, 1, 2, 14, 66, 71, 79, 91, 139, 143, 148, 175, 196, 198
     legitimacy and law, 1, 2, 3, 5, 8, 10
     legitimacy and legality, 1, 2, 3, 8, 10, 184
     legitimacy and legitimization, 1, 5
literacy, 5, 10, 11, 11n5, 12, 13, 13n16, 14, 14n17, 15, 15n22, 16, 17, 18, 20, 22, 23, 24, 25
     legal literacy, 5, 16, 17, 20
     literacy rate, 24, 184
     new literacy studies, 11, 11n5

litigant experience, 7, 109, 110, 126, 128
liva, 112
local experts, 54, 56, 59, 60, 62, 63
locals, 181, 186, 188, 191, 197, 198, 199

madhhab, 14n18, 16, 100, 129, 132, 136, 137, 138, 141, 146, 148, 149
mahkama, 24
mahlul land, 113, 115
Mahmudlar, 189, 191, 196, 197, 198
Malikane (tax farming contract to be held for life), 6, 47, 51, 52, 52n31, 57, 64
Maliki school of law, 7, 17, 70, 95, 96, 96n12, 97, 98, 99, 101, 102, 105, 106
Mamluk-Ottoman transition, 5, 10
Mamluk Sultanate, 10, 14, 18, 97
manāfi' (profitable utility), 146
manufacturing contract (*istisnā'*), 142
market(s)
     free market policies, 65
     market as public space, 68
     market as a site of veridiction, 79, 90
     market inspection (*ihtisab*), 6, 66, 69
     market inspector (*muhtasib*), 6, 16, 23, 65, 66, 68, 69, 69n12, 70, 71, 75, 80, 87
     market intervention/control, 6, 65, 66, 70, 75, 77
     market mechanisms, 69
     market spontaneity, 78, 81, 87
     market spontaneous order, 78
     natural order (functioning) of markets, 66, 76, 78, 91
marriage, 7, 20, 53, 93, 94, 96, 97, 98, 99, 100, 101, 102, 103, 104n38, 105, 106, 106n44
     marriage guardian, 98, 99
     marriage registrars (*ma'dhun*s), 100, 101
     registration of marriage, 101
     stipulations in marriage, 98, 99
Mecelle, 7, 8, 88n111, 129, 130, 130n2, 131, 132, 132n13, 132n18, 133, 134, 134n23, 135, 136, 137, 138, 139, 140, 141, 141n62, 142, 143, 144, 144n69, 145, 146, 147, 148, 149, 150, 151–52, 153–55, 162, 162n18
mezraa (communally owned arable land), 55, 55n48, 56, 60
Ministry of Finance, 181, 184, 185, 190, 191, 195, 196, 197, 198, 199
Ministry of Internal Affairs, 184, 188, 189, 190, 191, 192, 195, 196, 197, 198
miri land, 44, 111, 115, 116, 120, 121n56, 121n57, 122, 123, 124, 125, 127
modernity, 13, 132, 149, 156, 157, 157n4, 162, 177

morality, 22, 106
mortgage, 7, 44, 110, 114, 115, 119, 122, 123, 124, 128, 186, 187, 199
mu'ayene 26
Muazamiye, 47, 49, 50, 52, 54, 55, 56, 57, 59, 61, 63
mübadil, 180, 186, 187, 188, 189, 191, 192, 196
mufti (jurisconsult), 56, 85, 86, 95, 98, 99, 100, 106, 116, 131n10, 139n50
Muhammad Ali, Viceroy of Egypt (1805–48), 99, 100
muhasıllık councils, 84, 85, 88
mukataa (state revenue source), 51, 52, 57, 59, 60, 61, 62, 63
mukhtar, 119, 120, 127
Mülk, 6, 44, 45, 47, 49, 50, 53, 55, 57, 58, 59, 60, 61, 63, 64, 115, 121n56, 122, 123, 186, 190
Mustafa II, 48, 50, 53, 54, 57, 59, 61, 63

Naima, 66, 72, 72n30, 73, 73n37, 74, 75, 76, 77, 90
Nelly Hanna, 12, 14, 24
North Africa, 97
notary, 17, 18, 41, 100

ocaklık, 57, 58, 58n63, 59, 63, 64
oppression (zulm), 66, 71, 73, 74, 75, 89, 164
    oppression and economic inefficiency, 75
orality, 12
Ottoman Empire, 2, 3, 4, 5, 6, 8, 9, 10, 11, 25, 47, 53, 65, 66, 68, 69, 70, 71, 72, 76, 77, 78, 79, 80, 81, 82n86, 88, 89, 90, 92, 93, 96, 98, 111, 129n1, 130, 131, 132, 133, 135, 136, 140, 156, 157, 157n3, 159, 160, 162, 166, 169n38, 170n42, 173, 175, 183
Ottoman judicio-administrative sphere, 66
Ottoman land regime, 44n6, 45, 47
Ottoman language, 23
Ottoman Law of Family Rights (OLFR), 93, 96
Ottoman Parliament (Grand Assembly), 163, 167, 168, 169, 172, 173, 175

Palestine, 94, 96, 111, 113
pastoral nomads, 114n26, 116, 119
penal code, 8, 156, 157, 158, 159, 160, 161, 164, 167
    1810 French Criminal Code, 161, 170
    1840 Penal Code (Ceza Kanunnamesi), 158, 159, 160, 161
    1851 New Penal Code (Kanun-i Cedid), 159, 160, 161
    French Criminal Code, 161
    Imperial Ottoman Penal Code (IOPC), 158, 160
petitions, 8, 124, 182n19, 184, 184n31, 193, 194, 196, 198

police/policing (zaptiye), 26, 27, 38, 41, 76, 163, 166, 167, 168, 181
population exchange, 8, 179, 180, 182, 184, 185, 185n31, 186, 187, 190, 191
preferred opinions (rājiḥ), 97, 140
price-ceiling (narh), or setting/fixing prices, 6, 65, 66, 69, 70, 71, 72, 75, 76, 77, 78
prison (hapishane), 8, 33, 86, 86n104, 156, 157, 158, 159, 160, 162, 164, 164n27, 165, 166, 167, 168, 169, 169n39, 170, 171, 172, 173, 174, 175, 176, 177
    prison administration (hapishane idaresi), 164, 165, 167
prisoner (incarcerated, inmate), 86, 86n104, 156, 159, 165, 166, 168, 169, 169n38, 173, 176
    accused (mahbus), 156, 158n6, 166, 167, 168, 169, 170, 172, 174, 176,
    convicted (mahkum), 169, 170, 172, 174, 176
    rehabilitation, 156, 164
professionalization, 81
property, 5, 6, 7, 26, 27, 32, 32n31, 34, 35, 36, 41, 43, 44, 46, 47, 48, 49, 51, 52, 54, 56, 57, 59, 60, 61, 63, 64, 65, 75, 77, 80, 87, 92, 103, 104, 108, 110, 111, 111n11, 112, 115, 116, 118, 119, 120, 121, 121n56, 122, 122n60, 123, 124, 125, 126, 127, 128, 144, 144n67, 144n69, 146, 148, 158n5, 159, 161, 163, 164, 166, 173, 174, 175, 179, 180, 181, 184, 185, 186, 187, 188, 189, 190, 191, 192, 193, 194, 195, 196, 197, 198, 199
    attacks on property, 76
    private property, 6, 44, 47, 52, 57, 61, 64, 148, 163, 164, 173, 174, 175, 186, 190, 194
    property administration, 7, 115, 116, 119, 120, 121, 122, 123, 124, 126, 127
    property registers, 7, 108, 116n33, 121, 122n60, 123
    property rights, 8, 41, 43, 64, 75, 186, 195, 197, 199
province (vilayet), 3, 4, 36, 46, 47, 52, 55, 57, 58, 59, 61, 63, 68, 75, 82n87, 84n95, 87, 92, 95, 96, 97, 112, 112n20, 115, 117, 125n69, 138, 168, 169n39, 172, 181, 193
provincial administration (valilik), 67, 81, 87, 89n118, 109, 184, 188, 192
provincial administrative councils, 6, 66, 110, 127
provincial administrative regulation of 1849, 83
provincial administrative regulation of 1864, 67
provincial councils (eyalet meclisi), 66, 67n7, 80, 83, 84, 86, 88, 89, 91
provisioning, 66, 76, 79, 80, 86, 112
punishment (ceza), 1, 5, 8, 37, 38, 39, 41, 75, 136, 140, 156, 157, 158, 158n6, 159, 160, 161, 162, 163,

punishment (*ceza*) (*continued*)
   164, 165, 165n29, 167, 168, 169, 170, 171, 172, 173, 174, 175, 176, 177, 178
   banishment and exile, 158n6, 159, 162, 165n29
   corporeal punishment, 159, 160, 177
   discretionary punishment (*ta'zir* and *siyaset*), 158, 158n6, 159, 161, 162, 175, 177
   diyet, 158, 158n6, 159, 161, 175, 177
   fines, 53, 158n6, 159, 160, 162, 164, 165n29, 177
   hadd, 158, 158n6, 159, 161, 175, 177
   incarceration (imprisonment), 8, 23, 39n55, 94, 106, 156, 157, 158, 158n6, 159, 160, 161, 163, 164, 165n29, 166, 167, 168, 169, 170, 172, 173, 174, 176, 177
   kürek (hard labor), 159, 161, 162, 165n29, 173, 175, 176
   qisas (retaliation), 36, 38, 158, 158n6, 159, 161, 175, 177

Qadifeh, 55, 56
Quesnay, 76, 90

rationalization, 5, 148, 156, 161
reaya, 10, 27, 28n8, 71n29, 73
refugees, 82, 82n86, 82n87, 83, 111, 113, 114, 118, 125, 179n3, 181, 185, 187, 189, 192
right to property, 75
Rubin, Avi, 2, 3, 85, 85n99, 109, 110, 162, 171n45
rule of law, 28, 29, 29n12, 40, 159

salt, 7, 47, 49, 50, 51, 57, 59, 60, 61, 62, 63, 64, 108, 110, 111, 112, 112n15, 113, 114, 114n26, 115, 116, 116n33, 116n36, 117, 117n42, 118, 119, 119n52, 120, 121, 121n56, 121n57, 121n58, 122, 122n59, 122n60, 123, 124, 125, 126, 127
sancak, 45n8, 57, 58, 59, 112
scribe, 16, 17, 18, 35, 38, 40, 116
secondary causality (*tasabbuban*), 145
Second Constitutional Period, 163, 164, 168, 171, 172, 175, 176
secular, 7, 70, 109, 133, 140, 162, 177
secularization, 4, 109, 157, 161, 174, 177
Selçuk, 191, 196, 197, 198
settlement, 8, 34, 36, 43, 45, 62, 113, 124, 126, 180, 181, 182, 184, 185, 187, 188, 189, 191, 192, 193, 194, 195, 196, 197, 198
Shafi'i school of law, 7, 95, 96, 97, 98, 99, 101, 102, 105, 137
sharecroppers, 190, 197, 199
shahid (pl. *shuhud*), 17, 24

Sharia court, 3, 5, 6, 7, 92, 93, 93n5, 94, 95, 96, 97, 100, 102, 103, 104, 104n38, 105, 106, 108, 109, 110, 115, 116, 117, 117n42, 118, 118n44, 119, 120, 121, 121n56, 121n57, 121n58, 122, 123, 124, 126, 127, 134, 138, 140, 148, 162, 171
shar'i codes (*al-qawānīn al-shar'iyya*), 135
sicil, 3n7, 6, 21, 27, 28, 32, 34, 35, 36, 38, 39, 41, 46
Smith, Adam, 73, 90
socio-legal, 1, 5, 8, 157, 157n3
Söke, 192, 193, 198, 199
Spanish Empire, 19n36, 22n46
squatting, 199n63
standardization, 5, 148, 156, 161, 162
state-customary taxes (*tekalıf-i örfiyye*), 53
state lands (*miri*), 44, 59, 111, 115, 116, 120, 121, 121n56, 121n57, 122, 122n60, 123, 124, 125, 127, 186
state officials, 29, 69, 138, 158, 164, 165, 167, 168, 169, 181
statistics, 81n82, 112, 158, 164, 169, 170, 171, 172, 175, 177
subaşı, 36, 37, 37n47, 38
Sublime Porte, 135, 136, 160
sultanic decree, 43, 121n58, 146, 147
Syria, 7, 15, 97, 98, 108, 112, 113, 114, 116, 117, 117n42, 121n58, 125n69, 125n71, 127, 130

takhayyur, 95, 96, 107
Tanzimat, 4, 22n47, 67n2, 67n7, 86, 92, 112, 131, 158n5, 160
taxation, 7, 45, 52, 75, 88, 112m20, 115n29, 121, 128, 158n5
tax farmer (*mültezim*), 51, 52, 114, 115
tax farming (*iltizam*), 45, 47, 50, 51, 52, 52n31
tefviz (granting of revocable property rights), 8, 186, 193, 194, 195, 196, 198, 199
temlik (formal possession of property), 49, 186, 193, 195, 196
temlikname (deeds to formal possession of property granted by the Sultan), 47, 50, 53, 54, 57, 59, 63, 64
testimony (*shahāda*), 3, 17, 22, 35, 40, 45, 54, 56, 63, 100, 104, 118, 119, 120, 126, 134n23, 147, 148
timar system, 44, 45, 50, 51, 58
tithe, 20, 45, 53
transgression (*al-ta'dī*), 6, 29, 41, 145
transactions (*mu'āmalāt*), 32, 72, 100, 110, 111, 115, 116, 118, 119n50, 120, 121, 121n56, 121n58, 122, 122n59, 126, 127, 136, 138, 140, 141, 142
translator, 24
Tucker, Judith, 98
Tuğ, Başak, 104

Turkey (1922–), 1, 8, 46, 157n3, 179, 180, 180n6, 181, 182, 185, 190n45

ulema, 30, 32, 35, 38, 42, 52
Urla, 187, 188, 189, 193, 196, 197, 198
usurped (*maghsūb*), 144, 145, 146

Vidin, 82, 82n87, 88, 89, 89n117, 89n118
village boundaries, 5, 6, 45, 46, 47, 62, 63

waqf, 16, 23, 23n53, 25n61, 26, 27, 31, 31n26, 32, 32n30, 34, 35, 36, 41, 43, 44, 45, 48, 49, 55n48, 57, 58, 60, 61, 63, 64, 71
Westernization, 133, 134, 157, 161, 174
witness, 16, 17, 17n26, 17n28, 19, 19n38, 24, 24n57, 26, 27, 28, 32, 35, 45, 54, 55, 56, 59, 64, 82, 85, 100, 101, 117n42, 118, 119, 120, 122n59, 134n23, 147, 166, 172
wives, 105, 106n44, 170
    desertion of, 7, 94, 96, 97, 99, 102, 103
    maintenance and non-maintenance, 93, 97, 101, 102, 103, 103n34
    obedience and disobedience, 101, 102, 103
women, 6, 7, 28, 30, 41, 93, 94, 95, 96, 97, 98, 99, 100, 101, 102, 103, 104, 104n38, 105, 106, 106n44, 107, 170, 170n43

Yedikule Fortress, 6, 32, 33, 33n38, 34
Yusuf, Ali, 105

zawā'id (natural outgrowth), 146

www.ingramcontent.com/pod-product-compliance
Lightning Source LLC
Chambersburg PA
CBHW070401240426
43661CB00056B/2490